Following God

LEARNING LIFE PRINCIPLES FROM THE WOMEN OF THE BIBLE

LEARNING LIFE PRINCIPLES FROM THE WOMEN OF THE BIBLE

A Bible Study by

Wayne Barber
Eddie Rasnake
Richard Shepherd

AMG *Publishers*™
Chattanooga, TN 37422

Following God

LEARNING LIFE PRINCIPLES FROM THE WOMEN OF THE BIBLE

ISBN: 0-89957-302-9

Cover design by Phillip Rodgers
Editing and layout by Rick Steele

Printed in the United States of America.
06 05 04 03 02 01 –E– 9 8 7 6 5 4

This book is dedicated to our wives:

Diana Barber

Michele Rasnake

Linda Gail Shepherd

It is a joy to follow God through life with you!

Acknowledgements

This work goes forth to those who have encouraged us in the publication of the first two books in this series: Life Principles from the Old Testament and Life Principles from the Kings of the Old Testament. We are especially grateful to the body of believers at Woodland Park Baptist Church in Chattanooga, Tennessee, who have walked through many of these studies with us and have been a continual source of encouragement as the writing of new studies progresses. Thanks to the folks at AMG, especially Warren Baker, Trevor Overcash, Dale Anderson, Phillip Rogers, and Rick Steele. Special thanks to Debbie Bates, Linda Gail Shepherd, and Becky Autry, who assisted us with research and added a "woman's touch." Thanks to Robin Currier for her help with proofreading. Most of all, we remain grateful to the Lord Jesus, who continues to teach us and lead us in what it means to follow Him with a whole heart.

 THE AUTHORS

Wayne Barber

WAYNE BARBER is the director and keynote speaker for To Live is Christ Ministries, headquartered in Reno, Nevada. A renowned national and international conference ministry speaker, the primary goal of Wayne's ministry is in spreading the message of "the sufficiency of Christ." People around the world connect with Wayne's unique ability to make God's Word come alive through his honest and open "real-life" experiences. Wayne has authored or co-authored several books, and his most recent book, *The Rest of Grace*, was published in 1998. He also authors a regular column in AMG's *Pulpit Helps* monthly magazine. For eighteen years he served as the Senior Pastor-Teacher of Woodland Park Baptist Church, in Chattanooga, Tennessee, and for many of those years in Chattanooga, Wayne co-taught with noted author Kay Arthur of Precept Ministries and has studied under Dr. Spiros Zodhiates, one of the world's leading Greek scholars. Wayne and his wife Diana have two grown children and now live in Reno, Nevada.

Rick Shepherd

Richard L. Shepherd has been engaged in some form of ministry for more than twenty years, focusing on areas of teaching, discipleship, and prayer. He has served in churches in Alabama, Florida, Texas, and Tennessee and now serves as Director of Prayer and Spiritual Awakening with the Florida Baptist Convention. For nearly seventeen years (1983–2000), Rick served as an associate pastor at Woodland Park Baptist Church in Chattanooga, Tennessee. The Lord's ministry has taken him to several countries, including Haiti, Romania, Ukraine, Moldova, Italy, Israel, England, and Greece, where he has been involved in training pastors, church leaders, and congregations. Rick has also lectured on college and seminary campuses. He graduated with honors from the University of Mobile and holds a Master of Divinity and a Ph.D. from Southwestern Baptist Theological Seminary in Fort Worth, Texas. He and his wife Linda Gail have four children and make their home in Jacksonville, Florida.

Eddie Rasnake

Eddie Rasnake met Christ in 1976 as a freshman in college. He graduated with honors from East Tennessee State University in 1980. He and his wife, Michele, served for nearly seven years on the staff of Campus Crusade for Christ. Their first assignment was the University of Virginia, and while there they also started a Campus Crusade ministry at James Madison University. Eddie then served four years as campus director of the Campus Crusade ministry at the University of Tennessee. In 1989, Eddie left Campus Crusade to join Wayne Barber at Woodland Park Baptist Church as the Associate Pastor of Discipleship and Training. He has been ministering in Eastern Europe in the role of equipping local believers for more than a decade and has published materials in Albanian, Greek, Italian, Romanian, and Russian. Eddie serves on the boards of directors of the Center for Christian Leadership in Tirana, Albania, and the Bible Training Center in Eleuthera, Bahamas. He also serves as chaplain for the Chattanooga Lookouts (Cincinnati Reds AA affiliate) baseball team. Eddie and his wife Michele live in Chattanooga, Tennessee with their four children.

AMG
INTERNATIONAL

With operations of ministry in over 50 countries, AMG stands for Advancing the Ministries of the Gospel. Since 1942, AMG International has operated on the premise that God works primarily through the local church, and through individual Christians. Therefore AMG is dedicated to helping advance the gospel both locally and worldwide. Some areas of AMG's worldwide ministry include: missionary outreach, child care facilities, hospitals and clinics devoted to helping the poor, orphanages, church planting, training national workers, and Christian publishing.

Further information concerning AMG International can be obtained by calling 1-800-251-7206, or by writing us at: AMG International, 6815 Shallowford Road, Chattanooga, TN, 37421.

Our internet address is:
www.amginternational.org

Preface

Women are important to the plan of God. This may seem like an unnecessary statement of the obvious, yet often this important message gets clouded by our culture. There are even those in the body of Christ that so promote an imbalanced view of submission, that they leave little room for women to do anything in the service of God except take care of the nursery. Yet God makes it clear that women are important to Him

In Genesis 1:26–28, when the Trinity initiated the creation of mankind, we read, *"Then God said, 'Let us make man in Our image, according to Our likeness; and let THEM rule over the fish of the sea and over every creeping thing that creeps on the earth.' And God created man in His own image, and blessed them, and God said to THEM, 'Be fruitful and multiply, and fill the earth, and subdue it; and rule over the fish of the sea and over the birds of the sky, and over every living thing that moves on the earth'"* [emphasis added] In the plan of God, it takes both male and female to reflect His image.

[handwritten margin notes: ☐ Our Represents the Trinity ☐ Them represents man & woman]

It was Miriam, the sister of Moses, who ministered alongside him and was called a prophetess. God used the woman Rahab to save the lives of the two spies Joshua sent into Canaan. During the dismal period of the Judges, it was Deborah who God used in a mighty way to deliver His people. Young Esther was God's chosen agent to save all the Jews from extermination. God uses women, plain and simple.

Jesus affirmed women in His public ministry. He reached out to the Samaritan woman at the well, and then used her to take the gospel to a whole village. He rescued the woman caught in adultery from unjust justice. He gave women a prominence in His life and ministry that the culture did not. In fact, His public ministry was financed in large part by a group of women.

What is the message from all of this? Women are important to God. You may be asking, "how can three men write a book of Bible studies about women?" The fact is, what you will learn in the pages of this book is not about what we know of women, but what God's word has to say regarding women. Our goal is to take you to the word, specifically those passages that introduce us to the prominent female characters of the Bible, and let you see for yourself what God has to say. Through these women of Scripture He has a message for men and women alike about what it means to follow God. It is our prayer that this study will help you to follow Him more closely.

Following Him,

WAYNE A. BARBER   RICHARD L. SHEPHERD

Wayne A. Barber   *Richard L. Shepherd*

EDDIE RASNAKE

Eddie Rasnake

Table of Contents

THIS MAP IS PROVIDED TO ASSIST THE READER IN LOCATING THE VARIOUS BIBLICAL CITIES
MENTIONED THOUGHOUT THIS BOOK

Eve

FOLLOWING GOD AFTER FAILURE

Although she is the mother of us all, we know very little about this "first lady," Eve. She was the final creative act of the first week on earth, the complementary companion for Adam, the first man. She resembled Adam enough for companionship, yet she was very different in a complementary way. Her strengths blended with his so that together they were something neither could be separately. In fact, Genesis 1 shows us that it took both Adam and Eve to accurately reflect the image of God.

But all did not end well in the Garden of Eden. Through attacking Eve's contentment, Satan was able to incite rebellion in mankind and sin entered into the world. Eve led her husband into direct violation of God's revealed will to them, and as a result, mankind was banished from paradise. As we look at Eve this week, we will see a very human portrait of falling into sin, and the process of picking up the pieces of faith. Through her, we will see our faith in a fresh way.

> "... From any tree of the garden you may eat freely; but from the tree of the knowledge of good and evil you shall not eat, for in the day that you eat from it you shall surely die."
>
> Genesis 2:16, 17

THE SIX DAYS OF CREATION
WHERE DOES EVE FIT?

Day One	Day Two	Day Three	Day Four	Day Five	Day Six
GENESIS 1:1–5	GENESIS 1:6–8	GENESIS 1:9–13	GENESIS 1:14–19	GENESIS 1:20–23	GENESIS 1:24–31
God created the heavens and the earth God created light Separation of light from darkness	Creation of the sky Division of the waters	Dry land created Gathered the waters into seas Vegetation created	Creation of the sun, moon, and stars Separation of day and night	Sea creatures and birds created	Adam created in God's image, and established as ruler of God's Creation God created Garden of Eden Land creatures (cattle, beasts, creeping things) created God created Eve

2/22/03

CREATED FOR A PURPOSE

> **Eve was created to help Adam fulfill God's purpose for mankind. He couldn't do it alone.**

Eve was created to fill a unique and special role in creation. Not only was she to minister *with* Adam in his assignments in the garden, but she was also given specific ministries *to* Adam. She was his "help-mate." She was designed to assist and to complete him. We will see in the days ahead that some of her responsibilities changed after the fall. Today we want to briefly view Eve's purposes in the Garden before the fall, and look at life in Eden.

📖 In Genesis 1 we have an overview look at mankind in the Garden, and then in chapter 2 we see more of the details. Read Genesis 1:26–28 and write three things you learn there about God's purposes for mankind.

1) _He was to reflect God's image_

2) _He was to rule over creation_

3) _He was to reproduce_

In verse 26 we see that God created mankind first of all to be like Him, to *reflect* His image in creation. (Note that God is mentioned in the plural, probably a reference to the whole of the Trinity's involvement in creation.) The second purpose we see listed here is to *rule* over creation. Man is positioned as the pinnacle of creation, and is given authority over all the earth. In verse 27 we see that it takes both male and female to fulfill God's purposes. Then in verse 28 we see the third purpose: They are to *reproduce*—be fruitful and multiply (raise children who will also reflect God's image), and "fill" the earth. The task of ruling over creation was too great for them to do alone.

📖 Not only does God have a purpose for Adam and Eve, He also has a plan and purpose for the rest of creation. Look at Genesis 1:28–31 and write down everything you learn there about God's purpose for the rest of creation.

They are to subdue the earth. All
the plants are to be man's food

God instructs Adam and Eve that the earth is to be "subdued." The Hebrew word has the idea of being conquered and brought into subjection. In other words, the earth is to *serve* mankind. In verses 29 and 30 we see that all the plants are to be food for man and the animals. This does not mean man must be a vegetarian, for in Genesis 9:3, Noah is commanded to eat animals as well. What tremendous commentary verse 31 holds, revealing that the plan was "good" in God's sight!

📖 In Genesis 2 we see further specifics being given to God's unique purpose for mankind and also for Eve herself. Look at Genesis 2:18–22. Write out in your own words God's purpose for Eve listed there.

She was to be Adam's helper

Did You Know?

DID GOD INTEND FOR MANKIND TO BE VEGETARIANS?

Looking only at Genesis 1—2 it would seem that mankind's diet was limited to vegetables. This was apparently the case until after the Flood, but two things argue against that being God's permanent intent. From doctrine, in Genesis 9:3 we see God instruct Noah to begin eating meat. From design, we see that God made mankind by creating them with the teeth of omnivores. He gave them the molars of herbivores (vegetable eaters) and the incisors (front teeth) of carnivores (meat eaters).

_____

_____

Adam was not complete by himself. What an amazing statement it is here that even in the perfection of Eden before the fall there could be something that was "not good." What a contrast with the continuous refrain of creation up to this point; seven times in chapter 1 we read *"and God saw that it was good"* (1:4, 1:10, 1:12, 1:18, 1:21, 1:25, 1:31). But it was not good for man to be alone. He was created with need. He was created incomplete so that God could complete him with Eve. She was to be *"a helper suitable for him."*

Looking at Genesis 2:22–24, what principles about the marriage relationship do you see in Adam and Eve?

Eve was part of Adam. She was "bone of his bone and flesh of his flesh" – they were one. When couples marry they are to leave their parents and become one.

Some practical principles about relationships we find here are: **a)** that God brought Eve to Adam (it wasn't his job to find a mate); **b)** that, unlike the animals, she corresponded to him *("bone of my bones, flesh of my flesh")*; **c)** that their relationship necessitated him "leaving" father and mother (obviously looking forward to future generations since Adam had no father and mother); **d)** marriage requires "cleaving" (the Hebrew word implies pursuit and attachment, "to be joined by commitment"); **e)** marriage should result in oneness ("one flesh" points to the physical body, but in principle would include all that a person is—mind, emotions, will, etc.); and **f)** marriage results in nakedness without shame (again, this would go beyond just the physical side).

TEMPTATION IN THE GARDEN

One can only imagine what life was like in the Garden before sin. Adam and Eve had tasks to perform, but work was not by the sweat of the brow. They not only enjoyed intimacy with each other that was unstained by sin, but more importantly, they enjoyed unhindered intimacy with God. But Eve entered into a discussion with the serpent, and, through being deceived, she gave in to temptation, and all of that changed. Today we want to look at how Eve was tempted, and see what we can learn about our own temptations.

In Genesis 3:1 we see Eve engaging in a conversation with the serpent. Why, from what the text says about what he is like and what he does, is that a bad idea?

Because Satan was crafty (he was a liar and a deceiver) and he questioned God's will.

Satan succeeds in getting Eve to doubt the truthfulness of God's word and the goodness of His motives.

The text reveals two negative realities about Satan: **what he is like** – *"more crafty than any beast of the field, . . ."* and **what he does**—he calls into question the revealed will of God. He asks, *"Indeed, has God said. . .?"* He also exaggerates the limitations that God's will imposed on mankind. He misquotes God as saying, *"You shall not eat from any tree of the garden."*

📖 Compare Genesis 3:1–6 with each of the passages below, writing down what you learn about Satan's activities.

2 Corinthians 11:3

Satan is the deceiver. He operates by deception

2 Corinthians 11:12–15

He disguises himself as an Angel of light and all his servants masquerade as servants of righteousness.

1 Timothy 2:14

Eve ate the fruit and gave it to Adam - but he also had a choice - and he also was disobedient

We see in 2 Corinthians 11:3 that the serpent **"deceived** *Eve by his craftiness."* This idea is also picked up on by Paul in 1 Timothy 2:14 where he says that she was *"quite* **deceived."** Satan (along with his workers) operates through deception and disguise. In fact, we are told in 2 Corinthians 11:14 that he disguises himself as an angel of light. When dealing with an enemy who doesn't deal in truth, one must be especially careful to not take anything at face value. Eve should have let God's words be her authority, but as soon as Satan tricked her into calling what God said into question, it was only a matter of time before she went her own independent way. When we make ourselves the judge of whether God's words are true, transgression is inevitable.

📖 As you look closely at Eve's responses to Satan's questions, it looks at first like she accurately represents God's will, but if you look more closely you will discover some important differences. Compare how Eve quotes God in Genesis 3:2–3 with what God actually said in Genesis 2:16–17. On the chart below, mark the differences you see and write your observations on what she adds and what she leaves out.

HOW EVE QUOTED GOD (GENESIS 3:2–3)	WHAT GOD SAID (GENESIS 2:16–17)
From the fruit of the trees of the garden <u>we may eat</u>	<u>From any tree</u> of the garden <u>you may eat freely</u>
but from the fruit of the <u>tree which is in the middle of the garden</u>	but from the <u>tree of the knowledge of good and evil</u>
God has said, 'You shall not eat from it or *<u>touch it</u>	<u>you shall not eat</u>
lest you die.'	for in the day that you eat from it you shall surely die.

✱ Eve added this - God never said this

It is incredibly revealing when we look closely at the subtle but significant differences in how Eve quotes God compared to what He actually said. God had actually instructed that they could eat *"From **any** tree . . ."* and that they *"**may eat** freely."* Both statements emphasize the liberty of the Garden. Eve, by leaving these out, seems to be minimizing or making light of her liberties. God's sole restriction in the Garden was specific—they were not to eat *"from the tree of the knowledge of good and evil."* Eve doesn't focus on what the tree is, but on where it is. She avoids the reminder that the tree is associated with evil. In restricting them, God had only said, *"you shall not eat."* Eve adds the phrase, *"or touch it,"* and in so doing, seems to maximize the restrictions or limitations God had placed on them in the Garden. Finally, Eve quotes the consequence as *"lest you die."* She leaves out the term *"surely,"* and the phrase *"in the day that you eat from it,"* apparently making light of the certainty and immediacy of the consequences. When we shade God's truth just a little bit, it can have disastrous impact.

TRUTH OR CONSEQUENCES

When Eve began her conversation with the serpent, she had no idea how far–reaching the consequences would be. Likewise, we often treat our own temptations with equal disregard. We fail to realize that sin has consequences that reach for generations. Every time I sin someone else is affected. They may be affected directly through some consequence of the sin, or they may be affected indirectly through the loss of the ministry and life I would have given if I had continued walking with God. We learn painfully from Eve that talking with the devil and walking with the Lord do not go hand in hand.

If we stray from the truth of God's Word, there are always consequences.

📖 Looking at Genesis 3:4–5, How does Satan cast doubt on the things God had said concerning the forbidden tree?

First he says: "You surely shall not die." - he suggests that God wasn't truthful w/ them then he says they will be like God suggesting that God's motives aren't good

Satan calls into question two significant things in these verses. First, by saying, *"You surely shall not die,"* he casts doubt on the truthfulness of what God said. Second, by saying, *"For God knows that in the day you eat from it your eyes will be opened, and you will be like God, knowing good and evil,"* Satan invites Eve to doubt the goodness of God's motives. He suggests that God is withholding something good from Eve.

Every time I sin, someone else is affected. Either they share in the bad that results, or they are robbed of the good that would have come if I had not sinned. . . .

📖 Compare Genesis 3:6 with 1 John 2:16 and identify the parallels in Satan's temptation.

"The lust of the flesh — When the woman saw the tree was good for food

"The lust of the eyes" — and that it was a delight to the eyes

> *"For all that is in the world, the lust of the flesh and the lust of the eyes and the boastful pride of life, is not from the Father, but is from the world."*
>
> **1 John 2:16**

"The boastful pride of life" — <u>And that the tree was desirable to make one wise</u>

Looking closely at Genesis 3:6 in the light of 1 John, the parallel is obvious. The statement, *"When the woman saw that the tree was good for food,"* would seem to correlate with *"the lust of the flesh."* The phrase, *"and that it was a delight to the eyes,"* connects directly with *"the lust of the eyes."* Finally, *"and that the tree was desirable to make one wise,"* appears to be the same issue as *"the boastful pride of life."* It would seem that all temptation could be traced to these three enticements (see also Jesus' temptation in the wilderness in Matthew 4). The sin in the Garden was more than eating forbidden fruit, it was disobeying the revealed Word of God, believing the lies of the enemy, and Adam and Eve placing their own will above God's will.

📖 Where, according to Genesis 3:6, was Adam during Eve's temptation?

<u>He was with her</u>

The text tells us that Eve, after eating of the fruit, *". . . gave also to her husband **with her**, and he ate"* (emphasis added). It would appear that Adam was with her all the time, but said nothing. This would make him just as guilty as she was, not only because he ate of the fruit also, but because he failed to fulfill his leadership role in the relationship.

Eve **DAY FOUR**

The main reason for consequences to sin is not the sin itself, but our unwillingness to deal with that sin God's way.

A FLESHLY RESPONSE TO FAILURE

The problem of the Garden begins with the forbidden fruit, but it does not end there. In fact, it would seem from the continuation of the story that the consequences of Genesis 3 have as much to do with how Adam and Eve responded to their failure as they do the failure itself. As we see in the difference between king David and king Saul, having a heart after God's heart is not the absence of failure, but the willingness to deal with failure in a biblical way. Today we want to examine more closely the problems with how Adam and Eve dealt with their failure.

📖 Look at Genesis 3:7–8 and identify Adam and Eve's first approach to dealing with their sin.

<u>They recognized they were naked & covered themselves w/ fig leaves & hid from God</u>

We see in verse 7 that Adam and Eve start by hiding from each other. They try to cover their nakedness with fig leaves. Next, in verse 8, they try to hide from God among the trees of the Garden (where they should have stayed in the first place). It is our natural flesh response to try to hide when we sin. Pride never wants to be found out. Humility, on the other hand, is quick to take responsibility for failure. In Adam and Eve we see our own tendency to hide when we sin. It is this very tendency that alienates us from other believers and from God, and which gets in the way of putting the sin behind us.

📖 What do God's questions to Adam and Eve in Genesis 3:9–11 reveal about His method of confronting our sins?

He comes to us hoping we will admit our sin

Perhaps the most profound lesson here is that God comes to man. We see here that God calls out to Adam asking, *"Where are you?"* Of course, God knows where Adam is, but He wants Adam to admit where he is and why he is there. It is an invitation to repent. God comes *"in the cool of the day."* He waits until the sin is done and there is time to reflect. He comes personally (*"Where are **you**?"*). He also comes with accountability. He will not let Adam and Eve succeed in their hiding. He comes in judgment, but with it there is a mingling of mercy, for He promises to send a deliverer. Clearly from the narrative here, God holds Adam more accountable than Eve even though she was the first to eat of the forbidden fruit. Failing to lead rightly is sin.

📖 Look at where Adam and Eve place the blame for their sin. What can we learn from this about our own tendencies in dealing with sin?

Adam blamed Eve, Eve blamed the serpent
we tend to blame others instead
of being accountable for our sin

We see in Adam's response that with one statement he tries to shift the blame for his sin to both Eve and God. He says, *"that woman* (blaming Eve) *that You gave me . . ."* (blaming God). Eve takes the same approach, for she tries to shift the blame onto Satan (*"the serpent deceived me . . ."*). Our human tendency is to blame someone else, instead of taking responsibility for our sins.

📖 Briefly list all the consequences of sin that are found here in Genesis 3:14–24.

To the serpent: _You will crawl on your belly and eat the dust the rest of your life. (enmity between the serpent & Man)_

To the woman: _Painful childbirth under your husband's rule_

To Adam and the ground: _Hard labor would be required to grow food & the ground would produce thorns_

To the animals: _Animals were immediately killed to produce clothing_

To mankind: _He was banished from the garden_

The Consequences of Man's First Sin:

To the Serpent
- ✓ To crawl in the dust.
- ✓ Enmity between him and mankind.
- ✓ Ultimate judgment (the *seed* will crush his head).

✏ *Did You Know?*

❓ **THE CURSE UPON CREATION**

All of creation suffered consequences when Adam and Eve rebelled against the Lord. Romans 8:20, 22 tells us, *"For the creation was subjected to futility . . . for we know that the whole creation groans and suffers the pains of childbirth together until now."* Fortunately, when the Lord returns he will lift that curse.

To the Woman
- ✓ Pain in childbirth
- ✓ Subjection (would always be under husband's rule)

To Adam and all of Creation
- ✓ Hard labor and sweat would now be required to grow food.
- ✓ The ground would now grow thorns and thistles.
- ✓ Ultimate physical death for both mankind and the animal world. (Animals were immediately killed to provide clothing for Adam and Eve.)
- ✓ Expulsion from the Garden of Eden into a harsh and forbidding world.
- ✓ The consequence of a sinful nature.

📖 Compare how Adam and Eve covered their sin in Genesis 3:7 with how God dealt with it in Genesis 3:21. What observations can you make?

First time where it is clear that there is no remission of sin w/o the shedding of blood (the animal which provided garments for them)

✳ In Genesis 3:21 we have the first suggestion of animal sacrifice in the Bible. The *"garments of skin"* God clothed them with cost some animals their lives. Though the text does not say, it appears that God had already revealed to Adam and Eve that an innocent animal must die for them to live. Without the shedding of blood there is no remission of sin (see Hebrews 9:22). ✳

> "...One may almost say, all things are cleansed with blood, and without shedding of blood there is no forgiveness."
>
> Hebrews 9:22

Eve | **DAY FIVE**

FOR ME TO FOLLOW GOD

In First Corinthians 10:11 we are told, *"Now these things happened to them as an example, and they were written for our instruction, upon whom the ends of the ages have come."* We must recognize that the biographical sketch of Eve we find in Scripture is not simply a matter of history, but is written for our instruction. This means her life makes demands on our lives. We must be willing to ask the hard question, "How does this apply to me today?"

Eve was created to help Adam fulfill God's purpose for mankind. She was to be his helpmate for life. Together they would reflect the image of God to all creation, reproduce that image by filling the earth with their descendants, and fulfill God's plan for mankind by ruling over the created realm. From her life we can ascertain that Christianity is a team effort. There are no "Lone Rangers" in the body of Christ!

 As you think about your own life, take a few minutes to evaluate how you are doing at fulfilling God's purposes for mankind.

Reflecting the Image of God . . .
Like the world ⬅ 1   2   3   ④   5 ➡ Like God

Reproducing a Godly Heritage . . .
Separate faith from
family and friends ⬅ 1   2   3   ④   5 ➡ Passing the faith on to others

Ruling over Creation . . .

Serving creation   Faithful steward
or abusing creation   ← 1   2   ③   4   5 → of creation

Satan was successful in getting Eve to doubt the truthfulness of God's word and the goodness of His motives. What are some ways that you are tempted to doubt the truthfulness of what God has said in the Bible?

I don't doubt anything that the Lord says in the Bible

What are some things that tempt you to doubt the goodness of God's motives toward you?

When bad things happen I often feel discouraged. But I know that God is sovereign & has allowed it to accomplish His purposes & that He loves me and does nothing contrary to his nature.

APPLY If we stray from the truth of God's Word, there are always consequences. Take a few minutes to see if you can think of some of the consequences of sin that you have seen either in your life or in the lives of those you know.

Marrying an unbeliever

We saw from Eve's experience that the main reason for consequences from our sin is not just the sin itself, but our unwillingness to deal with that sin God's way. What are some ways you have seen this personally or with others?

If we are wise, we will learn from Eve's mistakes.

It was through our great, great, many times great grandparents, Adam and Eve, that we had our introduction into sin. The rebellious tendencies of our nature have their beginning with them. Yet as we have seen this week, there is much we can learn from their mistakes. If we are wise we will learn from how they made their mistakes and guard ourselves from repeating them.

Spend some time with the Lord in prayer right now.

 Lord You have created me in Your image—You desire to be seen in me. Yet so many times I choose to go my own independent way. I choose my will over Yours. Guard me, I pray, from mishandling Your truth—from making too much of the limitations Your Word places on me, and too little on the freedoms You give. Help me to trust the truthfulness of everything You say and the goodness of all your motives toward me. Help me to look to Your Word for answers when the enemy sends temptation my way. Most of all, when I do blow it, help me not to hide my sin or blame others for it, but to come back to you and make things right. Thank you for Your love, Your grace, Your forgiveness, and most of all for Your empowerment. Help me to walk with you. Amen.

Take a few moments to write down a prayer of application from the things that you have learned this week.

> Father
> Help me to always accept
> responsibility when I sin.
> And help me come to
> you quickly and admit
> my sin and ask for
> your forgiveness.
>
> Thank you Jesus
>
> Amen

Notes

Notes

Sarah

A WOMAN OF FAITH

Someone once said, "Behind every great man, there is a great woman." Though we don't know all we would like to know about Sarah, Scripture has more to say about her than it does almost any other woman. Her husband, Abraham, is the father of the faithful, but she too is a model of faith in God. Like Abraham, she was of the Chaldeans, whom Scripture calls a "fierce and impetuous people" (Habakkuk 1:6). The Chaldeans eventually became known as the Babylonians (modern day Iraq). She married Abraham before the journey to Canaan began (Genesis 11:31). They were not Israelites, for Israel (Jacob), their grandson had not yet been born. They were not Jews; that name would come from Judah, their great-grandson. Yet, God called them and they obeyed, and through them He established a new people—the people of God. As we look at Sarah's life this week, we see, as we did with Abraham, a flawed and imperfect pursuit of God. Yet we see a faith great enough to make it into the Old Testament "hall of fame" in Hebrews chapter 11. And we will see lessons in her life that will help to guide our own attempts to follow God.

In Sarah's life, as with Abraham, we see a flawed and imperfect pursuit of God. Yet we see a faith great enough to make it into the Old Testament "hall of fame."

WHERE DOES SHE FIT?

2200BC	1950	1700	1450	1200	950	700	450	100
SARAH 2155–2028		MIRIAM 1533?–1405				Daniel 619–534?		MARY and MARTHA 10BC?–60AD?
		DEBORAH 1300?–1200?		Solomon 991–931		ESTHER 504?–450?		
		Judges Rule 1385–1051		David 1041–971				
						Nehemiah 480?–400?		MARY, Mother of Jesus 20BC–60AD?
Jacob 2005–1858		Joshua 1495–1385		RUTH 1135?–1050?				
Isaac 2065–1885		Moses 1525–1405		HANNAH 1135?–1050?	VIRTUOUS WOMAN Prov. 31			
Abraham 2165–1990		RAHAB 1445?–1385?		Samuel 1105–1022				Jesus Christ 4BC?–30AD?

FOLLOWING IN FAITH

Sarah, like most women of her culture was a follower. She followed her husband to Canaan, then to Egypt, and back to Canaan once again. She also followed her husband's advice. When Peter taught on the subject of a wife's submission to her husband, he used Sarah as his positive example:

> *"In the same way, you wives, be submissive to your own husbands so that even if any of them are disobedient to the word, they may be won without a word by the behavior of their wives, as they observe your chaste and respectful behavior. And let not your adornment be merely external—braiding the hair, and wearing gold jewelry, or putting on dresses; but let it be the hidden person of the heart, with the imperishable quality of a gentle and quiet spirit, which is precious in the sight of God. For in this way in former times the holy women also, who hoped in God, used to adorn themselves, being submissive to their own husbands. Thus Sarah obeyed Abraham, calling him lord, and you have become her children if you do what is right without being frightened by any fear."—1 Peter 3:1–6*

Although we may look negatively from the vantage point of our culture at Sarah's submission and Abraham's authority over her, we still have much to learn about trusting God with the circumstances of our lives. Today we will look at how God dealt with Sarah when she submitted to Abraham even when he was wrong.

Once Abraham and Sarah made it to Canaan, they discovered that there was a famine in the land (Genesis 12:10). So they went down to Egypt to sojourn where there was food. Take a look at Genesis 12:11–20 and answer the questions below.

What did Abraham ask Sarah to do?

_____

_____

Was Sarah wrong to do what Abraham asked?

_____

_____

Did Abraham's plan protect Sarah from harm?

_____

_____

How did God take care of Sarah?

_____

_____

We see in the downward turn to Egypt the fledgling nature of Abraham's faith. Instead of trusting God to protect them in Egypt, he told a half-truth—that Sarah was his sister. She was his half-sister (Genesis 20:12), but by

Did You Know?

WHAT ABOUT "WOMEN'S LIB?"

Most people don't recognize the fact that Jesus was a great liberator of women. When Christ came on the scene, women were hardly more than possessions. They had no rights or identity. Jesus valued women in a way unusual to their society. The biblical directive for wives to submit to their husbands is often taught without the balancing truth of the husband's responsibility to sacrificially and unconditionally love his wife, and to live with her in an understanding way. It speaks not of her being of less value, but of her being given a different job description. The teachings of the New Testament, rather than being repressive, give women many more rights and much more value than ever before.

neglecting to say that she was also his wife, he put her in harm's way. It is worth mentioning that of all the turns in Abraham's journey, the turn from Canaan to Egypt was the first time Abraham neglected to build an altar to seek the Lord. Perhaps Abraham was wrong to go to Egypt. Certainly he was wrong to lie and to ask Sarah to lie for him. But was Sarah wrong? Peter did not think so. As already mentioned in 1 Peter 3:1–6, Peter uses Sarah's obedience to Abraham as an example to the church. God did not hold Sarah accountable for Abraham's mistakes, only for her obedience to Abraham. God honored her submissive heart and supernaturally protected Sarah from harm by warning Pharaoh.

TRYING TO HELP OUT GOD

Sarah was a sharer in the promise to Abraham. She too, longed for the fulfillment of God's promise of an heir. Genesis 11:30 tells us the tragic words that Sarah was barren. No cry echoes so deep as that of a woman whose longings for a child go unanswered. To the people of Sarah's day, her barrenness was a matter of shame—an evidence not of God's hand being on her marriage, but against it. As we look at Sarah's mistake regarding Hagar, we must not judge her too harshly, for the 20/20 vision of hindsight we enjoy was not her's to draw on.

📖 Take a look at Genesis 16:1–2. What was Sarah's idea, and where do you think she got it?

_____

_____

_____

_____

God does not want our help, He wants our obedience— Sarah's mistake is in not seeking God's plan.

It had been a long time since Abraham heard from God. Verse 3 seems to indicate they had been waiting ten years. The biological clock was ticking. Sarah was at this time in her seventies and had given up on having a child herself. So she suggested that Abraham have a child using her maid as a surrogate mother. This was not a new idea. It was a common practice in the Chaldean region they had come from. But it was not God's design. Monogamy was His plan from the very beginning.

📖 As you read the account of Hagar's pregnancy (Genesis 16:3–16), write down the changes in her attitude toward Sarah.

_____

_____

_____

"... and Abram listened to the voice of Sarai."
Genesis 16:2

In verse four we see that once Hagar is pregnant, her boss is _"despised in her sight."_ Later in verse 9 we begin to see a hint of what the problem was. The angel of the Lord instructed Hagar to return to Sarah and submit to her authority. Apparently once Hagar was bearing Abraham's child, she began to see herself as Abraham's wife and as superior to Sarah. Sarah very quickly regretted ever suggesting her idea concerning Hagar to Abraham.

Looking at Genesis 16:5 and 6, write what you see there about how Sarah handled the situation, and give your opinion on the right and wrong aspects of her response.

_____

_____

_____

_____

When Hagar began to flaunt her pregnancy in Sarah's face she was incensed and complained to Abraham. He had followed Sarah's lead so far in this mess, and he wasn't about to change now. He basically says in verse 6, "Do whatever you want to her." In her anger, Sarah treated Hagar so harshly that she fled. Sarah was not wrong for feeling hurt by Hagar's attitude, but she was wrong in how she dealt with it. James 1:20 states, *"for the anger of man does not achieve the righteousness of God."* Whenever we respond out of our anger we respond wrongly. Again we see Sarah reacting without seeking God.

Read the rest of Genesis 16 and record how the situation was resolved.

_____

_____

_____

After an encounter with the "angel of the Lord," Hagar returned and submitted to Sarah's authority. The child she carried was born and named "Ishmael." This child was not a child of blessing, however. He grew up to be *"a wild donkey of a man"* (Genesis 16:12). Everyone in Abraham's household had to adjust to this wild child's presence.

Sarah DAY THREE

Sarah struggles with the challenge of believing God or believing her circumstances.

HELP MY UNBELIEF

For thirteen years after the birth of Ishmael, Abraham and Sarah heard nothing from God. The heavens were silent. But finally God broke the silence when Abraham was ninety-nine years old. God restated His promise, and then the stage was set. In fact, God in His perfect timing and infinite wisdom had set the stage in such a way that He would get the greatest glory—He had made it impossible apart from Him. When the child finally came there would be no doubt who did it. The challenge that faced Abraham and Sarah here is significant though. While what they were hearing from God pointed in one direction, their circumstances pointed the opposite way. Humanly speaking, producing a child at such an old age is an impossibility. Like the father whose demon-possessed son the disciples could not help, Sarah's cry is, *"Lord, I do believe. . . . help my unbelief"* (Mark 9:24).

Today we want to look at Sarah's response when the promise was given again. Read Genesis 18:1–8 to get an idea of the context, and then look at 18:9–10 and identify what the message is for Abraham and Sarah.

_____

_____

_____

_____

_____

We see from Genesis 18 and 19 that apparently the three men of 18:1 are the *"angel of the Lord"* and the two angels who would rescue Lot from Sodom (19:1). Most theologians interpret the term "angel of the Lord" to mean the pre-incarnate Christ—verse 13 indicates it is "the Lord" speaking. Their message is that in a year Sarah will be pregnant. Like any clever busybody, Sarah was eavesdropping outside the tent and heard all that was said.

📖 Looking at 18:11–12, write what you learn about the circumstances and how Sarah responded to this message from God.

_____

_____

_____

Verse 11 tells us that Abraham and Sarah were very old—in fact, she was past childbearing (literally, "past the manner of women"—she has been through menopause). Abraham was ninety-nine years old and Sarah was eighty-nine.

Circumstantially, the promise of God looked impossible. It is not surprising that Sarah laughed. She says, "can two old people like us have pleasure?" In other words, she is saying, "We are too old even to make love—how could we have a child?"

📖 Now look at Genesis 18:13–15. What do these verses reveal about God and about Sarah?

_____

_____

_____

_____

When Sarah laughed in disbelief, God heard. This truth reflects the Lord's omniscience. He knows everything about us. Nothing in our hearts is hidden from Him. Even though we may have been taught this as a child, we often don't live our lives as if it is true. We also see here a very human portrait of Sarah. Not only did she laugh in disbelief, but when confronted she also lied about it. Yet this did not change God's plan and purpose. He affirmed His plan and made it clear that Sarah's untruth was not ignored.

📖 As you read Genesis 18:13–15 again, what is significant about the phrase, *"... at the appointed time..."*?

_____

_____

_____

Word Study
HOW DID ABRAM AND SARAI BECOME ABRAHAM AND SARAH?

It was God who changed Abram's name to Abraham. The name "Abram" literally means *"exalted father"* which must have been painful to a man who was childless until he was eighty-six. "Abraham" means *"father of a multitude."* God also changes "Sarai" (*"my princess"*) to "Sarah" (*"princess"*). At a casual glance, the change of Sarah's name seems much less significant, but there is a point to the change. No longer is Sarah to be Abraham's princess only. Now he will share her with a family that will multiply beyond belief.

"Is anything too difficult for the Lord? At the appointed time I will return to you, at this time next year, and Sarah shall have a son."
Genesis 18:14

What an awesome thought it is that God had appointed a time for Isaac to be born. He was not sitting in heaven waiting to see what Abraham and Sarah would do., but the child of promise arrived just when He planned: *"at the appointed time."*

📖 As we finish today's study, read Hebrews 11:11. We have seen Abraham's faith applauded, but this verse is a fitting balance, showing us the conclusion from the vantage point of Sarah. What does this verse reveal about what Sarah did and what the result was?

_____

_____

_____

Hebrews 11:11 shows us that Sarah *"considered Him faithful who had promised."* She was not leaning on Abraham's faith; she had faith of her own. And as a result, she was given the ability to conceive a child well beyond the proper time of life. Both Abraham and Sarah had to exercise faith in order for a child to be born, and they had to take action on what God had said. Theirs was no immaculate conception. They had to have relations in order to get pregnant, and that took faith. Faith in its purest form is simply taking God at His word—that what He says will happen really will happen, that what He says He will do, He really will do—and acting accordingly.

Sarah DAY FOUR

Faith Mixed with Flesh

Past faith is no guarantee of future victory—every day we must trust God.

There is a fundamental reality each of us must wrestle with: we cannot live today on yesterday's faith. Each day brings new challenges and new choices. Each day we must decide if we will walk in faith or in flesh. Today we will look at some smudges on the portrait of Sarah's faith. Although we will see some mistakes, we should be encouraged that the Scriptures do not succumb to the temptation toward hero worship. God's word paints these portraits of faith in a very honest fashion, complete with mistakes and messes. Yet it is this honesty which insures these portraits can minister to us today. For failure is a reality in each of our lives, and seeing the mistakes of these saints of old should encourage us that when we fail we are not alone. It should also remind us that, once we have failed in an area, we are ever vulnerable to make that mistake again. We should never be surprised at what shows up in our lives when we choose not to walk by faith.

📖 Take a few minutes to read through the narrative in Genesis 20. Clearly Abraham has made the same mistake he made in Egypt (Genesis 12:10–20). Sadly, he did not lead in the direction of faith. But what was Sarah's part in this? Look at Abimelech's response to God in verse 5 and identify Sarah's role.

_____

_____

Both Abraham and Sarah could plead ignorance the first time, but not this time. They should have known better. They should have learned from the earlier mistake. Abraham led Sarah in the wrong direction, but her lie shows she was a willing participant as well. Clearly we see God's grace manifested in His supernatural protection of Abraham and Sarah—God intervened and did not allow Abimelech to touch Sarah. But this was God's doing, not Abraham's or Sarah's. Their lies, instead of protecting them, put Sarah in harm's way. Even when we are faithless, God remains faithful, for He cannot deny who He is (2 Timothy 2:13).

📖 Now take some time to read Genesis 21:1–8. Summarize the details of what occurs here, and compare the change in Sarah's laughter from 18:12 to 21:6.

_____

_____

_____

_____

_____

God did what He promised, and Sarah had her son. In obedience they named him Isaac, which means "laughter." Every time they called his name they were reminded of the laughter of unbelief, but the memory was not painful. In 21:6 we see that the laughter of unbelief had been turned to the laughter of joy and delight. You might say, "God had the last laugh." There is a point we must notice from the last two passages. In both we see that Sarah in her pursuit of God had followed the mistakes of her husband. When he lied (20:2), she lied (20:5). When he laughed in unbelief (17:17), she laughed in unbelief (18:12). The failures of those we follow can easily become our own failures if we are not careful.

📖 Let's look today at one more incident in Sarah's life. Read Genesis 21:9–13 and record how Sarah responds to Hagar and Ishmael after Isaac's birth.

_____

_____

_____

_____

It is difficult to interpret Sarah's actions at this point. In her dealings with Hagar and Ishmael, was she right or wrong? We have no commentary other than that God told Abraham to take her advice and cast them out. This does not mean that Sarah was completely right in all that she did. Clearly, Ishmael was wrong in what he did, and like his mother before him he had voiced his animosity toward Sarah. But even in this, we see God's instructive reminder of the folly of fleshly effort, for Ishmael was Sarah's idea.

We close out the story of Sarah in Genesis 23 where we are told that she lived one hundred and twenty-seven years. That means she had thirty-seven years with Isaac. She saw him grow up, and in him she could catch a glimpse of the promise of the future. She walked with God. She made mistakes as all of us do, but she saw God's grace, and she saw growth. She left behind a legacy of faith for us to follow.

Put Yourself In Their Shoes
WHICH DIRECTION ARE YOU TAKING?

As we look at Sarah's life, we see a life governed by choices that resulted in life-changing consequences, both good and bad. The good consequences in her life were results of her choices based on faith. However, bad consequences came to her when her decisions were motivated by the flesh. Are your choices in life based on your faith in God, or are they actually rooted in fleshly desires?

FLESH   FAITH

FOR ME TO FOLLOW GOD

Faith is a journey, a pursuit. It is not something we conquer all at once. It is a process of growth. In Sarah we see the reality that it is an imperfect pursuit. But we also see that God's grace is sufficient even for our mistakes (see 2 Corinthians 12:9). As we look at Sarah's journey of faith, we see much of ourselves. What makes her faith more amazing is that she did not have the benefit of the Word of God as we do now. Today we want to look at how we can apply the lessons from Sarah's life to our own faith.

One of the things we saw this week was that, for Sarah, faithfulness to God meant being faithful to Abraham. She had been placed in relationship to him and was accountable. Each life has accountable relationships, and some of those relationships are to those God has placed in authority over us. Our obedience to those in authority is important to God. This does not mean that we cannot point out when we think authority is wrong, but regardless, we are accountable to the authorities in our lives. When we try to determine if we think authority is right before we are willing to obey, we have placed ourselves as judge, and we are wrong.

APPLY Are there any authorities in your life that you are not submissive to?

_____

_____

_____

_____

_____

God does not want our help—He wants our obedience. Sarah made a mistake when she tried to help out God with a worldly plan. Can you think of a time you tried to help out God with your own plan instead of seeking Him for His plan?

_____

_____

_____

_____

What were the consequences?

_____

_____

_____

_____

When a child did not come in Sarah's timing, she began to doubt the promise of God. God kept Sarah waiting until a child was humanly impossible. At that point, Sarah struggled with the challenge of believing God or believing her circumstances.

If we are wise, we will learn from the lessons of Sarah.

APPLY Have you been there? Are there any situations in your life right now, where your circumstances seem to be saying one thing though God's Word says another?

_____

_____

_____

_____

_____

Sarah's life shows us that past faith is no guarantee of future victory. Every day we must trust God, and we cannot face the challenges of today on yesterday's faith. Have you been surprised to discover that your old way of doing things is still around? Are there some examples in your own life of old failures creeping up again?

_____

_____

_____

_____

Remember that it is God who must work through us if faith is to be realized. When we fail, we must confess our failure to trust Him, and we must yield ourselves afresh to His will and way.

Spend some time with the Lord in prayer right now.

Lord, I want to know you. You have called me out unto that purpose. Yet so many times I stumble along the way. I struggle with trusting you and your promises. I take life into my own hands and try to help you out with my striving. When I fail, it makes it harder for me to trust You. I laugh in unbelief. Lord, help me to take You at Your Word—to believe that You will do all that You say. Amen.

Take a few moments to write down a prayer of application from the things you have learned this week.

_____

_____

_____

_____

_____

_____

_____

_____

_____

_____

HOW DO WE DEAL WITH FAILURE?

Failure is a reality. There is no Christian alive who has ceased from sin. James writes, *"we all stumble in many ways."* The victorious Christian life is not accomplished by never making a mistake, but by always coming back to God when we do make mistakes. When we fail (and we will) we must confess the sin of trusting ourselves, of pleasing ourselves, of obeying our own will and way, and we must yield afresh to God.

Notes

Miriam

TRUSTING GOD WITH YOUR POSITION IN LIFE

*S*omeone once said that "the hardest instrument to play is 'second fiddle.'" It was this assignment that God gave to the woman, Miriam. Though she was the oldest child in the family, Miriam grew up in the shadows of her two younger brothers, Aaron and Moses. She would become one of the most prominent and respected women in Israel, but she would struggle with following the lead of her baby brother. The focus of her life was both national and patriotic, and she served for years as a faithful public servant. But it was also Miriam who became jealous of her brother's position and publicly voiced her dissent. As a judgment for her covetousness, she was struck with leprosy as an example to all.

Miriam recovered from the result of her rebellion against Moses' authority, but the incident would be remembered for generations as an example of how God deals with those who will refuse to trust authority He places in their lives. Like her brothers, she would help to lead Israel to the borders of the promised land, but she would not live to see it herself. At her death, the entire nation of Israel mourned for her thirty days. Clearly she was a beloved national figure, and there is much we can learn from her life about following God.

Miriam would prove to be one of the great women among the people of God, but she had to learn to trust and follow God according to His ways, not hers.

WHERE DOES SHE FIT?

2200BC	1950	1700	1450	1200	950	700	450	100
SARAH 2155–2028		MIRIAM 1533?–1405				Daniel 619–534?		MARY and MARTHA 10BC?–60AD?
			DEBORAH 1300?–1200?	Solomon 991–931		ESTHER 504?–450?		
			Judges Rule 1385–1051	David 1041–971				
						Nehemiah 480?–400?		MARY, Mother of Jesus 20BC–60AD?
	Jacob 2005–1858		Joshua 1495–1385	RUTH 1135?–1050?				
	Isaac 2065–1885		Moses 1525–1405	HANNAH 1135?–1050?	VIRTUOUS WOMAN Prov. 31			
	Abraham 2165–1990		RAHAB 1445?–1385?	Samuel 1105–1022				Jesus Christ 4BC?–30AD?

THE PROTECTIVE WORK OF MIRIAM

Few women in history have held a more significant babysitting job than the elder sister of Moses. Our introduction to the woman, Miriam, is perhaps one of the most familiar narratives in the Old Testament. Most of us learned as children the Sunday school story of baby Moses floating in the Nile River in a basket. It speaks of a desperate act of trust on the part of a family fearing for their son's life. It speaks also of the miraculous deliverance of one destined to be a deliverer. Only God could have engineered so incredible a circumstance as the daughter of Pharaoh happening along at just such a time as this and taking responsibility to raise the one God would call to lead His people out of slavery to Pharaoh. The child Miriam protected would grow up to write the first five books of the Bible and would lead Israel from Egypt to the borders of the promised land. For forty years he would be the mediator between man and God. What a significant impact was born in this simple act of faithfulness!

Take a few moments to read Exodus chapter 1, and write down what you observe about the context of our introduction to Moses and Miriam.

_____

_____

_____

_____

What happened to Israel after Joseph and his generation died out (v. 7)?

_____

_____

_____

How did Egypt respond to Israel's growth as a people (vv. 8–12)?

_____

_____

_____

What was Pharaoh's plan to try to keep the Hebrews from multiplying (vv. 15–16)?

_____

_____

_____

How well did his plan work (vv. 17–20)?

_____

_____

_____

_____

Did You Know?

? HOW DID ISRAEL END UP IN EGYPT?

God initiated setting apart a people for Himself by calling Abraham out of Ur of the Chaldeans (Iraq) to the promised land of Canaan. Here his son Isaac and his grandson Jacob would be born. Jacob, who was renamed "Israel" would have twelve sons who would become the twelve tribes of Israel. It was because of jealousy that Joseph was sold by his brothers into Egyptian slavery. While there, his faithfulness and divine interpretation of dreams earned him the respect of Pharoah, and he served as Prime Minister. When famine came to the promised land, Joseph's brothers had to come to him for food and there the family was reunited. At first, Israel lived as sojourners in Egypt, but eventually they became slaves. After 400 years of slavery, Moses led them back to the promised land.

When his plan did not work with the midwives, how did Pharaoh attempt to deal with the growing population of Hebrews (v. 22)?

_____

_____

_____

The people of Israel were welcomed into Egypt in the days of Joseph. His God-given foresight spared them from destruction when famine came, and he was greatly loved by the people. But after Joseph and his generation died out, the next generation forgot the favor they enjoyed because of God's people, and the Hebrews began to be discriminated against. They were forced into hard labor and affliction. Yet in these dire circumstances God continued to prosper them, and they became more numerous than the Egyptians who enslaved them. Out of fear of this great multitude of people, the king of Egypt unsuccessfully tried to have the midwives kill all male Hebrew newborns. When that didn't work, he enlisted the aid of all the people of Egypt, and commanded that they cast every newborn Hebrew male into the Nile River.

It was in these dark circumstances that Moses was born to Amram and Jochebed of the tribe of Levi. He was successfully hidden for three months, but the king's strategy must have been having some measure of success—for something else had to be done. Hebrews 11:23 tells us that it was *by faith* that Moses' parents hid him, not fearing the consequences of the king's edict. Since their role was one of faith, we can assume that they were seeking God for wisdom, and that He was behind the idea. In faith, Jochebed made a little boat of a basket, and set Moses in the river, trusting him to God. The text tells us that she didn't set him afloat and let him drift, but rather, placed him *among the reeds* at the river's edge where it would appear he had drifted up to shore.

📖 Read Exodus 2:1–10 and record all you learn about Miriam's role in Moses' rescue from death.

What was Miriam's part to play in the rescue attempt for Moses?

_____

_____

_____

_____

When did she approach Pharaoh's daughter (vv. 6–7)?

_____

_____

What do you think would have happened to Miriam if their plan were discovered?

_____

_____

_____

Did You Know?
WHO WAS THE DAUGHTER OF PHAROAH?

The "daughter of Pharoah" mentioned here was most likely Thuoris, daughter of Ramses II. The historian Josephus tells us that she was a grown woman, who for political reasons was married to Si-Ptha, the infant heir to the throne of lower Egypt. She effectively ruled the region until the death of her brother, Amenephthis, made her regent over all of Egypt. This would explain how she was able to set aside her father's edict requiring death of newborn Hebrew males even in the full view of her attendants. It also suggests a powerful reason why she would be motivated to adopt the infant, for her marriage afforded no prospect of a legitimate heir in a son of her own.

What was the outcome of their strategy (vv. 8–10)?

_____

_____

When the plan was put into action and Jochebed placed Moses in the water to save him from death, Miriam *"stood at a distance to find out what would happen to him."* When it was evident that Pharaoh's daughter was not going to put Moses to death, but rather, *"had pity on him,"* even though she knew he was a Hebrew child, Miriam ran up and offered to find a nurse for the baby. Scripture doesn't tell us whether the idea to offer to find a nursemaid originated with Miriam or her mother, but in either case, Miriam risked her life by her role in the plan. If she were found out, the king's wrath would have meant certain doom. What bravery from a girl who was probably only ten to twelve years old! God's hand is clearly seen in the success of this plan which not only insured Moses' safety and protection from the death-edict of Pharaoh, but also allowed Moses to be trained in the best schools of Egypt at Pharaoh's expense. Best of all, he would still be allowed to grow up at his mother's knee and be taught the nurture and admonition of the Lord, and his mother would even get paid for it!

Little is said about Miriam's relationship to Moses during his adolescent years, but we know from Exodus 2:9–10 that the relationship began not in Pharaoh's house, but his own. Pharaoh's daughter instructed that Jochebed take the baby home and nurse him. At least until he was weaned (and perhaps longer) Miriam would have been intimately involved in Moses' life.

THE POSITION MIRIAM HELD

After her role in the deliverance of baby Moses, we hear nothing of Miriam's life until after Israel leaves Egypt. Yet from what little details we have of that period in Israel's history, we can draw a few assumptions about what her life would have been like. She grew up in poverty and prejudice. Hebrews in Egypt were viewed as little more than property. They were slaves—forced laborers. She likely experienced hard work all of her life. She surely saw injustice and learned compassion for those who had no voice. Her character was molded in the fires of adversity. In fact, the root meaning of her name is "bitterness." In a society dominated by men, Miriam obviously developed into a woman in the limelight. She exhibited responsibility and leadership. Clearly, she earned the respect of the people. Today we want to focus on trying to give some definition to Miriam's role in society and in the governmental role of her brother.

📖 Take a few minutes to read the song of deliverance found in Exodus 15:1–18. Now, read Exodus 15:20–21 and write down how Miriam is described and what she did.

_____

_____

_____

_____

Did You Know?

⌀ WAS MIRIAM EVER MARRIED

Scripture offers no account that Miriam ever married. Some historians have suggested that she was the wife of Hur, one of the judges of Israel and Moses' right hand man along with Aaron. This would make her the grandmother of Bezaleel, the famous artist involved in constructing the Tabernacle (Exodus 31:2). There is, however, no clear-cut evidence in the biblical record to either support or dispute this theory. It is quite possible that she remained single and gave her life in service to her country.

Our first introduction to Miriam by name is found in Exodus 15, immediately after Israel's miraculous deliverance from Pharaoh's army through the Red Sea. Here she is identified as *"Miriam the prophetess."* She is also described as *"Aaron's sister,"* which would obviously make her the sister of Moses also. As Moses and the men sang the song of deliverance (which many historians believe she wrote), Miriam led the women with the timbrel (similar to a tambourine) and dancing, and answered the men with what was probably a chorus that was inserted at intervals during the song. What stands out from this incident is that Miriam was clearly viewed as a leader, especially by the women. She used her giftedness to exalt God and to draw the people's attention to Him.

📖 Now look at 1 Chronicles 6:3 and record what you learn there about the makeup of the family Miriam grew up in.

_____

_____

_____

_____

We see here that Moses and Aaron were the only siblings Miriam had, so far as we see in recorded Scripture. It is possible that Miriam had sisters, who were not mentioned, for often in genealogies such as these, women were only mentioned if they were prominent and well-known to the reader. Miriam is the only female mentioned in this rather lengthy list, indicating that her inclusion was an exception because of her significance in the life of Israel. It is a compliment of sorts that she would be included here.

📖 Now look at Micah 6:4 and write who you see listed as the leaders of Israel.

_____

_____

_____

_____

It is significant that here the Lord says He *"sent"* before Israel, Moses, Aaron, **and Miriam**. Here we have it on sound scriptural authority that Miriam was sent as a leader in the same sense that Moses and Aaron were sent. The word "sent" indicates a formal calling from God. They did not appoint themselves as leaders, but were placed as such by God.

We don't know exactly how much older Miriam was than Moses, but we can guess that she was somewhere around ten to twelve years old when he was born. We know from Exodus 7:7 that Aaron was three years older than Moses. That would mean that Miriam was the first-born child, and Moses the baby of the family. That they were separated for a time while Moses lived with Pharaoh's daughter is probable. Miriam and Aaron probably saw nothing of Moses during the forty years he spent in Midian. But once they were reunited, they journeyed the wilderness together as family.

Word Study
PROPHETESS

The term, *"prophetess"* is used only a handful of times in the Bible. In addition to Miriam, it is applied to Deborah who functioned as a judge in Israel (Judges 4:4), to Huldah who spoke. *"Thus says the Lord,"* just as the male prophets did (2 Kings 22:14, 2 Chronicles 34:22), and to Anna in the New Testament (Luke 2:36). The term is also used of two women who prophesied falsely, Noadiah (Nehemiah 6:14), and Jezebel (Revelation 2:20). The Hebrew word, *"Neviah,"* is the feminine form of the word "prophet," which means "a speaker of oracles, one who spoke not his own words, but those which he had received from God."

THE PRIDE OF MIRIAM

Proverbs 16:18 tells us, *"Pride goes before destruction, And a haughty spirit before stumbling."* Even someone as godly as Miriam was not immune to this spiritual snare. Although her repentance kept her pride from bringing her to destruction, her "haughty spirit" certainly brought her to stumbling. Sadly, her failure was a very public one. Pride and haughtiness toward those who God has placed in leadership over us is sin. But it is worse still when those who are leaders of others vent their disagreements with those who lead them in a public way. Even if Miriam's concerns were legitimate, they should have been handled in private. But her concerns were not legitimate. As we will see today, the pride of her heart was masked behind a disguised motive. There is much we can learn from Miriam's mistake!

📖 Take a few minutes to carefully read Numbers 12:1–3. Looking at verse one, identify the first complaint brought against Moses and write your thoughts on the validity of this concern.

_____

_____

_____

_____

At a surface glance it appears that there may have been valid reason to question Moses' marrying a foreign woman. Arabia was commonly referred to as the land of Cush. The descendants of Cush, the grandson of Noah, who were viewed by the Hebrews as a contemptible people, populated the Arabian region. Some have considered this to mean that Moses' first wife had died and now he has taken a second wife, though the term, *"Cushite woman"* could simply be referring to Zipporah. In either case, the concern was valid regarding the danger of a foreign wife turning one's heart to other gods. Clearly this did not happen however, in Moses' case.

📖 Now read Numbers 12:2 and write the concern expressed here and your thoughts on the motive behind it.

_____

_____

_____

_____

The second concern seems to be a complaint directly against Moses and his leadership. Remember that verse one stated that Miriam and Aaron *". . . spoke against Moses. . . ."* Their argument seems to be that they had just as much right to lead Israel as Moses did. At the core of the grievance was jealousy for Moses' position as the main leader of Israel.

To fully understand the disagreement between Miriam and Moses, it is important that we see it in its context. Numbers 12:1 begins with the important word, *"Then,"* indicating a link with the preceding chapter.

Word Study
WHO WAS THE LEADER?

Although the English text reads *"Miriam and Aaron spoke against Moses . . ."* the Hebrew verb is feminine singular, making it clear that it was Miriam who was the leader of this criticism. This idea is further clarified by the fact that she is mentioned first as the instigator, and that only she is struck with leprosy as a consequence from the Lord. Probably Aaron agreed with the initial concern about Moses' wife, but did not have the same motive of jealousy as did his sister.

📖 Read Numbers 11:16–17; and 24–30. Identify what happened in the leadership structure of Israel, and write your thoughts on how that might have affected Miriam's attitude.

_____

_____

_____

_____

There had come a fundamental shift in the leadership structure of Israel. Up until this point, Moses, Aaron, and Miriam had been the sole leaders in Israel. Now Miriam and Aaron have been bypassed in favor of these seventy newly-appointed elders who had prophesied (hence Miriam's argument that the Lord had spoken through her and Aaron as well). They would still have a leadership role, but it would no longer be an exclusive one. If the wife spoken against in Numbers chapter 12 is in fact Zipporah, then, quite possibly, an additional motive is her father Jethro's counsel to Moses that the leadership responsibilities be divided among able men (Exodus 18). That counsel was just now beginning to be implemented, and clearly Miriam disapproved. She had succumbed to jealousy, the same temptation Moses had warned Joshua against in verses 28 and 29.

What a contrast we see here between Moses and Miriam! She viewed these seventy newly-appointed elders and prophets as a threat to her position, while Moses saw them as a much-needed asset. Numbers 11:17 tells us that this plan (which God clearly affirmed) would raise up a body of elders who would *"bear the burden of the people"* alongside of Moses. His heart, reflected in verse 29, was, *"Would that all the Lord's people were prophets, that the Lord would put His Spirit upon them!"* He saw no need to jealously cling to power, perhaps because he realized that the true power belonged to God.

The Punishment of Miriam

 DAY FOUR

Sin always has consequences, and the more public the sin, the greater the consequence. Miriam allowed her fleshly attitude to be seen in a very public way. Hebrews 12:15 warns us, *"See to it that no one comes short of the grace of God; that no root of bitterness springing up causes trouble, and by it many be defiled."* When bitterness takes root in our hearts, unless it is removed, it will eventually "spring up" and when it does, it will cause trouble and many **will** be defiled. Miriam gave vent to a bitter heart, and in so doing, publicly attacked and embarrassed her brother. She also dragged her brother Aaron into the fray, staining his attitude with her own malice. As a leader, she used her giftedness and her position to lead others into doubt, criticism, and questioning, instead of support and encouragement. Consider the contrasts this story presents to us. The seventy elders were given, in part, to *"take their stand"* with Moses (Numbers 11:16), while Miriam takes her stand against him. When others in the camp began to prophesy (speak for God), Joshua was jealous for Moses' sake (Numbers 11:29), while Miriam was jealous for her own sake. Today we will see that God deals strongly and swiftly with leaders who manifest self, instead of following God.

📖 Read Numbers 12:4–16 and answer the questions below.

When and how does God begin dealing with the controversy (vv. 4-5)?

_____

_____

_____

_____

What is the main point of His message to Miriam and Aaron (vv. 6–8)?

_____

_____

_____

_____

Looking closely at verses 9 and 10, record everything you learn about the consequences to Aaron and to Miriam.

_____

_____

_____

_____

_____

Did You Know?
LEPROSY

The leprosy referred to in Scripture was a highly infectious and communicable disease with differing stages of development spelled out in Leviticus 13. Miriam's onset of the disease appeared instantly as a fully symptomatic case at the peak of its ravaging effects. Her skin immediately took on a totally white appearance. Because of its contagious nature, those inflicted were required to separate themselves from other people, and had to cry out "Unclean! Unclean!" when anyone came into view.

Verse 4 tells us that *"suddenly"* God spoke. The Hebrew word in its root means "in a wink" or "instantly." God wasted no time in dealing with this insurrection. He called the three leaders to the tent of meeting, and then called Aaron and Miriam to stand before Him. The main point of God's response in verses 6–8 seems to be to remind them that He had a different relationship with Moses than He did with them or any other prophet. Both Miriam and Aaron were identified in Scripture as prophets (Exodus 4:16–17; 15:20), and as such had experienced the kind of communication the Lord refers to here. God had already defined a different role for Moses by virtue of the special relationship He had with Moses. There was absolutely no equality of service between Moses and his siblings, but neither was there equality of consequence for Miriam and Aaron in this rebellion. Both were rebuked—*"The anger of the Lord burned against* **them**, . . ." not just against Miriam. However, since her role was greater, so were her consequences. It was she, and not Aaron, who was struck with leprosy.

📖 Look at Numbers 12:11–12 and write down everything you see that has changed in Aaron's perspective as a result of his meeting with God and the consequence to Miriam.

_____

_____

_____

_____

_____

Perhaps most prominent in Aaron's response is the phrase, *"my lord,"* which he applies to Moses. He had gone from arguing his equality to expressing his submission. We also see in his response that he now recognizes the rebellion he participated in was both foolish and sinful. What a beautiful picture of what true repentance is: a change in thinking which results in a change of action. There is no blaming of others in Aaron's words, but rather, an acceptance of responsibility for his own sin.

📖 Now read through Numbers 12:13–16 and summarize what you learn about Moses' intercession and the outcome to Miriam.

_____

_____

_____

_____

_____

Moses cried out to the Lord for Miriam's healing, but God was not willing to do so immediately. Clearly part of the consequence for her rebellion against Moses' authority (which was really rebellion against God), would be seven days of public shame. Charles Ryrie, in the Ryrie Study Bible, comments: "If a father had to rebuke a daughter [by spitting on her face], a period of shame would follow (cf. Deuteronomy 25:9; Isaiah 50:6); how much more should Miriam be shamed seven days for flouting God's authority. The public nature of her sin called for public punishment (cf. 1 Timothy 5:20)."

In the end Miriam was healed of the leprosy with which God had inflicted her. After seven days of shame outside the camp, for which the whole company of Israel was forced to wait, she was again received into the fellowship of God's people. Her disease, which was instantly manifested at its peak of malignancy, was gone just as quickly. We can infer from this outcome that like Aaron, Miriam was repentant of her rebellion against God's authority structure.

FOR ME TO FOLLOW GOD

Miriam DAY FIVE

From Miriam's embarrassing excursion into rebellion until her death (Numbers 20:1), nothing more is said of her in Scripture. Like Moses, she would help lead Israel to the promised land, but not enter it herself. Does this mean that she never repented or that God removed her from leadership in Israel? We simply cannot say, and we err if we try to read anything into that silence. Tradition holds that in death Miriam was given a costly funeral and there was public mourning for her some thirty days—as was fitting the public leader she was. Though she is portrayed in all of her human frailty, Miriam was a beloved figure in the history of Israel and was remembered more in honor than in shame. From her successes we learn practical lessons about the power of influence and faithful service, and, even by her mistakes, we are tutored in what it means to follow God. As we reflect back on what we have learned from Miriam's life, we must recognize that she stands as a God-given example for our own faith.

📖 Look at Deuteronomy 24:8–9 and identify the context and significance of this reference to Miriam.

_____

_____

_____

_____

_____

Held within the requirements of the law regarding leprosy is this reminder of what God did to Miriam. Clearly God did not want Israel to forget her judgment. When Moses records the legal instructions about leprosy, he sets Miriam as a perpetual example both of the seriousness of the disease, and of God's ability to heal it.

As we look toward applying what we have learned, we must first recognize how easily we could succumb to her mistakes. As Miriam's public rebuke of Moses illustrates, if we do not watch closely over our hearts, it is easy to say one thing and mean another. Often, even our correct criticisms of other people are motivated by an incorrect attitude of the heart. If we nurse petty grievances and do not deal with them, they will end up being expressed in some other way. Jesus said in Matthew 12:34, *"the mouth speaks out of that which fills the heart."* A critical heart that is grounded in fleshly attitudes will even express a right criticism in a wrong and fruitless way.

APPLY Can you think of a time when wrong attitudes in your heart made you overly critical of another person?

_____

_____

_____

_____

What was the outcome?

_____

_____

_____

What do you think you should have done differently?

_____

_____

_____

_____

One of the key realities of Miriam's mistake was her struggle with Moses' authority. Romans 13:1 tells us, *"Let every person be in subjection to the governing authorities. For there is no authority except from God, and those which exist are established by God."* If we understand Scripture, then we must understand that a struggle with the authority structure is a struggle with God. The prophet Daniel stated, *"He removes kings and establishes kings"* (Daniel 2:21). This does not mean that authorities always do the will of God, but it does mean that even their evil is something He uses for good in our lives for as long as He allows them to rule.

APPLY Take a moment to identify all the authorities God has placed in your life.

___ Employer   ___ Police   ___ Husband   ___ Church Leaders
___ Supervisors   ___ State Govt.   ___Parents   ___ Teachers
___ Management   ___ Local Govt.   Other_____
___ Club Officers   ___ Federal Govt.

Now, look over this list again, and identify the authorities you have trouble trusting God with.

___ Employer   ___ Police   ___ Husband   ___ Church Leaders
___ Supervisors   ___ State Govt.   ___Parents   ___ Teachers
___ Management   ___ Local Govt.   Other_____
___ Club Officers   ___ Federal Govt.

Take some time to pray through this, and ask God to give you a heart of trust in what He is doing by allowing that leader to remain over you. And don't forget that Scripture exhorts you *"that entreaties and prayers, petitions and thanksgivings, be made on behalf of all men, for kings and all who are in authority, in order that we may lead a tranquil and quiet life in all godliness and dignity"* (1 Timothy 2:1–2).

One of the things which was at the heart of Miriam's mistake was her own pride. Certainly she was a gifted and capable leader. She believed that she could do as good a job as Moses could do in leading the people. But there is one fundamental problem with that line of thinking—even if she could have done a better job at what God wanted accomplished, He had not placed her in that role.

Some years later another challenge would rise up against Moses' leadership. Korah incited others to rebel against Moses. His argument was simple, and very much like Miriam's. In Numbers 16:3 we read, *"they assembled together against Moses and Aaron, and said to them, 'You have gone far enough, for all the congregation are holy, every one of them, and the LORD is in their midst; so why do you exalt yourselves above the assembly of the LORD?'"* In other words, they exclaimed, "we are just as qualified to lead as you are!" Moses' response is very telling. He doesn't try to defend his credentials or his training or his expertise. He simply says, *"the Lord has sent me to do all these deeds; for this is not my doing."* Moses' only qualification was the calling of God, and ultimately, that is the only qualification that counts.

APPLY Like Miriam, have you ever coveted another's position?

_____

_____

How did that affect your attitude?

_____

_____

_____

> **Ask God to give you a heart of trust in what He is doing by allowing that leader to remain over you.**

What actions resulted on your part?

_____

_____

_____

Are there any attitudes and actions of which you need to repent?

_____

_____

_____

Is there any restitution or apology you need to make to set things right with someone?

_____

_____

_____

Trust God in where He has placed you and in where He has not placed you.

It may be that you need to have some quiet time just between you and the Lord, and reaffirm your trust in where He has placed you and where He has not placed you.

Spend some time in prayer with the Lord right now.

Lord, You are the King of every king in my life and Lord of every lord. All men and women in positions of authority are placed in those positions by You. Help me to trust Your choices. Help me to watch my heart with all diligence and root out any attitudes of jealousy, pride, and covetousness. Help me to be satisfied with where You place me (and where You do not). Most of all, help me to be faithful to the tasks you give me, and humble in every position of authority I hold under Your authority. Amen.

Prayer of Application . . .

Take a few moments to write down a prayer of application from the things that you have learned this week.

_____

_____

_____

_____

_____

_____

_____

_____

_____

_____

Notes

Notes

Rahab

A Fresh Start with Faith

Some believers are born into Christian homes and grow up with godly parents and healthy training in the Word of God. They have never known anything but the fellowship of the people of God. Others are not so blessed. They are left to fend for themselves. Yet what a trophy of grace such people are when they come to faith. Jesus said in John 10:16, *"And I have other sheep, which are not of this fold; I must bring them also, and they shall hear My voice; and they shall become one flock with one shepherd."* Rahab was one such trophy of grace who was not in the fold of Israel, yet she heard the voice of the Good Shepherd and believed. Though she grew up as a stranger to the covenants of promise, an immoral outcast, what she had heard of God she believed. And God rewarded her faith. Her family alone was spared in the conquest of Jericho, and when she embraced Israel as her people and Jehovah as her God, she was welcomed. She would be an ancestor of king David and of Jesus Christ. The message from her life is powerful—it is never too late to begin following God. When we choose to believe, we find a fresh start with faith.

> **Rahab was a trophy of grace who was not in the fold of Israel, yet she heard the voice of the Good Shepherd and believed.**

Where Does She Fit?

2200BC	1950	1700	1450	1200	950	700	450	100
SARAH 2155–2028		MIRIAM 1533?–1405				Daniel 619–534?		MARY and MARTHA 10BC?–60AD?
		DEBORAH 1300?–1200?		Solomon 991–931		ESTHER 504?–450?		
			Judges Rule 1385–1051	David 1041–971				
						Nehemiah 480?–400?		MARY, Mother of Jesus 20BC–60AD?
	Jacob 2005–1858		Joshua 1495–1385	RUTH 1135?–1050?				
	Isaac 2065–1885		Moses 1525–1405	HANNAH 1135?–1050?	VIRTUOUS WOMAN Prov. 31			
Abraham 2165–1990		RAHAB 1445?–1385?		Samuel 1105–1022				Jesus Christ 4BC?–30AD?

A WOMAN WHOSE WORLD IS ABOUT TO CHANGE

Rahab was a harlot. She grew up in the pagan Canaanite culture of Jericho with all of its idols and worship of Baal. She was a woman of the world! Yet, as a child she began hearing stories of a people whose God had ransomed them out of Egypt with a mighty deliverance. We know not how old she was when the spies visited Jericho, but we know that forty years had passed since the miraculous plagues caused Pharaoh to relent and release God's people. Four decades had come and gone since the Red Sea opened for Israel and swallowed up Pharaoh's pursuing army. Yet still, this incident was talked about among the pagans. God had done something marvelous in their time. Rahab had never seen such manifested power from the impotent idols her culture revered. Deep inside her heart, those stories were united with belief—and a seed of faith sprouted that would one day blossom into maturity. Today we want to introduce this woman named Rahab, and try to paint a portrait of the kind of life from which God saved her.

We find our introduction to Rahab in the book of Joshua. Moses had already died, and Joshua was the new leader of Israel, trusted with the responsibility of leading the nation in its military conquest of the land of Canaan. In preparation for this assault, Joshua sends men to spy out the land. Having learned from his experience forty years earlier (see Numbers 13—14) when he went into the land as a spy, he keeps their mission a secret even from the Israelites, lest the spies bring back a bad report and the people's faith become shaken.

📖 Read Joshua 2:1 and identify what you learn of Rahab and why Joshua's spies happened to meet her.

_____

_____

_____

When the two spies crossed the Jordan River and entered the land of Canaan, their first stop was the thriving city of Jericho. We are told they found lodgings at the house of a harlot named Rahab. In this one sentence, we find two of her sources of income: prostitution and innkeeping. Since the Law clearly identified harlotry as "an abomination" we can assume that the spies were at her house for lodgings and not sexual favors. Though we would be quick to look down on such a woman, we must understand that having no revelation from God, her occupation would not have been seen in the same light in Jericho as we would view it. It was, none the less, sinful.

📖 Though the mission of these two men from Israel was supposed to be covert, somehow their secret was discovered, and the king of Jericho came searching for them. Read Joshua 2:2–7 and briefly summarize what you learn.

_____

_____

_____

Word Study
WAS RAHAB REALLY A HARLOT?

Some historians have tried to soft-sell Rahab's occupation and suggest that "harlot" should be translated "innkeeper." However, there is no support for such an idea, in either the meaning of the Hebrew word (*zoonah*) or of the Greek word with which she is identified in the New Testament (*porne*- root of our English term, "pornography"). This idea seems to be more rooted in the desire for her to be seen in a more favorable light, than in the facts themselves.

When the king of Jericho heard of the spies, he sent word to Rahab to turn them in. Instead, she misled the representatives of the king, telling them that the men had already left. In fact, she had hidden them among stalks of flax drying on her roof. The soldiers pursued the false lead and headed out toward the Jordan River where Israel had camped on the other side.

📖 In order to protect the lives of the two spies, Rahab lied to the soldiers sent to her by the king. Was she wrong to do this?

_____

_____

_____

_____

The question is often debated of Rahab's deception to protect the lives of the spies. On the one hand, lying is clearly forbidden in the Law. Yet, Rahab had no knowledge of the Law. It could also be said, as Herbert Lockyer argues, "under the rules of war, Rahab is not to be blamed for her protection of those righteous forces set against the forces of evil." Scripture makes no attempt to either condemn or condone Rahab's methods. Instead, what is affirmed is the underlying faith that motivated her. We are on solid ground if we have that kind of faith.

📖 Now take a look at Joshua 2:8–13 and answer the questions below.

What evidences of faith do you see in verse 9?

_____

_____

_____

_____

What had she heard of the God of Israel (v. 10)?

_____

_____

_____

What was her response (v. 11)?

_____

_____

_____

What request did she make of them in return for hiding them from the king's men (vv. 12–13)?

_____

_____

_____

It is amazing that at this point Rahab is more certain of God's coming deliverance than the spies are. She says, _"I know that the Lord has given you the_

Did You Know?

STALKS OF FLAX

Joshua 2:6 indicates that Rahab hid the spies in the stalks of flax which she had laid out on her roof, presumably for the purpose of drying them out. Flax is a plant with a meter-long fibrous stem which when beaten was used for making rope or for dyeing and weaving. Apparently this was another of her side-businesses. Though we would not applaud her harlotry, she certainly gives evidence of a work ethic and ingenuity.

land. . . ." She refers to God not just as a god, but "The LORD," using the Jewish national name for God, "Jehovah." She had heard of God's miraculous deliverance at the Red Sea, which had wiped out Pharoah's army and robbed Egypt of its military might (Ex.14). She knew of the Israelite victory over the Amorites, who were destroyed when they opposed Israel (Num. 21). Rahab had rightly concluded that the God of the Jews was the one true God. Because she believed in God, she had already cast her lot with His people against her own king, and now she asked that when they came to destroy Jericho, they would spare her and her family.

Rahab   DAY TWO

A PROMISE OF PROTECTION

Rahab's decision had been made, and her lot was cast firmly with the family of faith. She rejected the desires of her pagan king, and protected the representatives of the King of Kings she had chosen to serve. She had heard of Him when she was a child, and what God had revealed of Himself in that pagan environment, she had believed. As a result of her belief, she would see a new life begin, with a new way of living. As 2 Corinthians 5:17 reminds us, *"Therefore if any man is in Christ, he is a new creature; the old things passed away; behold, new things have come."* Today we will continue looking at the first encounter Rahab had with her new people, Israel.

📖 Look at Joshua 2:14. What is the overall attitude of the spies toward Rahab?

_____

_____

_____

_____

_____

Rahab chose the God of Israel and discovered that as He had protected Israel so He would protect her.

The spies vowed to deal kindly with Rahab in return for her protection of them. The Hebrew word for "deal kindly" (*chesed*) is the same word used of God's steadfast, loyal, covenant-keeping love for His people. Clearly they recognized the genuineness of her faith in their God.

📖 What additional details do you learn about Rahab's house from verse 15?

_____

_____

_____

_____

_____

In verse 15 we catch yet another glimpse of why Rahab's house was chosen for their lodging. Not only did its position on the city wall give them a good view of the entire city, but it also afforded them a quick get-away.

📖 Take a few minutes to read Joshua 2:14–21 and answer the questions that follow.

Looking at verses 17–20, identify the conditions of the agreement between the spies and Rahab.

_____

_____

_____

_____

When did she act on the conditions the spies had set (v. 21)?

_____

_____

_____

To guarantee her protection, Rahab first must tie a scarlet cord in the same window she had lowered the spies from. She must also stay in her house and hide her family there as well. Any who ventured outside this covenant-house would not receive its protection. The third condition was that she must not tell anyone about the spies. That Rahab believed is reflected in the fact that she immediately tied the cord in her window. What a beautiful picture we have here of faith in Christ! It is not enough simply to intellectually agree with the idea—we must act. The blood of Christ is reflected in the scarlet color of the cord, and like the Hebrews' deliverance at the Passover, that blood had to be applied. She acted in faith and received her deliverance as a reward.

Think about what we have here—an immoral woman from a pagan city that is about to be destroyed. Yet because of her faith—not her ancestry or morality—she is spared. What a trophy of grace Rahab is!

📖 Looking at Joshua 2:22–24, write down what you learn about what the spies did after leaving Rahab.

_____

_____

_____

_____

_____

Word Study
RAHAB'S NAME

Rahab's pagan family named her with a mythological and symbolic term meaning "the raging monster" or "the impetuous one." In the book of Job, the oldest book of the Bible, this beast is introduced (Job 9:13, 26:12). It is also referred to twice in the Psalms where it is used metaphorically of Babylon (Psalm 87:4, 89:12), and in Isaiah 30:7 it is applied to Egypt. In Isaiah 51:9 we read, *"O arm of the LORD; Awake as in the days of old, the generations of long ago. Was it not Thou who cut Rahab in pieces, Who pierced the dragon?"* Yet, because of her faith, commended in the New Testament, this once gruesome term is ever associated with the woman who believed God.

The spies followed Rahab's advice, and hid out in the hill country for three days until their pursuers gave up chasing them. Then they went directly back to Joshua to give a report. Joshua and the spies recognized the hand of the Lord in their providential circumstances, and rightly concluded that God had given the city into their hands (see Joshua 3). Think of the impact Rahab's faith has had on these two spies, and now, on the leader of Israel. When we trust God, He will always use our faith in someone else's life as well. Would Israel still have invaded Jericho without the encouragement from Rahab? We will never know, for the fact is, God chose to use her faith for this very purpose.

A CONQUERED KINGDOM

In Joshua chapter 6 we see the details of Israel's conquest of Jericho. Through God's supernatural dealings, the walls of Jericho came tumbling down, and the army of Israel marched in. Everyone in the city was devoted to destruction. Only Rahab and her family survived. Yet they, too, were conquered by Israel. Their faith in Jehovah made their hearts a conquered kingdom as well. What a contrast though! There really are ultimately only two options in life. Either we will bow our knee to Christ in surrender, or we will bow our knee to Him by force, but sooner or later *"every knee"* will bow, and *"every tongue"* will confess *"that Jesus Christ is Lord, to the glory of God the Father"* (Philippians 2:10, 11). May we join with Rahab in bowing by the choice of faith.

Joshua chapter 6 opens with Israel laying siege to Jericho. God had led them to this point. He had parted the Jordan River for them just like He parted the Red Sea for the generation before them. He had fed them for forty years on manna, but once they had entered the land and eaten some of its produce, the manna ceases. Retreat is not an option, for the Jordan will not open for them to run. To do nothing is not an option, for unless they move forward and conquer, they will have no food. Now they must act in faith on all that God has promised them.

📖 Read Joshua 6:1–5 and respond to the questions that follow.

Taking into account ancient methods of warfare, what does verse 1 suggest about the first phase of the conquest of Jericho?

_____

_____

_____

_____

What is God's promise to Joshua in verse 2?

_____

_____

What was God's strategy for phase two of the conquest of the city (vv. 3–5)?

_____

_____

_____

What effect do you think Israel's marches around the city and the trumpet blasts and shouts of the people had on the army of Jericho?

_____

_____

_____

_____

Did You Know?

❓ THE WALLS OF JERICHO

Archaeological excavations have discovered that Jericho actually had two walls about thirty feet high. The outer wall was six feet thick, and the inner twelve feet, with a twelve to fifteen foot space between them. The city itself was relatively small, and, as it became crowded, people built their houses between the walls. Rahab's house was obviously one of these, with a window on the outside wall. The excavated walls and city show signs of violent destruction.

Verse one tells us that Jericho was *"tightly shut"* because of Israel. This means the gates were closed, and everyone was hidden within the walls of the city. This reflects the fact that Jericho's army didn't believe they were able to win a direct fight with Israel. Without modern methods of warfare, a walled city was easy to defend and difficult to penetrate. Often the most effective method of attacking such a city was to surround it, cutting off supplies of food and water, and starve the inhabitants out. Starvation would eventually force them to come out and fight. We do not know how long this phase of the conquest lasted, but God uses Jericho's reaction to encourage Joshua that He had indeed given the city into their hands. Phase two of God's plan was equally important. Specific instructions were given to Israel requiring obedience and faith. They were to march around the city walls, carrying the ark before them. Can you imagine what Jericho's soldiers were thinking? They had heard of God's miraculous deliverance of Israel in the parting of the Red Sea. They were accustomed to fighting soldiers, but how could they fight a God who could part waters? This army was acting like none they had ever seen, and with each day their confidence was further eroded as fear filled their hearts.

What God had instructed, Joshua and the people obeyed. When the march was finished and the trumpets sounded, the people shouted in unison, and God caused the walls of Jericho to fall to the ground. Once the wall was breached, the soldiers rushed in, and the city was quickly taken. Only Rahab's part of the wall remained standing, and only her family was allowed to live.

📖 Read Joshua 6:15–25 and answer the questions that follow.

What were Joshua's instructions about the city and Rahab (v. 17)?

_____

_____

_____

What did the people do to Jericho (vv. 21, 24)?

_____

_____

_____

Who rescued Rahab and her family, and where did they take them (vv. 22–23)?

_____

_____

_____

_____

What happened to Rahab after the battle was over (v. 25)?

_____

_____

_____

Doctrine
FIRST FRUITS

The firstfruits of the land were to be devoted wholly to the Lord as a mark of His ownership over all the land. Thus, Jericho was the firstfruits of the Promised Land, and the firstfruits of each harvest were offered to the Lord.

This concept continues in our lives today through a lifestyle of giving. The firstfruits of all we receive from God are offered to Him as a mark of His ownership over all we have. The principle applies not only to our possessions, but also to our time and our very lives.

Word Study
DEVOTED

The Hebrew word *charam* or *cherem* means "devoted" or "under the ban." Something "put under the ban" referred to something set aside totally for God's purposes. The spoils of Jericho were "devoted" or literally, "under the ban"— set apart, as it were, as firstfruits belonging to the Lord (Joshua 7). Leviticus 27:28 speaks of a devoted offering, and 27:29 speaks of a person under the ban, meaning that person was set apart for judgment to be executed for his sin. Amalek was among those under the ban (*"utterly destroy"*—1 Samuel 15:3, 8–9, 18, 20) whose crimes merited execution as did the Canaanites of Joshua's day.

Joshua told the people that everything in the city was "under the ban" because it belonged to the Lord. This city was the "first fruits" of their conquest of Canaan, and as such, must be offered back to the Lord. Rahab and her house alone were to be spared. The people were obedient, and killed every man, woman, child, and animal, and then burned the city. Joshua put the two spies in charge of rescuing Rahab and all that were with her. They were taken from Jericho and placed *"outside the camp"* of Israel (v. 23). This positioning indicates that she was not yet considered holy, for no unclean person was allowed into the camp. Yet in verse 25 we see the ultimate result being that she was eventually permitted to live *"in the midst"* of Israel as a reward for her faith-motivated protection of the spies.

Many see in Rahab a beautiful picture of the Church. Rescued from out of the sin-stained world, with a compassion to bring others with her, she would eventually enjoy full status in the family of God alongside Israel.

Rahab DAY FOUR

A Faith Affirmed

Hebrews chapter 11 is often called, "God's Hall of Fame." In it, many of the Old Testament champions of faith are listed. There are only two women mentioned by name in this chapter on faith: Sarah, the wife of Abraham, and Rahab. Three times Rahab is mentioned in the New Testament. In each instance we find an affirmation of the belief that motivated her, and we gain valuable insight into this scarlet-lettered sinner who was redeemed by grace through faith. In her we see the beautiful reality that no life is beyond the reach of God's saving mercy, and we are reminded that it is never too late to repent and enjoy a new way of living. Today, as we look to what the New Testament teaches us of Rahab, we will see in her life a faith that is affirmed.

📖 The first mention of Rahab in the New Testament is found in Matthew 1:5. Read Matthew 1:1–16 and answer the questions below.

What is the purpose of this listing of people?

_____

_____

_____

_____

_____

What details do you learn about Rahab specifically?

_____

_____

_____

_____

_____

What other women are mentioned in this list?

_____

_____

In this list we see the genealogy of Jesus Christ traced all the way from Abraham. We are told here that Rahab was the wife of Salmon, the son of Nahshon. We are also told that Boaz, who married Ruth, descended from Rahab. That makes Rahab an ancestor of king David. There are only three other women mentioned or referred to in this list: Tamar, Ruth, and *"her who had been the wife of Uriah"* (Bathsheba [v.6]). All four are featured prominently in the Old Testament, and would be familiar to the Jewish readers of Matthew's gospel. Since clearly the mention of women in this list is the exception rather than the rule, it would seem that only those wives well-known in their own right are included. This argues against this being anyone other than the same Rahab of Joshua's day.

📖 Rahab is also mentioned in Hebrews 11:31. Read this verse and record what details you see there about Rahab.

_____

_____

_____

Most prominent in this verse is the term *"by faith."* It is used 19 times in the chapter of such notables as Abel, Noah, Abraham, Sarah, Moses, and king David. When applied to Rahab, it places her in tremendous company. We also see in this verse that she *"did not perish along with those who were disobedient,"* indicating that, in contrast, she was obedient. For this to be true, she had to have experienced a prompting which she obeyed. Third, we are reminded once again of what she was, a harlot. Yet grace transformed her into a model of faith. Finally, we see that her receiving of the spies was based not on them, but on the God they served and in Whom she believed.

In James chapter two we see the final NT reference to Rahab. The context of the chapter is significant. James is trying to answer the question "What kind of faith is saving faith?" He has already shown us that true saving faith is more than mere intellectual assent, for even the demons have an intellectual belief in Christ (2:19), though certainly they are not saved. He is not, as some have mistakenly interpreted, trying to teach salvation by works. Rather, he is teaching that the right kind of faith (the only kind that is saving faith) is shown valid by works. As James develops and defends his thesis, he lists two examples of those in the Old Testament who exhibited saving faith: Abraham and Rahab.

📖 Take a moment to read James 2:14–26 and then answer the questions that follow.

When in the Old Testament was Abraham *"reckoned righteous,"* and what is the context? (You can probably find the verse by cross-referencing from James, or by looking it up in a concordance.)

_____

_____

_____

_____

Did You Know?
RAHAB'S HUSBAND

We are told here that Rahab was married to Salmon, the son of Nahshon. Tradition holds that he was, in fact, one of the two spies who lodged with her on their excursion into the promised land. Later these same two would be charged with rescuing her and her family and escorting them to the camp of Israel. What a wonderful thought that this providential encounter would be allowed to blossom into love. Salmon was a prince of the house of Judah, and thus, Rahab, the pagan harlot, would have married into one of the most prominent families of Israel.

Did this occur before or after the actions of James 2:21, and how does this affect the interpretation?

_____

_____

_____

_____

What was the source of Abraham's works (v. 23)?

_____

_____

_____

_____

Word Study

JUSTIFIED

James 2:21 seems to suggest salvation by works. However, a close look at the Greek word translated "justified" (*dikaióō*) reveals a different message. Verbs which end in *-óō* generally indicate bringing out that which a person is or that which is desired, but not usually referring to the mode in which the action takes place. In the case of *dikaióō*, it means to bring out the fact that a person is righteous. It is not that Abraham's works made him righteous, but that they revealed him to be righteous.

Abraham was *"reckoned righteous"* when he believed the promises of God (exhibited faith). This quote comes from Genesis 15:6, and follows God's promise to give Abraham a son and descendants as numerous as the stars of the heavens. Abraham was *"reckoned righteous"* thirty years or more before the actions listed in James 2:21 (recorded in Genesis 22:9) by which he was *"justified by works."* Therefore, since he was already righteous for thirty years, his works didn't save him; they merely proved the reality of his faith in Genesis 15. We see from James 2:23 that the source of Abraham's works was his intimate friendship with God (*"and he was called the friend of God"*). The more intimately we know God, the easier it will be for us to trust Him. The more we trust Him, the more works we will give as evidence of that trust.

📖 Now, lets look at how this statement about Abraham relates with Rahab. Read verses 24–26 again and answer the questions that follow.

What does Abraham have in common with Rahab according to James (v. 25)?

_____

_____

_____

Thinking from the mindset of a Jewish background (James is writing to Jewish Christians), how would Abraham be viewed differently than Rahab?

_____

_____

_____

What do these two examples teach us about the relationship between faith and works in salvation?

_____

_____

_____

_____

Abraham and Rahab both demonstrated by their actions that they had faith in God. There is no greater evidence of what we really believe than how we behave. Conversely, if what we say we believe does not affect our behavior, it is to be doubted. The selection of Abraham and Rahab as examples is a very unlikely pairing. To the Jew who would read this, Abraham would be the best possible example. If anyone made it into heaven, Abraham did. He was called *"the friend of God."* He was the father of the Jewish nation. Rahab on the other hand, would carry little clout with the Jews. She wasn't Jewish and she wasn't even moral. She was a Gentile prostitute. As far as Scripture records it, the only spiritual thing she ever did was to hide some spies of God. Yet James makes it clear that it was the fruit of her faith. He obviously is giving a "greatest and least" example. The issue on his mind is not how many works you have, but that at some point you show your faith by your works. He is saying that we are saved by faith **alone**, but not by faith that **is alone** (James 2:20, 26).

For Me to Follow God

R ahab, like Abraham, cultivated a relationship with God, and fruit was the result. What God revealed to her of Himself, she believed. In response to that belief, God revealed more of Himself. Look at what God did because her heart trusted Him. He supernaturally protected her from the judgment given to her city. He provided a new people, a new husband, and a new life. He even brought from her the kingly line of David. And even though she had a stained past, God gave her a glorious heritage as an ancestor of the Messiah. God even held her up as an example to all generations that He offers a new life to those who believe. Today we will begin looking at how we can apply the message of Rahab's life to our own faith.

APPLY Have you ever struggled with thinking that your past means that you can never be close to God or used by Him?

_____

_____

_____

_____

What encourages you most out of Rahab's story?

_____

_____

_____

_____

Rahab, like Abraham, cultivated a relationship with God. They followed Him, and fruit was the result.

One of the principles clearly seen in Rahab is that God holds us accountable only for how we respond to those truths to which we have been exposed. Is there any truth you are aware of that God has revealed, but you know in your heart you have not responded to yet? If so, do not delay. Your walk with God and your ministry to others is directly tied to what you do with what God has revealed to you.

Certainly, there was a measure of regret for her past choices when she learned the Law and how God viewed her immorality. But there was also a large measure of gratefulness as she reflected on all the things from which she had been redeemed.

📖 Read Luke 7:36–47 and reflect on how Rahab's past would have affected her relationship with God.

_____

_____

_____

_____

In Luke 7:47, Jesus says of the sinful woman who anointed His feet with costly perfume and wiped them with her hair, _"For this reason I say to you, her sins, which are many, have been forgiven, for she loved much; but he who is forgiven little, loves little."_ Certainly, Rahab's experience could not have been much different. Her sinful past would have given her more love for God and a deeper intimacy with Him.

APPLY Reflect on your own past. What are the things that God has saved you from that you appreciate most?

_____

_____

_____

_____

_____

_____

_____

Perhaps in the scenario we just looked at, you can identify more with the Pharisee, who had little love because he had little awareness of his own sins or of his need for forgiveness.

Take some time to look through this list of sins in which the Pharisee may have struggled, and mark the ones with which you can identify.

___ Pride	___ Selfishness	___ Independence from God
___ Lack of love	___ Judging others	___ Lack of gratefulness
___ Critical spirit	___ Boasting	___ Inability to forgive others
___ Other _____		

Why not take a few moments to thank God for forgiving you of the specific things you have identified here today?

Another lesson from Rahab is not simply appreciating our own forgiveness, but accepting God's ability to forgive others. Fortunately for all of us, God is quicker to forgive than man is. All of us should recognize that we stand before God always and only **by grace.** Yet sadly, though we recognize our need for grace from God, often we demand justice in our relationships with

All of us should recognize that we stand before God always and only by grace.

others. When they fail us, we become angry and embittered, and often those emotions are left to fester within us long after the person has repented and received grace and forgiveness from God. The great revivalist Roy Hession used to say, "Be careful what you say about the faults and mistakes of others—they may have already been to the cross about them."

James tells us that Rahab's faith was vindicated when she *"received the messengers and sent them out by another way,"* yet it took longer for Israel to accept her than it took God. When she was rescued from Jericho, she was placed *"outside the camp"* as one unclean. In time the Israelites lined up with what God had done though, for eventually she *"dwelt in the midst of Israel."* We all need to experience and embrace God's forgiveness in a great enough measure to become agents of grace in the lives of others.

A seed of faith was sown in Rahab's heart, as she heard of the mighty dealings of God on Israel's behalf. She responded in belief, and the seed sprouted. Eventually God gave her the opportunity to express that faith when He sent Joshua's spies her way. Think of how different her own life history would have been if she had not protected the spies. Instead of a new life, a new people, and a new husband, she would have perished in Jericho. God desires our faith to bear fruit in our lives. Abraham's faith matured and was completed when it began to be expressed by his works. His works flowed out of his friendship with God. Perhaps you are new in Christ, or newly-growing. Or perhaps, there is some staleness in your walk with God. Good works are called "fruit" for a reason. Jesus compared us to branches connected to Him, the Vine. He said, apart from Him we would be able to do nothing (see John 15:5). Consider what it takes to grow a tree that bears fruit. . . .

How to Grow a Tree That Bears Fruit

- ✓ Plant the seed. (If you have not yet trusted Christ, do so.)
- ✓ Care for the root. (Water it with God's Word and cultivate it with prayer.)
- ✓ Care for the fruit—pick it when it is ripe. (Be obedient to what God calls you to do in the opportunities He gives you.)
- ✓ Prune it. (Be willing to let go of things that hinder your fruitfulness.)
- ✓ Wait. (There is no substitute for time—younger Christians should not be frustrated if they bear less fruit than older, more mature Christians.)

Perhaps you have been plagued with guilt from past sins, and have believed the lie that God could never use you because of your sinful past. You cannot **alter** your past, but you can put your past on the **altar**. If you surrender your past failures to God, you may be surprised to discover that instead of a hindrance to Him using you, they may become the very thing that makes you useable.

Why not spend some time with the Lord in prayer right now.

 Lord, thank you for revealing Yourself to me. I know that I did not seek You out. I only responded to what You revealed. Help me to see all the things for which you have forgiven me. Give me a grateful heart for my forgiveness, and guard me from judging the mistakes of others. I take my own sinful past and place it on the altar in surrender

Too often we want mercy for ourselves and justice for others.

You cannot alter your past, but you can put your past on the altar.

to you. Take it and turn it into something You can use. Send people my way that will give me the opportunity to express my faith. Thank You for the new life You give me in Christ. Never let me take it for granted. Amen.

Prayer of Application . . .

Take a few moments to write down a prayer of application from the things that you have learned this week.

_____

_____

_____

_____

_____

_____

_____

_____

_____

_____

_____

Lord, thank You for the new life You give me in Christ. Never let me take it for granted.

Notes

Notes

Deborah

THE BATTLE IS NOT YOURS, BUT THE LORD'S

God is faithful! Even in the dismal 350 year period of the Judges, when Israel was pulling away from God, He remained faithful to them. During Joshua's time Israel saw victory after victory, but in the period of the Judges they saw defeat after defeat. God used their trials to call them back to Himself. He would always faithfully provide a deliverer. Unfortunately, that deliverance would usually be short-lived, for as soon as Israel got comfortable again, they would wander away from the Lord. A new generation would arise in Israel that didn't know the God of their fathers. As a result, the nation declined spiritually. But God would not abandon His people. He would send another deliverer, and this time it was a woman. Anyone who believes that the only ministry a woman can have is in the nursery will need to cut these chapters out of their Bible. Not only did Deborah serve Israel as a Judge and a prophetess, it was her leadership that her co-leader, Barak, leaned on in what would be one of the greatest military victories of their generation. Through Deborah we see that God wants to use us. God can use you, and God can use me. But we must understand, if we are going to be used, we are going to have to do it His way and not ours. God uses those who understand that the battle is not ours, but the Lord's (see 2 Chronicles 20:15). At this dark time in Israel's history, Deborah was a torch-light of trust in God's power to deliver and a reminder of God's covenant love for His people.

At a dark time in Israel's history, Deborah was a torch-light of trust in God's power to deliver and a reminder of God's covenant love for His people.

WHERE DOES SHE FIT?

2200BC	1950	1700	1450	1200	950	700	450	100
SARAH 2155–2028		MIRIAM 1533?–1405				Daniel 619–534?		MARY and MARTHA 10BC?–60AD?
			DEBORAH 1300?–1200?	Solomon 991–931		ESTHER 504?–450?		
			Judges Rule 1385–1051	David 1041–971				
						Nehemiah 480?–400?		MARY, Mother of Jesus 20BC–60AD?
Jacob 2005–1858		Joshua 1495–1385	RUTH 1135?–1050?					
Isaac 2065–1885		Moses 1525–1405	HANNAH 1135?–1050?	VIRTUOUS WOMAN Prov. 31				
Abraham 2165–1990		RAHAB 1445?–1385?	Samuel 1105–1022					Jesus Christ 4BC?–30AD?

THE PROBLEM GOD ADDRESSES

Word Study icon (scroll)

Word Study
JUDGES

The term "judges" is from the Hebrew word, *shophetim,* whose root means "to put right, and so to rule." That is exactly what the judges did during this period. The period of the Judges is a sub-period at the end of the age of the Patriarchs, covering the turbulent era from around 1380 BC to about 1050 BC, and bridging the conquest of Canaan to the establishment of a monarchy. The last judge, Samuel, who also served somewhat as a prophet, provides a transition into the period of the kings.

Did You Know?
THE BOOK OF JUDGES

As one studies the book of Judges it is important to understand that it was not written in strictly chronological fashion. The first two chapters and the first six verses of chapter three give a political (chapter 1) and spiritual (2:1—3:6) background of the period. Then in 3:6 we begin to see the major judges laid out in a sequential manner—Othniel, Ehud, Deborah and Barak, Gideon (chapters 3—8), and then the seven overlapping judges (chapters 10—16). The last five chapters give a concluding overview of the apostasy of this period, but overlap chronologically with some of the previous chapters.

Deborah lived in the dismal days recorded in the book of Judges when *". . . there was no king in Israel, [and] every man did what was right in his own eyes"* (Judges 17:6). It was a period of Israel's history marked by continual straying. We know very little about Deborah's background except that she was married to Lappidoth and lived between Ramah and Bethel in the hill country of Ephraim. She served for some time as a judge, which in some ways functioned like a modern biblical counselor. Often, Deborah would sit underneath a palm tree and people would reveal their problems to her. She would offer advice, using the wisdom God had given her through her study of the Scriptures, along with the revelation God had given to her as a prophetess. Yet this ministry was not the only one God had planned for this faithful woman. God would use her as a catalyst to call the whole nation of Israel back to Himself. To fully appreciate the woman, Deborah, we must begin by looking at the days in which she lived. You see, God wanted to fight **for** Israel, but His first battle was **with** Israel. Today, we want to look at the spiritual climate of the days in which Deborah lived.

📖 Read Judges 2:1—3:6. A cycle of events occurs during the period of the Judges. Look particularly at chapter 2, verses 11–23, and identify the four main elements that make up this cycle.

2:11–13 _____

2:14–15 _____

2:16–18 _____

2:19 _____

Judges 2:11–23 demonstrates for us a spiritual pattern that is repeated over and over throughout the book and is illustrative of what God was trying to do through Deborah. The cycle would begin when Israel forsook the Lord for other gods (2:11–13). Then God would chasten Israel by sending other nations against them to plunder them (2:14–15). The conquered Israelites would then cry out to the Lord (2:18), and God's grace would be evidenced by His bringing up someone to deliver them from their enemies (2:16–18). The land would then enjoy revival and peace. Unfortunately, when the judge died, Israel would again forsake the Lord (2:19–23) and the cycle would begin all over again. Deborah was one of these deliverers the Lord raised up to call Israel back to Himself.

An important lesson about the Christian life is found in the book of Judges, and it is this: "Victory is not my overcoming sin, or the devil, or the world. True, lasting victory is only found when Jesus overcomes me." As we will see with Israel in the days of Deborah, God's toughest battle was not in overcoming the armies of Jabin, king of Canaan. His toughest battle was with wandering Israel.

📖 Let's look at Judges 4:1–3 and examine this "sin cycle" of Judges played out.

What did Israel do that reflected the "sin cycle" as seen in Judges chapter 2, and when did they do it (v. 1)?

_____

_____

_____

What did the Lord allow to happen, and what part of the cycle does it represent (v. 2)?

_____

_____

_____

_____

What did the sons of Israel do, and how long did their oppression last (v. 3)?

_____

_____

_____

_____

_____

In Judges 4:1 we see that, ". . . _the sons of Israel_ **again** _did evil in the sight of the Lord_" [emphasis added]. Although the text here doesn't specifically tell us, we can assume from the sin cycle of chapter 2 that part of the evil deeds they practiced was that they followed other gods from among those worshiped by the Canaanites (2:12). It is significant that this evil practice occurred **after** Ehud died. As the nation did with most of the judges, Israel followed the Lord while Ehud reigned, and the land had eighty years of peace under him (3:30). After they strayed into evil, the Lord's chastening was seen when He "_sold them into the hand of Jabin king of Canaan_" (v. 2). But eventually, when things got bad enough, the sons of Israel "_cried to the Lord._" Verse 3 seems to indicate that it took a while for Israel to get desperate enough to turn back to God, for their oppression lasted twenty years.

The story of Deborah is told in two chapters of Judges. Chapter four gives us a chronological narrative of sorts, and chapter five (written in the form of a song) gives us a brief commentary and overview of her life.

📖 Look at Judges 5:6–8 and identify the events that took place in Israel during the life of Deborah.

_____

_____

_____

_____

> **Victory is not me overcoming sin, or the devil, or the world. True, lasting victory is only found when Jesus overcomes me.**

In Judges 5:6 we are told that *". . . the highways were deserted, and travelers went by roundabout ways."* The Canaanites controlled the highways, making travel in that region so dangerous that people would go out of their way to avoid those routes. The statement in verse 7 that the "peasantry" ceased in Israel indicates that the region was so unsafe that no one lived in the rural, unwalled villages anymore. In verse 8 we see confirmation that *"new gods were chosen."* In other words, Israel began worshiping other gods. The ultimate result of the nation's straying was war. The end of verse 8 is not just saying that Israel numbered only 40,000 at this time, but that even one single spear or shield per forty thousand people was rare. Israel was defenseless in a dangerous land.

Israel was in deep trouble! They had nowhere to look except up. Often it is that way in our lives as well. As long as we can figure our way out of our problems, we don't look to God. I wonder how many times difficulties have come into our lives because the Lord has delivered us into the hands of trials to get us to the place where we will cry out to Him. Finally, after twenty difficult years, Israel did just that. In the midst of Israel's travail, we meet Deborah.

THE PERSON GOD CHOOSES

Deborah is introduced at a time of desperation in Israel. The picture becomes crystal clear. There is Sisera with nine hundred iron chariots, and here is Israel—who doesn't even have a sword or spear among 40,000 men. But God is about to deliver them. Remember that the lesson to be learned here is that the battle is His, not ours. If you will think about it, God continues to orchestrate circumstances in all of our lives to the point where we are so outnumbered and defenseless that if we don't trust Him, then there will be no answer for whatever we are dealing with. This is the way God teaches us. You look at what you are facing and it is absolutely overwhelming. You come to God, and that is when you begin to discover that it is *" 'not by might nor by power, but by My Spirit' says the Lord of hosts"* (Zechariah 4:6).

On one side you have an army with no weapons. On the other side you have Sisera, leader of the most heavily armed soldiers found in the entire book of Judges—900 iron chariots strong! And God finally said, "Enough is enough!" Aren't you grateful for that? Whatever you experience in the consequences of sin, God knows when enough consequences have been paid. I am so grateful for that! In Romans 12 it says, *"Vengeance is mine . . . says the Lord."* We are not to repay. The Greek word translated "vengeance" in Romans 12:19 (*ekdikesis*) does not mean revenge, but should literally be interpreted, "out of righteousness." This implies that God is the only One who knows how much we can take, and He is the only one who knows what kind of consequences to orchestrate in our lives when we have sinned. He is the one who brings us to brokenness and eventual repentance. I don't want to be in your hands if I have done something wrong. I would much rather be in His, because God is a merciful God and knows exactly when "enough is enough." When God determines that Israel has been chastened enough, He sends Deborah as their deliverer.

Did You Know?
WHERE IS HAZOR?

Judges 4:2 says, *"And the Lord sold them into the hand of Jabin king of Canaan, who reigned in Hazor; and the commander of his army was Sisera, who lived in Harosheth-hagoyim."* To get a little bit of the geographical setting here, Hazor was one of the cities conquered by Joshua, as recorded in Joshua 11:1–14, that had apparently been rebuilt. Hazor was located ten miles northwest of the Sea of Galilee on the main trade route from Egypt to Mesopotamia. Jabin's military commander, Sisera, had under his command 900 iron chariots. The idea of Israel fighting him with no weapons is comparable to a modern foot soldier going out against 900 tanks.

📖 Look at Judges 4:4–5 and write down all you learn about Deborah.

_____

_____

_____

_____

In these verses we see, first of all, that Deborah was a woman through whom God could speak. She was open and receptive to what God wanted to say. She was a prophetess. Now what is a prophetess? The word "prophetess" is simply the female title for "prophet." A prophet is a person through whom God could speak; one who could never add any words to what God had said, whatever God revealed. Old Testament prophets became mouthpieces to reveal what God wanted to say to His people. Deborah was not only a person who could receive what God revealed, but also a person through whom God could speak. Today, we have the whole Word put together. God still speaks to us today. We don't need prophets now, because we have the Holy Spirit who lives within us.

Secondly, we are told that Deborah was *"the wife of Lappidoth."* The name Lappidoth means "flame, torch, or lamp." It is the name for a strong man, or a strong leader. Now, here is a woman who is strong in her own right. She was a person through whom God could speak. She was married to a strong man; a man who stood out; a man who was a light; a man who was a leader in his day. Thirdly, Deborah was a judge of Israel. People came to her, and she made judgements under what was called *"the Palm Tree of Deborah"* (v. 5).

📖 Another important truth about Deborah is found in Judges 5:7. Read it and write what you see.

_____

_____

_____

_____

Deborah had compassion for her people. I love the way this is stated in Judges 5:7. You can't miss it. It says, *"The peasantry ceased, they ceased in Israel, until I, Deborah, arose, until I arose, a mother in Israel."* What a description— Deborah was "a mother in Israel." What is the picture here? She is one who is filled with care and compassion, as a mother would be for her own children. She loved the people of her nation. She cared very deeply about them.

📖 Why do you think God chose to use Deborah as a judge?

_____

_____

_____

_____

There are three things that stand out to me about why God may have chosen Deborah: her weakness, her faithfulness, and her availability. Peter said that the woman is the weaker vessel (1 Peter 3:7). This doesn't mean "worthless," but "fragile." In fact, in my house the "fragile" things are the most expensive.

Did You Know?
PROPHETESS

Deborah was not the only prophetess in the Old Testament. Exodus 15:20 calls Miriam "the prophetess." Huldah was a prophetess found in 2 Chronicles 34:22. Not all the prophetesses in the Old Testament were good, just like not all the prophets were good. There was one by the name of Noadiah who sought to hinder Nehemiah in his efforts to rebuild the walls of Jerusalem. Nehemiah 6:14 reads, *"Remember, O my God, Tobiah and Sanballat according to these works of theirs, and also Noadiah the prophetess and the rest of the prophets who were trying to frighten me."*

The fledgling nation of Israel is the epitome of weakness according to human eyes, and to see it pitted against one of the most impressive armies found anywhere in the Old Testament leaves little room for hope. But God is trying to show us something. This is the way God works in all of our lives. When there is absolutely nothing we can do about a situation, we are rendered weak and anemic. It is when we are up against unimaginable odds, then, in the midst of hopelessness, Christ's strength is made perfect. What is evident here is that God used this woman, not a military man like Barak, but a **woman** to manifest the power of what He can do, even in the most difficult situations. God chose her. Second, she was faithful. If she were not, God would have never used her. God chose what man would consider the weaker vessel—through her He would manifest His perfect strength. This wasn't just any weaker vessel. Deborah was a woman of great character; a woman who respected the Word of God and the will of God; a woman through whom God could speak; and a woman who was faithful in her family. Third, she was available. Her availability is the most appearing thing. This is true concerning all the people God chooses. We have seen this over and over in the characters we have studied so far. Deborah was a simple, ordinary person just like you and me, who made herself available for God to use.

Deborah DAY THREE

THE POWER GOD USES

God's wisdom is so awesome! At first glance, this passage might simply look like just another story of someone greater than us doing greater things than we could ever do. But if you look long enough, you begin to see what God has done here. The main point is not Deborah's power, but the power that He used to work through Deborah. Have you ever made this statement, "If that person gets right with God, God sure could use them"? I have. Every one of us ought to repent the very moment we make that statement. Though God may manifest His power through the gifts and talents He has given us, His power is not limited by our abilities, nor is it those talents that truly make us usable to Him; it is our availability. Remember that, and never, never forget it. Let's not take anything away from Deborah—she was someone who was faithful, available, one who trusted in God. Yet any of us could be just as useable to God (if we yield to Him and let His power work through us). God uses His power, not man's strength.

Read Judges 4:6–7 and make note of what you learn from Deborah concerning the details of God's plan as she shared it with Barak.

_____

_____

_____

_____

_____

The first thing we need to see is that this was not Deborah's plan. Notice the phrase, "... *the Lord, the God of Israel, has commanded....*" Deborah was a prophetess who could hear from God. She just simply took what God had said to her and told it to Barak. She didn't go to bed one night and have a vision and then run to Barak and say, "I have a wonderful way in which we could defeat this army." No, she heard from God. She said, "*. . . the Lord, the God of Israel, has commanded, 'Go and march to Mount Tabor, and take with you ten thousand men from the sons of Naphtali and from the sons of Zebulun.'*" Deborah told Barak to take ten thousand men to Mount Tabor. Surely, you get the picture here. Over on one side of the valley are Sisera and all of his nine hundred chariots. He was positioned by the River Kishon beside a huge plain, perfect for a battlefield, and many battles have been fought there. On the other side is Mount Tabor. God said, "Deborah, I have a plan. Go get Barak and ten thousand men." Remember that there were no weapons in Israel. What were they going to do—throw rocks at them? God had something up His sleeve. Why would God tell Deborah to tell Barak to take his troops up to Mount Tabor?

Well, verse 7 tells us why. It says, "*And I will draw out to you Sisera, the commander of Jabin's army, with his chariots and his many troops to the river Kishon; and I will give him into your hand.*" In other words, God had a plan to get Sisera out from his encampment—where the iron chariots were, where they couldn't be touched by anybody—and to get him and his troops out into that plain. But first of all Barak had to take ten thousand men up to Mount Tabor, which is on the other side of that plain. Again, Deborah didn't come up with that idea. She was not this brilliant military strategist trying to help out God. God told her to do that!

📖 What is Barak's response to Deborah, and why do you think he responded that way (4:8)?

_____

_____

_____

_____

_____

Barak respected the leadership of Deborah. There are some who suggest that Barak is expressing fear here, but I have come to think differently about that. Verse 8 says, "*Then Barak said to her, 'If you will go with me, then I will go; but if you will not go with me, I will not go.'*" To go out into battle against nine hundred iron chariots is arguably a fearful thing. Barak was no fool. He knew that God spoke through this woman, and he knew that, without any weapons, going against such a formidable foe would be absolutely overwhelming. He wasn't about to budge unless God in this woman went with him out into that battle. He understood who was going to have to give the power and the wisdom and the direction in this battle if it were ever going to be won. You see, the Christian life is not getting a "word from God" one time and then going out and acting on it. It is continually seeking God and hearing from Him every step of the way.

Actually Deborah and Barak made a pretty good team. Barak couldn't prophesy, but he could fight. Deborah couldn't fight, but she could prophesy. So the two of them went to battle together. Israel had the military man, but Deborah was essential too. She was the spiritual "warrior." You have got to know what God wants before you put any effort into it. Barak refused to do anything without the spiritual leadership of Deborah. For this reason if for no other, I respect Barak.

Deborah and Barak did what God told them to do. That was the key to victory.

How does Deborah respond to Barak's request (v. 9)?

_____

_____

_____

_____

_____

> "This is the word of the LORD to Zerubbabel saying, 'Not by might nor by power, but by My Spirit,' says the LORD of hosts."
>
> Zechariah 4:6

In verse 9 Deborah says, *"I will surely go with you; nevertheless, the honor shall not be yours on the journey that you are about to take, for the Lord will sell Sisera into the hands of a woman."* Then Deborah arose and went with Barak. In other words, God wasn't going to give the victory to a military man. God was going to assign the victory to a woman, whom man would say was the weaker vessel. First, God used Deborah, and now He would use another woman to show that it is *" 'not by might nor by power, but by My Spirit,' says the LORD of hosts"* (Zechariah 4:6). He was teaching Israel to fight God's way—in His strength instead of their own.

There is a little background information slipped in at this point that we need to mention. In Judges 4:11 we are introduced to a man named "Heber" who was a "Kenite." It almost appears as if the writer remembered that he had not introduced us to Heber, and so he "slipped him in" before he forgot. Why is Heber so important to this story? In verse 17 we are reminded that the Kenites (a tribe associated with the Midianites) were at peace with Jabin, the king of Hazor. Heber lived in close proximity to where the battle took place, and Sisera thought of Heber's house as a safe place to hide since there was some sort of peace treaty between the Kenites and Jabin, king of Canaan. We will come back to Heber a little later in our lesson.

Look at Judges 4:12–13 and write down what Sisera did when he learned there was an army from Israel headed his way.

_____

_____

_____

_____

Sisera got the news that Barak had taken the ten thousand men and gone over to Mount Tabor. Do you see what God is doing? He is luring Sisera, the mighty warrior out into the open. He may have mused to himself concerning Barak, "This joke of a commander has only ten thousand men with him, and he has gone upon Mount Tabor?" So he rallied his troops. Remember, God said, "I will draw him out on that plain. I have to get him out on that plain because that is where we are going to defeat him."

Verse 13 reads, *"And Sisera called together all his chariots, nine hundred iron chariots, and all the people who were with him, from Harosheth-hagoyim to the river Kishon."* Now, can you imagine what he was thinking right now? Sisera was convinced that this puny little army from Israel was no match for his hundred thousand troops and nine hundred chariots. And he was right. The only problem was, he didn't realize that the battle was not Barak's, not Deborah's, but the Lord's!

THE PRODUCT OF GOD'S POWER

Have you ever watched a movie that had really good sound effects? You can just feel the sound vibrating all around you. As we examine the text in Judges chapter four, imagine Israel's battle with Sisera displayed on "the big screen," with modern sound effects. This cinematic aid will help you get a better grasp of the miracle God performed on behalf of the children of Israel. Imagine the sounds of the horses and chariots rolling out— all nine hundred of them! The chariots begin to be mobilized, and they start heading over that plain of Jezreel over to Mount Tabor. There is excitement in the camp! God had drawn Sisera into His trap. We can see what Sisera could not see—God had just set him up for defeat. In prideful arrogance Sisera was so convinced that Israel did not stand a chance against him, that he moved his army out into the open in a very vulnerable position on the riverbed. What he could not see was that the weather was about to change.

📖 Read Judges 4:14 and answer the questions that follow.

What was Deborah's *"word from the Lord"*?

_____

_____

_____

How did Barak respond?

_____

_____

_____

Why, from this verse, do you think it was important for Deborah to be present during the battle?

_____

_____

_____

_____

Now, you see Deborah and Barak working together. Here was Barak—a warrior without weapons, but a warrior nonetheless. He was ready, waiting on Deborah to tell him when to move because she heard from God. He didn't dare move until God told him to move. Verse 14 of chapter 4 tells us, *"And Deborah said to Barak, 'Arise! For this is the day in which the Lord has given Sisera into your hands; behold, the Lord has gone out before you.'"* So Barak went down from Mount Tabor with his ten thousand men to face an army ten times as great. I love that picture! I can just feel the thrill inside of Barak, and I can just hear him saying, "God is going to do something today! God better do something because we don't have any weapons, and the enemy is out there in that valley." Deborah faithfully delivered the message from God, and Barak stepped out in obedient faith. Aren't you glad God had Deborah there? I know Barak was glad. Through her, God let Barak know exactly what to do and when to do it. There is another piece of the puzzle you have

> *"Behold, the LORD has gone out before you."*
>
> **Judges 4:14**

to glean from chapter 5. Remember that chapters 4 and 5 work intermittently. Chapter 5 is the poetic summary of chapter 4. It does add some things that are helpful in understanding this.

📖 Look at Judges 5:4, 20–22 and see what else is recorded about God's plan to conquer Sisera.

_____

_____

_____

_____

_____

Barak and his troops came down off Mount Tabor to the valley of Jezreel. Sisera's men had come out in the valley beside the Kishon River. That is significant. Verse 21 of Judges 5 reads, *"The torrent of Kishon swept them away, the ancient torrent, the torrent Kishon. O my soul, march on with strength."* Boy, did God ever have something up His sleeve! In Judges 5:4 we see that the "heavens" and the "clouds" dripped water. In other words, they had some serious rain!

The River Kishon could have been dry at that time, but doesn't necessarily have to have been. Whatever happened, there was a surge of water in the River Kishon where Sisera was stationed. The River Kishon borders the plain of Jezreel. Here were those chariots—those big, heavy, iron chariots going out on to the plain of Jezreel—and all of a sudden it was like a dam broke! God just said, "Watch this." Suddenly the water came and spilled over the banks and poured around those chariots. Of course, the sandy ground just became mud, and the nine hundred iron chariots went from being an asset to being a huge liability. Here come ten thousand Israelites shouting "Glory, God is on our side!"

I love these stories in the Old Testament. They make you stop and think, two plus two doesn't equal up to four with God. Two plus two is whatever He says it is—period. God said, "Now it is time." God had the timing down to the season, to the weather, to everything! Barak knew he needed Deborah to reveal God's timing, and Barak wasn't going to budge until she said, "It is time." That is what I love about this whole picture. Deborah shows us how God works in people's hearts.

📖 Moving back to chapter 4, look at vv. 15–16 and write down what you see of the results of Deborah and Barak's faith.

_____

_____

_____

_____

Well, it was no real feat for Barak to whip Sisera's army. Once Sisera's chariots got bogged down, evidently his troops threw their swords away and fled. It says in verse 16, *"But Barak pursued the chariots and the army as far as Harosheth-hagoyim, and all the army of Sisera fell by the edge of the sword; not even one was left."* Where did they get swords? I thought there were no weapons in Israel. I don't think there were. I think these were the very

Did You Know?
FLOOD!

The riverbeds in the Middle East are called "wadis." Matthew 24:20 says to pray that it won't be in winter when perilous times begin to happen to the nation of Israel, and those in the Holy Land flee towards the mountains, because the way they would have to go (most people believe they will go to Petra) is through a particular place where there are many wadis. They are usually dried up. But during winter, rains are often heavy, and flash flooding can occur because of the rocky terrain. Raging torrents in this region are often strong enough to overturn cars! It may have been that God sent a flash flood to entrap the chariots of Sisera. A similar thing happened in 1799 when Napoleon defeated the Turks in this very same place.

weapons of the people in the iron chariots. I believe they got so confused and so panic stricken when they realized that their source of power was gone, that the swords went by the wayside as they fled, and the Israelites were right behind them picking up those swords and killing them just as fast as they could! Not a single Canaanite was left! Thousands upon thousands of enemy soldiers were killed. Now, before you start heaping accolades upon Barak, make sure you notice the first statement of verse 15: *"And the LORD routed Sisera. . ."* [emphasis added]. God did this!

📖 Now read Judges 4:17–24 and summarize in your own words how God dealt with Sisera (It also may be helpful to read Judges 5:24–31).

_____

_____

_____

_____

Sisera fled from the battle on foot to the tent of Heber, whom we met earlier. Since Heber's family was of the Kenites, Sisera felt safe hiding there. While Sisera stayed at this tent, he was served by Heber's wife, Jael. Now if you look closely at 5:25 you will find an important clue: *"He asked for water and she gave him milk. . . ."* Think about the difference between the two. Milk has ingredients that fill you up, while water merely quenches thirst. Then our text says, *"In a magnificent bowl she brought him curds."* He really thought he was being honored, but she was just "fattening up the hog for slaughter." With a full stomach he fell asleep—never to awaken again—for while the exhausted Sisera took a nap, Jael took a tent stake and a hammer, and drove the stake into his temple, all the way through his head and killed him!

God was not finished yet, though. Judges 4:23 reads, *"So God subdued on that day Jabin the king of Canaan before the sons of Israel. And the hand of the sons of Israel pressed heavier and heavier upon Jabin the king of Canaan, until they had destroyed Jabin the king of Canaan."* God not only won the battle for them, He removed their enemy. That is some victory!

The final result of God's dealings with the Canaanites is reflected in the last statement of chapter 5, *"And the land was undisturbed for forty years."* Peace at last! You know, we may be able to get temporary relief some other way, but only when we turn to God, and He does what only He can do, will we ever find lasting peace. That, I believe, is the most important lesson we learn from this judge named Deborah.

FOR ME TO FOLLOW GOD

Deborah DAY FIVE

In a day when there was "no king in Israel," when leadership was lacking, God raised up a woman named Deborah, who for a time filled the vacuum. Who says God can't use women in mighty ways! She faithfully served Israel as a Judge, a settler of disputes, a mender of relationships, a counselor operating not in human wisdom, but in the attitude of "thus says the Lord." I believe it was because of her faithfulness in dealing with those interpersonal situations that God used her to tackle this international situation. She was someone who knew better than to try and help out God. She simply listened to Him, and told others what He was saying. You see, God doesn't want nor need our help—what He longs for is our trust and our obedience. "Trust and obey, for there is no other way to be happy in Jesus, but to trust and obey."

Today we want to bring this lesson down to the level where we live. What is it that is overwhelming you? What are the nine hundred iron chariots in your life? Let's just be honest. I guarantee you that there are some iron chariots in your path and they are overwhelming you. It might be a situation in your family, or possibly a financial situation you are facing. It might be a work-related problem such as job security. I don't know what it is, but you are overwhelmed.

APPLY Write down any difficult situations in your life that the Lord brings to mind.

_____

_____

_____

_____

_____

> **God doesn't want nor need our help— what He longs for is our trust and our obedience.**

Have you learned that you can't fight against these situations in your own power? You can't sit down and figure them out. You come to God. It says in 2 Corinthians 10:4, *"For the weapons of our warfare are not of the flesh. . . ."* Ask Barak. He could tell you. They are not of the flesh, *". . . but divinely powerful for the destruction of fortresses. . . ."*—those things that rob us of the knowledge of God which transforms our life.

What are some of the ways of "warring in your own power" that you are tempted toward?

_____

_____

_____

_____

What have we learned about our weapons in this lesson? What are our weapons? Well, one weapon is recognizing your enemy—how weak you are, and how strong they are. One of the first steps of living in the victory God has given to us is to realize what we can't do in our own strength. Many of us are so filled with pride that we can strut sitting down. Miles Stanford, in his classic book, *The Green Letters – Principles of Spiritual Growth*, makes an important statement about spiritual maturity. He says, "Maturity is learning to recognize the bankruptcy of self and our riches in Christ." We must see how bankrupt we are on our own, but we must also understand how rich we are with Him working for us.

Another weapon comes through realizing that you come to God on the basis of His terms and you come to His Word. Deborah was a prophetess. Through the prophetess the Word of God was spoken. So if you want to translate this situation to the New Covenant, Barak just took the Word of God with him and studied it. He didn't move until he heard from God. That is the key. The Word of God has got to be deep in your heart. Surrender to whatever it is that God wants you to do, waiting upon His bidding and His command.

 APPLY What do you need to do to make sure you are in a position to hear from God about your own situation?

_____

_____

_____

_____

What should you avoid to protect yourself from running ahead of God?

_____

_____

_____

Your job in any crisis is not "do all you can do and then worry that you didn't do enough." Your job is to simply walk with God and do what He says. When you hear, and God has spoken, step out on what He says and understand that victory is something you already have, but you haven't known it until you have obeyed. It is faith that accesses the grace of God. It is obeying Him that accesses the victory we already have in Christ Jesus. Whatever situation you have, God is bigger than that situation. Just write that down. We have great weapons but they are spiritual weapons. They require walking with God to be effective.

> **Whatever your situation, God is bigger than the situation.**

Look through the items listed below and identify which ones were not a part of God's deliverance through Deborah and Barak.

____ Seek to hear God.
____ Ask God to bless your plan.
____ Follow God's directions fully.
____ Step out in faith.

____ Come up with a great plan.
____ Wait on God's timing.
____ See what has worked for others.

One final thing to think about. Can you see any evidence in your own walk of the "sin cycle" we see in Judges? Do you tend to wander and only take your relationship with God seriously when He sends chastening circumstances your way? If so, the most important thing you need to learn from this lesson is that the person God chooses is the one who is faithful and obedient to Him. Or maybe more important, the power God uses is not our own energy, but Him working through us as we yield to Him.

As we close this week's lesson, make this prayer your own:

Lord, forgive me for those times when I have forsaken You for other gods, the god of money, the god of pleasure, or the god of self. Make me sensitive to Your chastening hand. Help me run **to** You in my troubles and not **from** You. Thank You for loving me too much to let me stray. Help me to be quick to cry out to You. Most of all, thank You for the grace and mercy You show. Take Your place on the throne of my heart and show Your power through me. Empower me to be faithful and obedient. Amen.

Prayer of Application . . .

As we close our lesson this week, take to heart any areas the Lord has singled out to you and express them in your own prayer to Him.

_____

_____

_____

_____

_____

_____

_____

_____

_____

_____

Notes

Notes

FOLLOWING OUR KINSMAN-REDEEMER

The story of Ruth is the true account of a woman who chose to follow the Lord God of Israel and found Him compassionate and faithful, full of grace and love. It is the chronicle of a walk of faith—of surrender to the Lord, of following Him and His ways. Ruth saw that the Lord is involved in the seemingly small events of a person's life as well as in the epoch-changing events of nations. She discovered this Lord to be the powerful and sovereign Lord over all nations as well as the caring redeemer of her life.

Ruth shows us that following God has its difficulties, its times of faith when there is little (if any) sight to go along with it. Her life reveals that following Him is the path of truest joy, of surest life, and of greatest peace. In Ruth's case it was also the path of greatest reward, for she would be in the line of the Messiah, the Redeemer of Israel. He would come for **all** who would surrender to Him in faith and trust. We can learn much from Ruth about the faithful Messiah she came to know, the one greater than Boaz, the true Root of David. As we come to know Him, we too can find new life and great reward, for He is the one who saves us from our old ways and leads us in following Him.

Did You Know?

RUTH'S GREAT-GRANDSON

Ruth was the great-grandmother of King David and one of the ancestors of the Lord Jesus Christ, the Messiah. She is one of only four women mentioned in the genealogy of Jesus in Matthew chapter one—Tamar, Rahab, Ruth, and Bathsheba.

WHERE DOES SHE FIT?

2200BC	1950	1700	1450	1200	950	700	450	100
SARAH 2155–2028		MIRIAM 1533?–1405				Daniel 619–534?		MARY and MARTHA 10BC?–60AD?
			DEBORAH 1300?–1200?	Solomon 991–931		ESTHER 504?–450?		
			Judges Rule 1385–1051	David 1041–971				
						Nehemiah 480?–400?		MARY, Mother of Jesus 20BC–60AD?
	Jacob 2005–1858	Joshua 1495–1385	RUTH 1135?–1050?					
	Isaac 2065–1885	Moses 1525–1405	HANNAH 1135?–1050?	VIRTUOUS WOMAN Prov. 31				
Abraham 2165–1990		RAHAB 1445?–1385?	Samuel 1105–1022					Jesus Christ 4BC?–30AD?

THE HAND OF THE LORD IN TIMES OF CALAMITY

> ### "In those days there was no king in Israel; everyone did what was right in his own eyes."
>
> ### Judges 21:25

The story of Ruth the Moabitess occurred *"in the days when the judges governed"* (Ruth 1:1). The period of the Judges covered from approximately 1370 BC (after the time of Joshua, 1495–1385) to around 1041 BC when Samuel, serving as the last of the Judges, anointed Saul as Israel's king, and the period of the monarchy began. The events of the book of Ruth took place during a ten to twelve year period between 1150 and 1100 BC.

📖 What do we know about this period of the Judges? Read the summary statement in Judges 2:8–22. What characterized this period of Israel's history?

_____

_____

_____

_____

_____

The period of the Judges was marked by the following cycle:

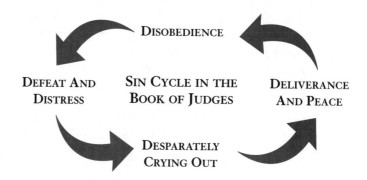

Over and over Israel repeated this cycle. The people did what they wanted, worshiped the way they wanted, made decisions based on their own desires and their own opinions. It was a time when there was no king in Israel. Judges 21:25 makes that statement and adds, *"everyone did what was right in his own eyes"*—letting himself be the sole judge of what was right. This is more than a statement about their form of government. It is a statement about the condition of the hearts of the people; for the people did what **each** thought was right, not what **God** or a righteous king said was right. It was in this kind of atmosphere that we find the events of the book of Ruth.

In Ruth 1:1, we find mention of a famine in Bethlehem. God spoke to His people concerning such conditions. Passages such as Deuteronomy 28:15, 23–24 and Deuteronomy 32:23–24 speak to this. Deuteronomy 28 describes God's blessings for obedience and His curses for disobedience. One of the curses was that there would be no rain and no crops. Deuteronomy 32 contains the "Song of Moses" given to teach the people of Israel the faithfulness

Did You Know?
? FAMINES IN ISRAEL

Famines in Israel occurred from time to time throughout the Scripture record. The first one we know of occurred in the life of Abraham and resulted in his move to Egypt for a short time (Genesis 12:10; 13:1). Isaac experienced a famine and the Lord instructed him not to go to Egypt (Genesis 26:1–6). Famine also occurred in the days of Jacob while Joseph ruled over Egypt and resulted in the move of his family there (Genesis 42:1–5; 47:1–27). They stayed for over 400 years (Exodus 12:40). In the famine recorded in Ruth, Elimelech chose to go to Moab. Famines also occurred in the lifetimes of David (2 Samuel 21:1), Ahab (1 Kings 18:1–2), and Elisha (2 Kings 4:38) among others.

of their covenant-keeping God alongside their faithless nature as His people. In the "Song of Moses" God warns the people of the dangers of idolatry and apostasy. One of the dangerous results would be famine. The book of Ruth does not say specifically that the famine in Bethlehem was God's judgment, but it is worth considering as a possibility.

We find that Elimelech moved his wife, Naomi, and their two sons, Mahlon and Chilion, from Bethlehem (where there was insufficient provision) to Moab (where they found adequate provision). It appears he tried to take care of his family in the midst of the famine. It is possible that the famine put an extraordinary strain on Elimelech's family. Consider that the sons were named Mahlon, meaning "weak" or "sick," and Chilion, meaning "failing" or "pining." This may be an indication of weaknesses traced back to their births and early years, conditions that made the famine even more severe for this family.

📖 What does this family face in Moab according to Ruth 1:2–3?

_____

_____

_____

_____

📖 What do you find in Ruth 1:4?

_____

_____

_____

_____

Soon after the family settled in Moab, Elimelech died leaving Naomi and her two sons, Mahlon and Chilion. These sons married Moabite women. Mahlon married Ruth (Ruth 4:10) and Chilion married Orpah. What is the significance of their marrying Moabite women? How were Moabites different from Israelites? The answers to those questions will help us get to know Ruth.

_____

_____

_____

_____

The Moabites descended from the incestuous union of Lot and his oldest daughter after the destruction of Sodom and Gomorrah around 2065 BC (Genesis 19:36–37). The Moabites eventually settled in the land east of the Dead Sea in what is today the country of Jordan. Many years later (1445 BC), after Israel came out of Egypt, Balak king of Moab hired Balaam to pronounce a curse on Israel. Obeying direct instructions from God, Balaam refused to curse Israel, but later influenced Balak in directing the Moabites to intermarry with the Israelites so that the children of Israel might be led to commit idolatry and face the eventual wrath of the Lord (Numbers 31:16; Rev. 2:14). As a result, Moab caused Israel to stumble into immorality and

Did You Know?

MARRIAGE TO A MOABITE

Marriage to a Moabite was not prohibited in the Mosaic Law. In Deuteronomy 7:1–3, the Lord prohibited marriage to any of the seven nations found in Canaan (Hittites, Girgashites, Amorites, Perizites, Canaanites, Hivites, and Jebusites). Moab was not one of these nations.

idolatry (Numbers 25:1–18; 31:13–16). The plagues of idolatry and immorality that swept over Israel drew them away from the Lord.

When Israel came into Canaan, the Lord instructed Israel to leave the Moabites alone (Deuteronomy 2:8–9). Their land was to remain their possession, not the possession of Israel. Furthermore, Deuteronomy 23:3–4 made it clear that no Moabite (nor Ammonite) was to enter the assembly of the Lord unto the tenth generation (around 1200 BC) because of the way they refused to help the Israelites when they came out of Egypt, and for leading Israel into immorality at Peor (see Numbers 25). The events of Ruth occurred after 1150 BC.

📖 What happened next according to Ruth 1:5?

_____

_____

_____

_____

📖 When did this occur?

_____

_____

_____

_____

After ten years in the land of Moab, the two sons of Naomi died, leaving Naomi and their widowed Moabite wives, Ruth and Orpah. This devastation would have been especially difficult in the culture of that day. A woman depended on her family relationships for her livelihood. With no husband, a woman would face many hardships unless other family members stepped in to provide and protect. Naomi, Ruth, and Orpah faced a dismal future if someone did not come alongside to help them.

📖 Let's skip ahead a few verses to see how Naomi viewed this time in her life. In Ruth 1:19–22, how does she describe the last twelve years of her life?

_____

_____

_____

_____

📖 How does she see the Lord's hand at work?

_____

_____

_____

_____

Did You Know?
MOABITE RELIGION

The Moabites worshiped a god they called Chemosh, and their religion was particularly vile. Worship rites sometimes included child sacrifice (I Kings 11:7, 33; 2 Kings 3:26–27).

Naomi spoke of the Almighty (*Shaddai*) dealing bitterly with her, so much so that she said her name should be Mara (the Hebrew word for "bitter") instead of Naomi (meaning "pleasant"). Not only does she speak of the contrast between a once-pleasant life that had now become bitter, but she also speaks of going from full to empty, of being afflicted by the Almighty rather than being blessed, and of the Lord testifying against her rather than for her. This was not a pleasant time in her life, but that was about to change.

THE HAND OF THE LORD IN TIMES OF PROSPERITY

 DAY TWO

There is a change in circumstances in Ruth 1:6–7. Naomi heard that *"the Lord had visited His people"* in giving them grain. Naomi was ready to return to Bethlehem and to her people there. The fact that verse 6 says the Lord visited His people in giving them food could indicate that they had been under His chastening hand for some time, and now they were experiencing His blessing.

📖 As Naomi prepared to return to Bethlehem, Ruth and Orpah chose to go with her. How did Naomi respond to this according to Ruth 1:8–9?

_____

_____

_____

_____

_____

_____

_____

Word Study

VISITED

"The LORD had visited His people in giving them bread" (Ruth 1:6). The word for "visited" *(paqad)* in Ruth 1:6 is the same word Joseph used twice when speaking to his brothers in Egypt, *"God will surely take care of (visit) you."* (Genesis 50:24, 25) It refers to the helpful actions of a superior to those under him, in Ruth 1:6 the Lord Himself bringing benefit to His people.

As they were on the way to Bethlehem, Naomi urged them to return to their own homes where they could find security and the opportunity to remarry and raise a family. They still wanted to go with her. It was at that point that Naomi referred them to an Israelite custom concerning remarriage after the death of one's husband. In Ruth 1:11–13, Naomi explained that she could not provide a husband for them from her offspring. She would have to marry, bear two sons, and Orpah and Ruth would have to wait until the sons grew to an adult age before they could marry and bear children of their own. This was known as a levirite marriage (from the Latin, *levir*, "brother-in-law"). In Deuteronomy 25:5–6, the Mosaic Law made provision that if a man died, one of his unmarried brothers was to marry the widow (his sister-in-law) in order to bear a son to maintain the name of the deceased brother. The son would also acquire the deceased's inheritance in the land of Israel.

As Naomi talked with Orpah and Ruth in verses 8–14, she saw the hand of the Lord in all that had happened to her. She had left her homeland and settled in a foreign land where her husband and two sons died. For Naomi, this was all at the hand of the Lord. She recognized the hand of the Lord in the entire calamity she had faced. This was no complaint. It was simply an acknowledgment of the sovereignty of the LORD Jehovah (or *Yahweh*), the personal covenant-keeping God of Israel.

At this point in the narrative we find that Orpah chose to go back to her people and to her gods, while Ruth *"clung"* to Naomi (v. 14). The word "clung" is the same word translated *"cleave"* in Genesis 2:24, and it means to stick together like clay or to be glued together.

📖 What do you find about Ruth's decision in 1:16–18? What was her commitment?

_____

_____

_____

_____

_____

How did she view the Lord in this decision?

_____

_____

_____

_____

WHEREVER YOU GO

"Entreat me not to leave you, Or to turn back from following after you; For wherever you go, I will go; and wherever you lodge, I will lodge; Your people shall be my people, And your God, my God. Where you die, I will die, And there will I be buried. The Lord do so to me, and more also, If anything but death parts you and me." Ruth 1:16–17

In one of the most beautiful statements in Scripture, Ruth reveals her heart. She made a clear-cut, well-thought-through choice. She would cling to Naomi whatever came their way. She would follow her, stay with her, adapt to her ways and the ways of her people. She would follow her God throughout her life until death. She so identified with Naomi that she never wanted to return to Moab, even wanting to be buried where Naomi was buried. She did so in submission to God, the LORD (Jehovah), and called on Him as witness and guarantor of this vow. Naomi knew that Ruth was indeed determined to stay with her.

From Moab, Naomi and Ruth traveled the sixty-plus miles back to Bethlehem where the women of the town met them. Many of them remembered Naomi and were somewhat surprised at her appearance. Perhaps the hardships of the years had taken their toll in her countenance.

Word Study
DETERMINED OR STEADFASTLY MINDED

The word translated determined *('amats)* in Ruth 1:18 literally means "to be strong" and could be translated "she made her choice having strengthened herself." In other words, Ruth set her heart and will to go with Naomi and did so with all her might and determination.

Naomi and Ruth arrived in Bethlehem at the beginning of the barley harvest in April, in time to take part in the harvesting of grain. One of the fields belonged to Boaz, a relative of Naomi through her husband Elimelech. We meet him in chapter 2 as Ruth and Naomi settle in. Let's trace the events of this new chapter in the lives of Ruth and Naomi.

📖 According to Ruth 2:1–2, how did Ruth respond to the circumstances in which she and Naomi found themselves?

_____

_____

_____

_____

_____

Ruth willingly offered to go and glean in the fields behind the reapers. Her servant's heart was evident. The practice of gleaning is rooted in the Mosaic law which instructs the Israelites to allow the poor, the stranger (a non-Israelite), the fatherless, and the widow to pick the grain in the corners of the fields and to go behind the reapers, gleaning what is left from the harvest (Leviticus 19:9–10; 23:22; Deuteronomy 24:19–22).

📖 What do you find about Boaz in Ruth 2:1, 4?

_____

_____

_____

_____

Boaz was a relative of Elimelech and a man of great wealth. When he came to his field he greeted his reapers with *"the LORD be with you,"* while they replied with *"the LORD bless you."* This shows something of the heart of Boaz. His first words are rooted in his relationship to the LORD, the God of Israel. In the time of the Judges, it is evident that he saw the Lord as King over his life. He had a good relationship with his workers who also recognized the Lord in their lives and in their work. It appears that Boaz knew that the harvest always comes by the providence and mercy of the Lord.

Ruth 2:5–7 presents us with the testimony Ruth bore to the workers in the fields. When Boaz came to his field, he recognized the presence of a young woman he had not seen before. The servant in charge of the reapers had ample time to see her at work and spoke well of her. She was known as the Moabite woman who came back with Naomi. The servant took note of her as a diligent worker. She had worked hard since morning with only a short time of rest in the field tent.

📖 How did Boaz treat Ruth according to Ruth 2:8–9?

_____

_____

_____

_____

Boaz urged her to stay in his field to reap with his young women, assuring her that she would be protected there. He had commanded the young men not to touch her. Furthermore, he made sure she knew water was available to drink whenever she might be thirsty. Here was protection and provision.

Ruth 2:10 shows us Ruth's response of deep humility and gratitude. She acknowledged that as a foreigner she had no rights in the land, but was grateful for the gracious provision and protection of Boaz. In her conversation with Boaz, Ruth displayed that same servant-like attitude that she had earlier revealed toward her mother-in-law, Naomi.

What was the testimony Boaz had heard about Ruth according to 2:11–12?

_____

_____

_____

Did You Know?

GRACE IN GLEANING

Leviticus 19:9–10; 23:22, and Deuteronomy 24:19–22 make provision for the foreigner, the fatherless, the poor, and the widow to glean in the fields of Israel. This was a provision of grace because the Israelites had been shown grace in the Lord's deliverance of them from Egyptian slavery. Boaz showed even more grace in his abundant provision for Ruth and Naomi (Ruth 2:8–19; 3:15–17).

What was the testimony of Ruth's relationship with the Lord?

_____

_____

_____

Did You Know?

 UNDER THE LORD'S WINGS

As in Ruth 2:12, the imagery of a young bird under the wing of its mother is often used in the Psalms of one seeking refuge in the Lord (Psalm 17:8; 36:7; 57:1; 61:4; 63:7; 91:4). It conveys a close relationship of protection, provision, and blessing. That is our relationship with the Lord.

Boaz knew of the death of her husband, of her servant-like attitude toward Naomi, of her commitment to stay with Naomi and the people of God—though it was in a new land away from her father and mother and the land of her birth. He blessed her with a blessing from the Lord. He desired for her a reward for all her hard work. He was quick to add his wish for the Lord's blessings upon her. Ruth's surrender to the Lord was evident. Boaz compared her relationship with the Lord to that of a young bird seeking refuge under the wings of its mother (v. 12). Ruth had come to Israel to seek refuge, protection, and security in the Lord.

APPLY Where are you seeking refuge? In a bank account? In a job or career? In sports? In your intellectual abilities? In your talents? In your social position? In amassing material goods? In popularity? There are many false roads to take to find security and protection. The Lord is our refuge. He can cover us with His wings so that we are truly protected forever.

 DAY THREE

THE HAND OF THE LORD WORKING THROUGH THE KINSMAN-REDEEMER

With the encounter between Ruth and Boaz found in Ruth 2:8–12, we are introduced to a man who followed the Lord, the God of Israel. We begin to see his heart and character as he speaks with Ruth. With this encounter we are also introduced to the one who could serve as a **kinsman-redeemer**. We see the word first mentioned in Ruth 2:20. It is translated "next kinsman" or "close (or closest) relative." Today, we will get to know Boaz better and with that knowledge also begin to learn some things about the kinsman-redeemer.

What do you find about Boaz in 2:13–16?

_____

_____

_____

_____

_____

Ruth stated that Boaz had comforted her and spoken kindly to her, which were two marks of the character of God. He apparently had a very tender, sensitive heart, for the phrase _"spoken kindly to"_ (v. 13) is literally "spoke to the heart of." He spoke in a way that touched Ruth's heart. Ruth acknowledged that he did so even though she was not at the level of even one of his maidservants. Not only that, Boaz also took special note of her at mealtime, giving her bread with vinegar (helpful to quench thirst), as well as an abundance of parched grain. (She had enough and some left over.) After eating, Boaz instructed the young men to allow her to glean among the full sheaves without reproaching her. Even more, he told them to purposefully let some of their grain fall that she might pick it up.

Ruth worked a full day, finishing in the evening and carrying home about an ephah of barley (equivalent to around 30 to 40 pounds). She carried it home to Naomi along with the left-over parched grain from lunch, evidence that she had indeed had a prosperous day.

Ruth 2:19–20 gives us Naomi's response to events of the day and to the hand of the Lord at work. It was evident to Naomi that this was no ordinary day's gleanings. Ruth had been blessed! Someone had taken notice of her and purposefully blessed her. Ruth reported about her day's labor in the field of Boaz, and Naomi saw more than just the kindness and generosity of this land owner. The word for "kindness" (*chesed*) is the word used of "covenant loyalty or faithfulness," and is often translated "lovingkindness" or "mercy." Naomi saw a deep-seated kindness as well as the hand of the Lord prospering her and Ruth, and she praised the Lord for such covenant kindness. Naomi knew this man was one of their kinsmen, one who could serve as a kinsman-redeemer to Ruth and to the family. She saw in Boaz one who not only had the **family ties** to serve as a kinsman-redeemer, but one who also had the **heart** of a kinsman-redeemer.

Boaz urged Ruth to stay with his reapers until the harvest was finished. Boaz knew that protection and provision could be found in the presence of the reapers. Naomi agreed that Ruth should stay in the field of Boaz. Ruth worked through the barley harvest and into the wheat harvest, which ended in mid-June. The hand of the Lord was at work to prosper Ruth and Naomi.

After two months of hard work in the harvest fields, the time for threshing was at hand. Naomi spoke to Ruth about seeking rest or security for her through a kinsman-redeemer (3:1–2). As we noted earlier, the Mosaic law provided for a levirite marriage to care for the widow of a brother and to raise up a child to assure the continuation of the deceased brother's name in Israel. The exact relation of Elimelech to Boaz is not known, but it was certainly one that could fulfill this need. He could serve as the close relative or kinsman-redeemer.

📖 In Ruth 3:3–4, what does Naomi tell Ruth to do?

_____

_____

_____

📖 What was Ruth's response in Ruth 3:5?

_____

_____

_____

Naomi spoke of Boaz winnowing (sifting) barley that night. This was customary since the Mediterranean breezes would blow across the hilltops in the

Word Study
KINSMAN-REDEEMER

Literally translated "redeemer," *go'el* is often translated "close relative" or "kinsman-redeemer." Its root, *ga'al* means "to redeem or buy back" and occurs 23 times in the book of Ruth, most notably in 2:20, 3:9, 12, 4:1, 3, 4, 6, 8, 14. The duties of a kinsman-redeemer could include avenging a murder (Numbers 35:19—he is called *"the blood avenger"*), marrying his brother's widow to raise up a son in the name of the deceased brother (Deuteronomy 25:5–10), redeeming any family land that had been sold (Leviticus 25:25), redeeming a family member sold into slavery (Leviticus 25:47–49), or caring for any of the family members in need (Leviticus 25:35). The role of a kinsman-redeemer would fall first to the brother of a man. After that it fell to an uncle, then to an uncle's son, then to any near relative (Leviticus 25:48–49).

early evening hours. These breezes allowed the workers to throw the grain into the air, catching the chaff and allowing the clean grain to fall to the ground. Naomi instructed Ruth to wash and anoint herself and put on her best clothes. Then she was to go to the threshing floor where Boaz would spend the night. Naomi instructed Ruth to follow a Middle-eastern custom of uncovering the man's feet as a way of making known to him that she was available to be married—to be covered or protected by him as her husband.

Ruth's response to Naomi was as would be expected, *"All that you say, I will do"* (v. 5). She followed Naomi's instructions and went to the threshing floor. After Boaz had eaten, he went to sleep at the side of the heap of grain. Ruth came in and uncovered the feet of Boaz and waited. There was no hint of impropriety in this custom, rather it was a clear picture of tender care, of loving commitment, and of the promise of faithfulness to one another. In the middle of the night, Boaz awoke to see her at his feet. She identified herself and then asked Boaz to take her under his wing—that place of protection and care.

📖 How did Boaz respond and what did he say about Ruth in 3:10–11?

_____

_____

_____

_____

_____

> ## "All that you say, I will do."
> ### Ruth 3:5

Boaz recognized the pure character of Ruth, her evident relationship to the Lord, and her kindness toward him. Though she could have sought a younger man to be her husband, Ruth came to the older Boaz desiring him as her kinsman-redeemer—as the one who would fulfill the levirite marriage. Boaz also recognized and mentioned Ruth's reputation as *"a woman of **excellence**,"* the same word that is used to describe the virtuous wife of Proverbs 31:10.

📖 What was Boaz' commitment to Ruth according to Ruth 3:12–13?

_____

_____

_____

_____

> **Boaz also recognized and mentioned Ruth's reputation as "a woman of excellence," the same word that is used to describe the virtuous wife of Proverbs 31:10.**

Boaz acknowledged that he was a close relative and able to be a kinsman-redeemer, if a closer relative to Ruth chose not to fulfill that role. He committed himself to go that morning and fulfill the requirements, if the closer relative did not want to do so. Boaz again centered all he did on his relationship with the Lord, even making his commitment to Ruth with an oath before the Lord—*"as the LORD lives,"* the personal, covenant-keeping God of Israel and of Boaz.

Early in the morning (apparently while it was still dark), Ruth went to Naomi and told her all that had happened at the threshing floor and about the promise of Boaz. She also showed her the wonderful provision of grain he had given her. Naomi wisely instructed Ruth to wait patiently on Boaz. Surely that morning he would go and seek to fulfill his desired role as the kinsman-redeemer.

THE HAND OF THE LORD FULFILLING HIS PURPOSES

When morning dawned, Boaz was determined to do all he could to redeem the land of Elimelech and the hand of Ruth. He went to the city gate very early that morning, for that was where business matters were cared for in the culture of that day. There he soon saw the relative of Naomi who stood in a closer relation to Ruth than he did and he called for him to join in a meeting. Then Boaz called for ten elders of the city, men who could witness the transaction between Boaz and this other relative.

📖 Review the details of Ruth 4:3–5 and record what happened. What do you see about Boaz?

_____

_____

_____

_____

Boaz very carefully presented the facts of the matter. Naomi had to sell the portion of land that belonged to Elimelech. We are not told why, but it is presumed that her poverty was a factor. Boaz and the other relative were kin to Elimelech in some way, though the exact relation is not certain. (The use of the term *"our brother"* in some translations does not refer to an actual brother.) Boaz used the emphatic "I" in verse 4 to point out that he was initiating this right of redemption. He wanted to know if this other kinsman would redeem the land before the elders and witnesses according to the custom of the day. If not, Boaz was ready, even eager, to redeem it. The man agreed to redeem the land. Then Boaz informed him, that to inherit the land, he must also agree to marry Ruth the Moabitess, the widow of the deceased Mahlon, son of the deceased Elimelech. With that bit of information the man refused because of the jeopardy in which it would put his own inheritance. He then offered his right of redemption to Boaz.

Was this refusal in keeping with the Mosaic Law? It appears there was an honorable way to refuse the role of kinsman-redeemer, especially knowing that there was another near-relative prepared to fulfill that role. According to the custom of that time-period, the near-relative then took off his sandal and gave it to Boaz—thus giving him the right of redemption for the land and Ruth. He was saying in essence, "I give you my right to walk on and possess this land. You may walk on it as yours." With his right to marry Ruth, he would also be entrusted with raising up a son in Mahlon's name, and thus, in Elimelech's name as well.

Did You Know?
LAND IN ISRAEL

Land in Israel was first of all owned by the Lord. He chose the land where Israel would live and He gave it to them to enjoy. He still owned it as Leviticus 25:23 made clear, *"The land is Mine."* That meant it could not be sold permanently. It was considered a vital part of each family. As such it was not to be sold or traded out of the tribe and if possible was to stay within the family. Numbers 36:7–9 clearly stated that land was not to be transferred from one tribe to another. Each tribe was to hold on to their inheritance. The Law in Leviticus 25:23 said that if the land was sold (not permanently), a family member was to redeem the land where possible (25:24–27). If it was not possible, then it was to revert back to the family in the Year of Jubilee (25:28).

With this, Boaz announced to all present that he was acquiring all that belonged to Elimelech, Chilion, and Mahlon. He also announced his marriage to Ruth that they might *"raise up the name of the deceased on his inheritance"* so that his name might be carried on among his family and in the city of his birth, Bethlehem (4:10).

📖 What was the response of the elders to the marriage of Boaz and Ruth, according to Ruth 4:11–12?

_____

_____

_____

They testified to the validity of Boaz' claim and then pronounced a blessing over the couple. In their blessing, they asked the Lord to make Ruth like Rachel and Leah, who built the house of Israel. This was a blessing of great worth! There was no home so honored as was the home of Jacob (Israel) with his twelve sons through Rachel and Leah. The twelve tribes of Israel came through them. They also wished, for Boaz and his family, wealth or power and a name of greatness and honor in Bethlehem. They did not stop there. They wished for their home to be like the home of Perez, son of Judah, through whom came the tribe of Judah, the tribe that was promised the scepter in Israel and the tribe of which Bethlehem was a part.

📖 According to Ruth 4:13, what do you see about the hand of the Lord in this family?

_____

_____

_____

_____

The Lord enabled Ruth to conceive, and she bore a son. Nothing is said of all the years of her marriage to Mahlon and the fact that no children came of that union. She may have been barren. It is significant that here we see clearly stated that the hand of the Lord blessed Ruth so that she could conceive. Verse 13 says literally that the Lord *"gave her conception,"* evidence of what Psalm 127:3 declares, *"Children are a gift of the Lord, the fruit of the womb is a reward."*

📖 What was the response of the neighbor women concerning this family and Naomi, according to Ruth 4:14–17?

_____

_____

_____

_____

How did they view the Lord's hand at work?

_____

_____

_____

Did You Know?

? THE SCEPTER IN JUDAH

Jacob made it clear when he prophesied over his twelve sons that the scepter or ruler's staff would not depart from the tribe of Judah, the tribe of Boaz. Ruth married into that tribe of Judah and became the great-grandmother of King David, the ancestor of Jesus, the Lion of the Tribe of Judah (Revelation 5:5).

The women of Bethlehem praised the Lord for giving Naomi a "redeemer," referring this time to the son born of Boaz and Ruth. They prayed that his name would become great in Israel and they longed for Naomi to know the restoration of life that a kinsman-redeemer could bring, not only for now, but also in Naomi's old age. They gave testimony of Ruth's love for Naomi and declared that she was better than seven sons would have been. Ruth's son was seen as much a gift to Naomi as he was to Boaz and Ruth. Naomi became the child's nursemaid, treating him as though he were her own. The neighbor women saw this and chose for this son the name Obed, meaning "servant," implying that this child would serve Naomi and the family as the true fruit of a kinsman-redeemer and as a kinsman-redeemer himself.

📖 Ruth 4:18–22 lists ten key figures in the line from Perez (son of Judah [Ruth 4:12]) to David, covering a period of about 850 years. This genealogy shows the evident place of David in the tribe of Judah. Compare this passage with Matthew 1:3–6. What is significant in this passage?

_____

_____

_____

_____

_____

_____

How do you see the hand of the Lord at work?

_____

_____

_____

_____

_____

The interesting thing in Matthew 1 is the place given to the four women in the genealogy of Jesus. These four women are as follows: Tamar (with Judah [1:3]); Rahab (with Salmon [1:5]); Ruth (with Boaz [1:5]); and Bathsheba (with David [1:6]). In each case there was something that scarred their lives, but the Lord chose them to be in the genealogy of His Son. Think of these facts: Tamar bore Perez through her trickery with Judah, her father-in-law; Rahab was a harlot in Jericho; Ruth was a Moabitess; and Bathsheba, who was the wife of Uriah, committed adultery with David. Each of these women had something that marred them in some way, yet God in His grace chose to use them not only in the life of Israel, but ultimately in the genealogy of Jesus. In each case we see the hand of God overseeing their lives and overruling their liabilities. Ruth was among them as one called out of Moab to join herself to the Lord and to His people. The hand of God in her life as well as in the life of Boaz and Naomi gives testimony to the grace, mercy, and love of God in using very ordinary people to fulfill His extraordinary purposes. That is the kind of Kinsman-Redeemer He is.

God uses very ordinary people to fulfill His extraordinary purposes.

FOR ME TO FOLLOW GOD

The book of Ruth presents us with the many ways God works to accomplish His purposes. We see the hand of God at work in Moab and in Bethlehem. Through calamities, through times of prosperity, through various relationships and events, He is ever working to accomplish His purposes. That occurred not only in the lives of those involved then, but also in the lives of generations to come. The Lord has not changed. He is still working in this way. Just as we see abundant grace through the life of a kinsman-redeemer like Boaz, so we see in infinitely greater ways that abundant grace in and through our Kinsman-Redeemer, Jesus Christ.

> *... so we see in infinitely greater ways that abundant grace in and through our Kinsman-Redeemer, Jesus Christ.*

APPLY Pause for a moment and think through the events of your life. What ways do you see the overruling hand of God at work?

_____

_____

_____

_____

_____

Can you think of some calamities you or someone close to you has faced? Perhaps it has been recent or even going on right now, and you are having a hard time seeing God anywhere. Are you where Naomi was, feeling afflicted, empty, like God was against her rather than for her? Many times there are no easy answers. However, many answers can be found in God's holy Word, and we have an Author at hand to walk us through the problems and questions we are facing. That requires faith in His loving heart rather than trusting our limited sight or feeling in the midst of dark circumstances.

Talk to the Lord about some of the difficulties you or those close to you face. You may want to write a letter to the Lord in the space below. Think back over the lives of Naomi and Ruth as you do so.

_____

_____

_____

_____

_____

_____

_____

> *Sometimes we have allowed our prosperity to fill us with the "junk food" of the world so that we have no appetite for Him and His Word.*

Sometimes we are in the midst of prosperity. In those times we must also look to the Lord. There is a necessity to use special caution in prosperous times, for it is in those times that He seems even further away from us—because we sense no need for Him. Sometimes we have allowed that prosperity to fill us with the "junk food" of the world so that we have no appetite for Him and His Word. Are you in this condition?

APPLY Stop and consider where you are and talk to Him about it. Write any thoughts in the space below.

_____

_____

_____

_____

_____

Perhaps you are seeing God meet your needs with a little surplus. Are you living like Ruth, following His directions in the "field" in which He has you? Are you acknowledging the hand of the Lord like Naomi and Ruth did? Are you grateful? Content? Perhaps you need to keep doing what He has you doing now, trusting that when it is time to change, He will take care of that as well.

Ruth was a Gentile idol worshiper, with no claims to greatness. Yet, she became the great-grandmother of king David. From her descendants would rise Solomon and all the kings of Judah. One day, from her family would rise the King of kings. But what did she do to find the purposes of God for her life? She had to put aside her old life and friends in Moab, and find a new place with the people of God.

Ruth chose to become a part of the life of Naomi, and with that, a part of the people of God. She sought refuge under the wing of Jehovah. Here is a beautiful picture of repentance and surrender. Ruth forsook her family, her homeland, but—most of all—she forsook the Moabite gods in order to follow the Lord, the true God. In so doing, she was also in a place to receive the redemption offered by the kinsman-redeemer (Boaz), and ultimately the redemption offered by the Lord to those who trust Him as their God. Orpah, on the other hand, was back in Moab apart from any relation to the true God or His people. She did not receive the redemption that could have been hers. We hear nothing more of Orpah.

When Ruth turned from her old life in Moab and surrendered her life to the God of Naomi, this penniless widow found the two things all of us spend our lives looking for: **security** and **significance**.

Let's take a few moments to review the security Ruth found when she left Moab and its idols for Israel and its God. (Check all that were true of Ruth.)

☐ Food   ☐ Protection
☐ Famine   ☐ The True God
☐ The family land of her first husband   ☐ A new husband
☐ A false god   ☐ Barrenness
☐ A child   ☐ Prosperity

APPLY Naomi told Ruth that she wanted to seek security or rest for her through a kinsman-redeemer. Where are you seeking your security? Review the lists on the following page and ask the Lord to help you honestly evaluate where you are.

> *For many in Ruth's day, to leave one's land was to leave one's gods. Ruth did this with a whole heart and never looked back.*

> *Ruth found true security in the Lord.*

In the Lord	In All the Wrong Places
☐ In the promises of His Word	☐ In the opinions of others
☐ In the provision He has given	☐ In getting more things/money
☐ In His strength	☐ In my best efforts
☐ In humbling myself under His hand	☐ In confidence in my abilities
☐ In His wisdom	☐ In the wisdom of this world

Perhaps the thing lacking in your life is designed by God to draw you toward Him. It is He who will bring you to the place of true satisfaction, of fulfilling all of God's purposes for your life. Are you seeking the Kinsman-Redeemer He has sent, the Lord Jesus? Are you listening to what He is saying to you or reading any of His letters—His Word?

Do you believe He is sufficient for your needs? Are you willing to wait on Him and trust Him to take care of all the details to accomplish your full redemption? Find your rest in Him as Ruth did in Boaz. Of course, ultimately Boaz, Ruth, and Naomi knew it was the Lord caring for them, carrying, guiding and redeeming them. **He** was their rest. He wants to be the same for you.

Not only did Ruth find **security** when she turned to the God of Israel, she also found a **significance** she had never known. She became a mother for the first time. Through this child, Obed, Ruth would see kings arise. And through this Biblical book that bears her name we have a record of her faithfulness and trust; thus, her ministry continues to this day.

 Where have you been looking for **significance**?

_____

_____

_____

_____

_____

_____

You will never find true **security** or **significance** until you surrender yourself to the Lord.

Spend some time with the Lord in prayer right now.

Lord, I thank You that You never change. You are the same yesterday, today, and forever. Your hand is ever working, fulfilling Your purposes. Thank You that You have included me in those purposes. Thank You that Your hand is at work, and that You are fitting together all the things in my life, even though I sometimes fail to see your hand working in my life. I thank You for the lean times as well as the times of plenty. Thank You that You have a redeeming, loving heart and that I can find rest in You. May I learn to trust You in all the circumstances of my life and wait on You as You fulfill Your purposes and lead me in the security of Your redemption. Amen.

> **Ultimately, Boaz, Ruth, and Naomi knew it was the Lord caring for them, carrying them, guiding and redeeming them. He was their rest.**

Write a prayer to the Lord, expressing your trust in Him where you are now.

_____

_____

_____

_____

_____

_____

_____

_____

_____

_____

Did You Know?

THE MEGILLOTH

The Book of Ruth is part of the *Megilloth*, five books of the Old Testament read in conjunction with five festivals of Israel. The Song of Solomon was read at Passover (March), Ruth at Pentecost/Feast of Weeks (May) in celebration of the spring grain harvest, Lamentations on the ninth of Ab (July) in memory of the destruction of Jerusalem in July of 586 BC, Ecclesiastes during the Feast of Tabernacles (October), and Esther during Purim (December).

The Life of Ruth the Moabitess

DATE	EVENTS	SCRIPTURE
ca. 1175 BC?	Boaz was born in Israel, a descendant of Salmon and Rahab (Joshua 2:1–21; 6:22–25).	Ruth 4:21; Matthew 1:5
ca. 1150? BC	Ruth was born in the land of Moab, east of the Dead Sea, in what is modern-day Jordan.	Ruth 1:4
ca. 1125 BC	A famine struck the land of Israel.	Ruth 1:1
	Elimelech, his wife Naomi, and his two sons, Mahlon and Chilion, left their home in Bethlehem (in the area known as Ephrathath) and moved to the land of Moab (a journey of about 60–70 miles).	Ruth 1:1-2
	Elimelech died in the land of Moab leaving Naomi and her two sons.	Ruth 1:3
ca. 1125 BC	The two sons married Moabite women. Mahlon married Ruth and Chilion married Orpah.	Ruth 1:4; 4:10
ca. 1115 BC	After about ten years in the land of Moab, Mahlon and Chilion died.	Ruth 1:4–5
	The land of Bethlehem experienced fruitful harvests. Naomi heard about this and prepared to return to Bethlehem.	Ruth 1:6
	Naomi, Orpah, and Ruth began the journey to Bethlehem.	Ruth 1:7
	Naomi released Orpah and Ruth to return to their respective families in Moab, and await the Lord's choice of a husband for them.	Ruth 1:8–9
	Orpah and Ruth chose to go with Naomi.	Ruth 1:10
	Naomi urged them to stay in Moab where they could be married once again. She would not be able to raise up sons to take the place of Mahlon and Chilion (Levirite marriage provision [Deuteronomy 25:5–10]).	Ruth 1:11–13
	Orpah chose to leave Naomi and stay in Moab with her people and her gods.	Ruth 1:14–15
	Ruth chose to cling to Naomi and go with her to Bethlehem.	Ruth 1:14; 16–18
	The people of Bethlehem gladly received Naomi. Naomi recounted her bitter circumstances.	Ruth 1:19–21
April, 1115	They returned at the beginning of barley harvest.	Ruth 1:22
First day in barley fields	Ruth went to glean barley in the fields, following the reapers and gleaning what was left after them and what was untouched in the corners according to Mosaic law (Leviticus 19:9–10).	Ruth 2:1–3
	Ruth came to the field belonging to Boaz, a relative of Elimelech, Naomi's deceased husband.	Ruth 2:1, 3
	Boaz observed her gleaning in his field and inquired about her. The servants spoke of her as the Moabitess who came with Naomi. She had been working since morning.	Ruth 2:4–7
	Boaz told Ruth to stay in his field with his servants. He promised her protection as she gleaned. Ruth responded with humility and gratitude.	Ruth 2:8–10
	Reflecting on how Ruth forsook her home and family in Moab, he spoke favorably of her commitment to come with Naomi. He blessed her by asking that the Lord God reward her, for she sought shelter and refuge under the *"wings"* of the Lord. Ruth again responded in humility and gratitude.	Ruth 2:11–13
	Boaz invited her to eat with him and the reapers. He gave her bread, vinegar, and grain. She ate till she was satisfied and saved back some of the grain. Boaz instructed his servants to let her glean among the sheaves and to purposefully allow extra grain to fall on the ground so she could glean it.	Ruth 2:14–16
	Ruth diligently gleaned until evening and brought home about an ephah of barley (20 quarts or 35 pounds). She also provided Naomi with grain she had kept back at lunch.	Ruth 2:17–18
	Naomi sought to know where Ruth had gleaned. She rejoiced and praised the Lord to hear of Boaz, because he was a relative to Naomi.	Ruth 2:19–20
Spring 1115 BC	Naomi advised Ruth to stay with the servants of Boaz in his field. Ruth gleaned there for the remainder of the barley and wheat harvests.	Ruth 2:21–23
On a certain night 1115 BC	Naomi instructed Ruth to go and meet Boaz after he finished winnowing (sifting) barley, proclaim herself to be available for marriage, and to follow what he said. This was according to the law of the kinsman-redeemer, a relative who could redeem her through marriage. Ruth agreed to this.	Ruth 3:1–5
	Ruth did as Naomi instructed. When Boaz discovered her at his feet, he listened to her request that he be her kinsman-redeemer (see Deuteronomy 25:5–10).	Ruth 3:6–9

DATE	EVENTS	SCRIPTURE
Certain night 1115 BC	Boaz spoke the blessing of the Lord upon Ruth. He agreed to be her redeemer if no closer, more qualified relative arose to fulfill that role.	Ruth 3:10-13
The next morning	Ruth went to Naomi with the blessing of Boaz. He had also given her six portions of grain. Naomi told her to wait on Boaz concerning these matters.	Ruth 3:14–18
	At the city gate (the place of official business transactions), Boaz spoke to the other relative who could claim the right of kinsman-redeemer. The man declined that right and gave it to Boaz.	Ruth 4:1–6
	The elders of the city witnessed the transaction of Boaz redeeming the land of Elimelech and acquiring Ruth as his wife to fulfill the law concerning inheritance. They blessed Boaz and Ruth and the offspring they would bear.	Ruth 4:7–12; Leviticus 25:25; Deuteronomy 25:5–10
ca. 1112 BC	The Lord enabled Ruth to conceive, and she and Boaz had a son.	Ruth 4:13
	The women of Bethlehem blessed the Lord for providing a redeemer for Naomi Naomi rejoiced in this child.	Ruth 4:14–16
	The neighbor women named this son Obed, meaning "servant."	Ruth 4:17
	Obed became the father of Jesse, who became the father of David. Ruth was David's great-grandmother.	Ruth 4:17

Notes

Hannah

BRINGING OUR BARRENNESS TO THE LORD

Many know of Hannah through her son, the prophet Samuel. It is said that much can be known about someone by the words they speak, because words come from the heart. If that is true, then the statement Hannah made at Samuel's birth reveals much about her heart. First Samuel 1:20 says she exclaimed of her newborn son, "*I have asked him from the LORD.*" Hannah had a heart to ask and receive, because she knew the Lord had a heart to give. She knew that if her barrenness was to end, it must end by the hand of God. That is why she brought her barrenness to the Lord.

If your heart is crying out because of some area of barrenness, then Hannah should become a true friend to you. She discovered much about asking as well as thanking, praising, and interceding. If you are facing some pains that won't go away, you will want to spend some time with Hannah and listen to her cries and her counsel. In the midst of all that she experienced, she discovered that God was at work doing more than she could ask or think. If you long to know God at a depth you thought was only for the "super saints," then Hannah will be an encouragement to you. She didn't have all the answers, but she learned to bring her questions to the Lord in prayer. There God met her and walked with her, and she followed Him.

Hannah lived as a barren woman at a time when the nation of Israel was experiencing spiritual barrenness. Her solution was Israel's solution: brokenness before the Lord.

WHERE DOES SHE FIT?

2200BC	1950	1700	1450	1200	950	700	450	100
SARAH 2155–2028		MIRIAM 1533?–1405				Daniel 619–534?		MARY and MARTHA 10BC?–60AD?
			DEBORAH 1300?–1200?	Solomon 991–931		ESTHER 504?–450?		
			Judges Rule 1385–1051	David 1041–971				
						Nehemiah 480?–400?		MARY, Mother of Jesus 20BC–60AD?
Jacob 2005–1858		Joshua 1495–1385	RUTH 1135?–1050?					
Isaac 2065–1885		Moses 1525–1405	HANNAH 1135?–1050?	VIRTUOUS WOMAN Prov. 31				
Abraham 2165–1990		RAHAB 1445?–1385?	Samuel 1105–1022					Jesus Christ 4BC?–30AD?

 **DAY ONE**

HANNAH'S CRY OF BITTERNESS

The events in the life of Hannah, recorded in 1 Samuel, occurred during the years 1135 to 1090 BC. This was during the close of the period of the judges, just prior to the period of the monarchy beginning with the choice of Saul as king (1051 BC). It was a period of spiritual decline and corruption. Israel was marked by a wandering heart. The final verse of Judges summarizes it well, *"In those days there was no king in Israel; everyone did what was right in his own eyes"* (Judges 21:25). It is during this time that we are introduced to the family of Hannah.

📖 We are first introduced to Hannah's husband. What do you find out about him in 1 Samuel 1:1–2 and 1 Chronicles 6:33–34, 38?

_____

_____

_____

_____

_____

Hannah's husband was named Elkanah. He lived in the city of Ramathaim-zohim, also known as Ramah (1 Samuel 1:19) in the hill country of Ephraim, about five miles north of Jerusalem. Although he lived in the territory of Ephraim, Elkanah was of the priestly tribe of Levi (1 Chronicles 6:38). When 1 Samuel 1:1 mentions Elkanah's ancestor Zuph as an Ephraimite, it is referring to his location in this territory—not to his tribe, since the Levites lived scattered throughout the twelve tribes of Israel.

📖 What do you discover about Hannah in 1 Samuel 1:2?

_____

_____

_____

_____

Hannah was one of two wives belonging to Elkanah. This was not God's design, since from the beginning He created one woman for one man (Genesis 2:18–25). This situation was tolerated even as it was with Jacob, who married both Leah and Rachel (Genesis 29). Since Hannah is mentioned first, it is most likely that Hannah was Elkanah's first wife and probably the older of the two. There is one crucial distinction between these two women. Hannah had no children; Peninnah had several children, perhaps as many as five or six (1:4). It is possible that Elkanah married Peninnah because Hannah was barren.

📖 What do you find about this family in 1 Samuel 1:3–5?

_____

_____

_____

_____

Did You Know?
✏ A LEVITE LIVING IN EPHRAIM

God provided in the Law that the Levites would not have a specific territory in Israel but would live throughout the land within the territory of each of the twelve tribes (Numbers 18:23–24; 35:1–8; Joshua 21:1–42). Therefore we find Elkanah of the tribe of Levi living in the territory of Ephraim.

"In those days there was no king in Israel; everyone did what was right in his own eyes."

Judges 21:25

Elkanah was a spiritual leader in his home. He continued to do what God commanded in spite of the time in which he lived (Judges 21:25; 1 Samuel 2:12–17, 22). As a devout man he traveled every year to worship and offer sacrifices at the three required feasts held at the tabernacle at Shiloh, which was located about twenty miles north of Jerusalem and fifteen miles from Ramah. There Eli, the high priest ministered along with his two sons, Hophni and Phinehas. At Shiloh, Elkanah and his family sacrificed and feasted before the Lord. Elkanah provided for Peninnah and her sons and daughters as well as for Hannah with this one difference: he gave Hannah a double portion because of his deep love for her.

In the midst of this picture of Elkanah's family, a grievous situation existed. Read 1 Samuel 1:5–7. What was at the center of Hannah's struggle?

_____

_____

_____

How did Peninnah fit into this situation?

_____

_____

_____

_____

What does the mention of Peninnah's actions tell you about her? How did Peninnah think of Hannah?

_____

_____

_____

_____

How did this affect Hannah?

_____

_____

_____

_____

At the center of Hannah's life stood the stigma of barrenness. She and the entire family knew that it was the Lord who blessed a husband and wife with children, and she above all others felt the burden of the truth—*"the Lord had closed her womb"* (vv. 5–6). Peninnah used Hannah's barrenness to ridicule her. Added to that was the evident favoritism Elkanah showed Hannah. Those things combined to make Peninnah a "rival," the Hebrew word referring to an adversary or enemy. This enemy (in Hannah's own house no less) often provoked her (literally, "thundered against her") to bring hurt feelings. Peninnah continually goaded Hannah, and brought her much grief. When they went to worship or to celebrate one of the feasts, it seems that Peninnah's insults over Hannah's barrenness intensified. Perhaps

Did You Know?
REQUIRED FEASTS

All men of Israel twenty years and older were required to travel to the place God chose to celebrate three feasts— Passover/Feast of Unleavened Bread [in Nisan (March/April)], Pentecost/Feast of Weeks [in Sivan (May/June)], and the Feast of Tabernacles or Booths [in Tishri (September/October)]. Exodus 23:14–17 and Deuteronomy 12:11–14; 16:1–17 (note vs. 16) give the regulations for these feast times.

Word Study
ELKANAH'S LOVE

The word translated "love" (*a'hab*) in 1 Samuel 1:5 speaks of a strong inclination of the mind and at the same time carries the idea of a deep and tender affection toward someone. It is often used of the love of a husband and wife for one another. This was the love Jacob had for Rachel (Genesis 29:30). In Deuteronomy 6:5 Israel is commanded to love God with this kind of love.

it was her way of berating Hannah by pointing out a supposed lack of spirituality or lack of favor with God. Perhaps she insinuated that she was more godly than Hannah was because she had been blessed with children. The words of taunting condemnation were extremely heavy upon Hannah. She often wondered, "Why can't I have children?" Those words and thoughts brought Hannah to the point of tears and a refusal to eat.

📖 What was Elkanah's response to his wife Hannah?

_____

_____

_____

Elkanah was one of the Kohathites, descendants of Kohath, one of the three sons of Levi (1 Chronicles 6:16, 33–38). His descendants ministered as Levitical musicians at the tabernacle in David's reign and at the Temple from Solomon's reign on (1 Chronicles 6:31–34).

Word Study

BETTER THAN TEN SONS

The meaning of "better" (*tov*) carries the idea of something beneficial, favorable, or good and often referred to economic or material benefits. How could this relate to Hannah? When Elkanah spoke to Hannah, his use of the word "better" may have pointed to economic benefits. If she became a widow, her only source of security was in having sons to provide for her in her old age. Elkanah had provided for Hannah better than ten sons could.

Elkanah wanted Hannah to know of his great love for her. He saw her tears and her refusal to eat. He asked her, *"Why is your heart sad?"* In the Hebrew language that question literally reads "Why is your heart bad?" The word translated "sad" is the Hebrew word *ra'a',* which can refer to an envious or selfish, begrudging eye or an angry, sullen, resentful eye. Elkanah wanted to know why Hannah was acting in such a fashion. He wondered if she might be angry and resentful because she had no children. He loved her. Wasn't his love for her better than giving birth to ten sons?

Through Elkanah's questions, God was getting Hannah's attention. Her resentful attitude revealed a wrong focus. She was intent on looking at her barrenness and her rival—not at her Lord and the evident love of her husband. Hannah had to deal with her heart attitude as well as with her despair. How would she do that? What could she do? We will observe that in Day Two.

 How about you? Are you in a situation of barrenness? Are you resentful, or are you simply burdened down with the weight of circumstances you never dreamed you would face? Or are you like Peninnah—on the giving end of grief, making sure others are suffering? It is time to ask those questions, but do so in the presence of the Lord.

 **DAY TWO**

HANNAH'S PRAYER OF BROKENNESS

Apparently Hannah listened to her husband's counsel. She ate and drank there at Shiloh. When she finished eating, she arose and went to the entrance of the temple area, a complex of dwellings that included the Tabernacle. Eli the priest was sitting on a seat near the doorway when she came.

📖 What do you read about Hannah in 1 Samuel 1:10? What was the condition of her heart?

_____

_____

_____

_____

Hannah was "greatly distressed," or literally, *bitter of soul*. The years and the tears had taken their toll. She was at a low point and knew that she must do something, but this time her focus was not on her physical barrenness nor on Peninnah. She recognized that her anguish was getting the best of her, producing in her a spiritual barrenness. She had been responding wrongly by focusing on her circumstances rather than on the Lord. The problem was in her soul. She was "bitter of soul"—resentful, anxious, striving—and she wept in brokenness before the Lord.

📖 How did she handle this barrenness in her heart?

_____

_____

_____

_____

Hannah came before the Lord in prayer with a broken and contrite heart. She knew she could pour out all of her heart to the Lord, and that He would understand. He had closed her womb, but because He was the Creator and the Giver of all life, He could open her womb and give her children if He chose to do so. She wept with many tears as she prayed. She recognized her condition, her circumstances, and her hurts, but her focus was now on her Lord.

📖 To whom does Hannah pray (1:11)? [Note the same name in v. 3.]

_____

_____

_____

_____

As Hannah prayed, she called on the name of the LORD of Hosts, signifying one of two things. The LORD of Hosts is the Lord who is over all the heavenly hosts, the angels, and the armies of heaven. It could also refer to His being Lord over all the hosts of heaven, that is, the stars, sun, moon, and the millions of galaxies. God controls their orbits and their positions like clockwork. In either case, He is the sovereign Lord. She recognized His sovereignty over everything. He rules over everything everywhere, and He was not oblivious to her situation. The Lord could give Hannah a son.

📖 What did Hannah pray (1:11)?

_____

_____

_____

_____

Hannah asked the Lord to "look," which carries the idea of examining or investigating, and thus fully perceiving. She desperately wanted Him to be fully aware of the *"affliction of Thy maidservant."* Here we see her humility and spirit of submission to the LORD of Hosts. She was His maidservant who willingly humbled herself before Him. Her pain and affliction produced

Did You Know?

BARREN WOMEN AND THE CHILDREN THEY BORE

Hannah was one of many barren women the Lord blessed with significant children. Those include Sarah with Isaac (Genesis 11:30; 21:1–3), Rebekah with Jacob and Esau (Genesis 25:21–26), Rachel with Joseph and Benjamin (Genesis 29:31; 30:22-24; 35:18), Manoah's wife with Samson (Judges 13:2–3), Ruth with Obed who became the grandfather of king David (Ruth 4:13), Hannah with Samuel (1 Samuel 1:2, 5, 19–20), and Elizabeth with John the Baptist (Luke 1:7, 24–25).

In the vow Hannah made, she offered to give Samuel back to the Lord so that he might serve the Lord all the days of his life. Her statement about a razor never touching his head was very similar to the requirements for a Nazirite. In addition to this stipulation, a Nazirite never ate or drank anything from the vine (grape juice, wine, grapes, raisins) and never touched anything dead. Hannah's devotion to her Lord led her to offer this son to the Lord for life as a Nazirite. (Numbers 6:1–8).

Word Study

DAUGHTER OF BELIAL

When Hannah spoke to Eli at the door of the temple, she urged him not to think of her as a daughter of Belial (*"worthless woman"*—I Samuel 1:16). The meaning of Belial has two possibilities. The first takes this Hebrew word as rooted in *bly*, "to swallow" referring to Sheol or Death as the "Greatest Swallower" of life thus bringing destruction. A second perspective combines the two words *beli* and *ya'al* to form a word *beliya'al* meaning "without value" or "worthless" and thus "wicked." Therefore Ben Belial would be translated "son of worthlessness." In the New Testament, Belial became associated with Satan (2 Corinthians 6:15). That was the furthest thing from the heart and mind of Hannah.

humility in her, even as the wilderness experience of the children of Israel was meant to humble them for their own good (Deuteronomy 8:2–5, 15–16). She asked the Lord to remember her, which meant to act on her behalf—*"give Thy maidservant a son."* Then she expressed her devotion and trust as she made a vow to the Lord. If the Lord would grant this gift of a son to her, she would in turn, give him back to the Lord all the days of the child's life. She also promised that no razor would come upon his head.

When Eli the Priest saw Hannah's mouth moving but heard nothing, he assumed she was drunk. At the feasts it was not uncommon for someone to feast a little too much and get drunk. The pagan nations around Israel certainly experienced drunkenness at their places of idol worship, and sadly, so had some in Israel. This woman, however, was not consumed with alcohol. She was consumed with her bitterness of soul. She was praying from her heart because of her deep anguish of soul.

📖 What was Hannah's answer to Eli (vv. 15–16)?

_____

_____

_____

Hannah focused on the depth of her anguish, on the weight of the oppression in her spirit. She had not even poured out one cup of wine. Rather, in her oppression, she had poured out her soul before the Lord. Her prayer flowed from the depths of her soul, from a humble submissive heart calling on her sovereign Lord to act on her behalf. She would not dishonor God by any drunkenness. She quickly urged Eli not to think of her as a worthless woman drunk on wine. She knew the Lord was her covenant-keeping LORD (Jehovah), and she was submitting her heart concerns to Him. All her thoughts, all her desires for a son, even all memories of Penninah's insults, she brought before the Lord.

🛑 **APPLY** Are there some issues that have been a torment to your mind, haunting you continually? Are these issues keeping your attention so focused on the pain that you find it hard even to think straight? Cry out to the Lord. He wants to hear. He waits to hear your earnest petitions.

_____

_____

_____

_____

_____

_____

In 1 Samuel 1:17, Eli responded very graciously, *"Go in peace"* (shalom—full tranquillity, harmony). He then proclaimed a blessing for Hannah, *"May the God of Israel grant your petition."* She pleaded with God as a needy soul coming to a sovereign Lord, knowing He was capable of granting her request. Now she could return with this word of peace in her soul.

📖 How did the statement of Eli in verse 17 affect Hannah (1 Samuel 1:18)?

_____

_____

_____

_____

Hannah took Eli's statement very seriously. She saw in his statement the grace of God. There was a new ray of hope for Hannah. When she left him, she went back to her family and ate a good meal. Her countenance no longer revealed a troubled heart. Hannah's encounter with the Lord and with His representative, Eli, had sent a message to her heart, and now she would wait in faith for the answer to her prayer. It is important to realize that her countenance changed after she met with God—not after she received the answer. Her heart was at rest regardless of the outcome.

HANNAH AND THE BLESSINGS OF SURRENDER

The next morning the family rose up early, worshiped the Lord, and then returned to Ramah. Would things be different now? Or would the grief caused by Peninnah continue?

📖 How did the Lord respond to the prayer of Hannah (1:19)?

_____

_____

_____

📖 What happened in her life (v. 20)?

_____

_____

_____

_____

Hannah had prayed that the Lord would remember her. Indeed He did! The Lord remembered her request and in His timing gave her the ability to conceive. She gave birth to a son, the precise desire of her heart and exactly what she had asked the Lord to give her. She named him Samuel.

There is significance in Samuel's name. When Hannah gave her son the name Samuel, she made the statement _"Because I have asked for him from the Lord"_ (1:20 NKJV). Samuel literally means "name of God," but in the Hebrew language, it sounds similar to the word that means "heard by God." This play on words reflected Hannah's heart in petitioning the Lord for a son. He had heard her cry, and He answered her prayer.

What do you find in 1 Samuel 1:21–23 about this family and about Hannah?

_____

_____

_____

_____

_____

_____

"Praise the LORD! Praise, O servants of the LORD. Praise the name of the Lord. . . . He makes the barren woman abide in the house as a joyful mother of children. Praise the LORD!"

Psalm 113:1, 9

As one looks at the interaction between Elkanah and Hannah, there is an evident oneness between them. Elkanah was in agreement that this child was a gift to the Lord and would be taken to Shiloh at the proper time. Elkanah went to Shiloh, not only to offer the regular sacrifices, but also to give the offerings in fulfillment of a vow he had made. This was possibly a vow in agreement with Hannah's vow. It is evident that he considered Samuel as a child devoted to the Lord (Leviticus 7:11–16; 27:28).

Hannah stayed in Ramah while the rest of the family traveled to Shiloh. There she would continue raising the infant, preparing him for the time he would go to be with Eli. She told Elkanah that she would wean Samuel before taking him to Shiloh. Children were usually weaned at about age two or three. The Lord had answered prayer, and Hannah and Elkanah were living in the blessing of that answer. They now experienced true contentment of heart. When we are surrendered to the Lord and His will, we will truly be satisfied from the inside out. That is what we see in Hannah.

After about three years elapsed, it was time to take Samuel to Shiloh. There were certain regulations to be observed in fulfilling a vow. In Numbers 15:1–3, 8–10, the Lord gave specific regulations for the various sacrifices and offerings of His people. For the fulfillment of a vow, one could bring a young bull. Along with that particular offering went a grain offering of three-tenths of an ephah of fine flour mixed with oil and a drink offering of wine. This would have been about six quarts of flour and about three or four pints of wine. The bull was sacrificed and burnt on the altar. With it the grain and oil were offered up in the sacrificial fire and then on all of that the offering of wine was poured out. In each offering is the picture of whole-hearted surrender and brokenness: a bull sacrificed, its life poured out on the altar, grain crushed into flour, oil from the crushed olives, and wine from the beaten grapes. As the offering was burned and the wine poured out, this would have produced a sweet aroma as the smoke ascended to the heavens, a very Jewish picture of the fully surrendered heart, offering a gift of love to the Lord in heaven.

Hannah brought more than the required offering according to 1 Samuel 1:24–25. Some translations state she brought three bulls, and some say that she brought a three-year-old bull. Verse 25 states they slaughtered one bull. In either case she was fulfilling her vow. She brought three times the needed flour and a full skin of wine. Some view the flour and wine as part of a meal to be eaten along with the sacrifice. Since there was evidently more flour and wine than needed for the sacrifice, this is a possibility. The central truth here is not whether they ate and drank, but how they worshiped. We will see that in the next verses.

What is Hannah's testimony to Eli (1:26–27)?

_____

_____

_____

_____

_____

Elkanah and Hannah brought the child to Eli after the bull had been offered. Hannah offered her testimony of answered prayer in the life of the boy, Samuel. She had asked for a son and the Lord had granted her request. What Eli had said to her over three years before, the God of Israel had done (verse 17).

📖 What did Hannah and Elkanah do in 1 Samuel 1:28?

_____

_____

_____

_____

Hannah "lent" or "dedicated" Samuel to the Lord for life. The root word in Hebrew for "lent" is the same as the word for "asked" in verse 27. Hannah had asked for this son. Eli had wished for her that God would grant what she **asked** (1:17). Her testimony was one of **asking** and receiving. When she brought the child she gave Samuel to the Lord. She recognized the Lord had given him to her and now she was giving him in service back to the Giver. That is the heart of worship—gratefully receiving the life God gives and, in turn, wholeheartedly giving that life back to Him. There at Shiloh, Elkanah and Hannah did just that. They and Eli worshiped the Lord, possibly eating a fellowship meal as part of this celebration of worship and giving.

> *The heart of worship is gratefully receiving the life God gives and, in turn, wholeheartedly giving that life back to Him.*

APPLY How is your worship? Are you living in the light of knowing that everything you have is a gift from God? Are you walking in surrender to Him moment by moment? Think about all God has given you—children, finances, opportunities for ministry, and relationships. In your heart, have you given them back to the Lord in surrender? Why not offer up a prayer of thanksgiving? Then, make a fresh surrender of all to Him. It will make life as it should be, at least in your heart.

Hannah's Song of Worship

Hannah DAY FOUR

There at the place of surrender and celebration, Hannah began to pray. Her appreciation for the Lord and His ways had certainly developed over the last four years. There, looking at her only son and sensing in her heart that God was doing something far-reaching and of great significance, her words began to overflow in praise and thanksgiving.

📖 Read Hannah's song in 1 Samuel 2:1–10. In verses 1–2, what is first on her lips? What is her focus?

_____

_____

_____

_____

_____

Hannah focused her attention first on the Giver who had given her a son. Her heart was exulting in the Lord, saying in essence, "My heart is full of praise for the Lord. He is the one who strengthened me, when no one else could. He has given me victory when all around and all within, all I knew, was defeat and despair. He is like no other. No one is holy and pure like Him. No other humbles himself to help those who are weak and downcast. I am full of praise for You, my Lord."

📖 In light of her praise and exaltation of the Lord, what does Hannah confront in 1 Samuel 2:3?

_____

_____

_____

_____

Hannah spoke of the proud and arrogant who should silence themselves. She recognized that the Lord Himself was watching and weighing all that was going on. The word "knowledge" (_de'ah_, rooted in _yada_) refers to knowledge gained by experience, a knowledge gained from interaction with someone or something. It was sometimes used of a sailor sailing a vessel, a hunter skilled in the hunt, or a musician playing his instrument. It was also used of the knowledge a husband and wife have of one another as one flesh. God is ever interacting with His creation—ever watching and weighing the actions and attitudes of men and women. He knows fully all they do, think, or say, as well as their motives. Therefore, no one should ever act or speak out of an arrogant heart.

In light of this, Hannah exalted the sovereign Lord. In 1 Samuel 2:4–9, she mentioned over a dozen types of people: the mighty, the feeble, the full, the hungry, and many others. The Lord is over all of them. Hannah experienced honor from this sovereign Lord when she humbled herself in prayer. He had shown Himself strong on her behalf. She became a joyful mother, no longer barren, no longer bitter, now blessed by the Lord Himself. She experienced the workings of the Lord in her life and knew that He was not finished with her nor with her son Samuel.

Hannah's song emphasized that no man can prevail by his own strength (2:9). He must depend on the Lord, a fact Hannah personally experienced. She knew the Lord would deal with the proud who sought to get their own way. In 1 Samuel 2:10, Hannah spoke about the Lord thundering from heaven against His adversaries. The phrase "thunder against" is the exact phrase used of Peninnah in her provocation of Hannah (*"irritate her"* [1:6]). Hannah heard the arrogant provocation of Peninnah time and time again and just as the Lord had vindicated her against the thundering of Peninnah, so He would deal with all His enemies to the ends of the earth (2:10).

The Lord would also raise up His king and His anointed. We know from the remainder of First and Second Samuel that Hannah's son, Samuel would be the one used to anoint and appoint Israel's first two kings, Saul and David. David, of course, was the king who foreshadowed the greater Son of David, the one who would come as the Lord's King and Anointed One—the Messiah, Jesus Christ! Her song of triumphant worship in the present was also a prophecy of the greater work the Lord would do in the future.

Elkanah and Hannah returned to their home in Ramah, and the boy Samuel began ministering before the Lord in Shiloh. He did so in the midst of the corrupt leadership of Eli's sons, Hophni and Phinehas, who had no desire to please the Lord. The sons of Eli were lawless, irreverent, and immoral. The Scripture calls them *"sons of Belial,"* or sons of worthlessness, also translated "worthless men," or "corrupt" (2:12). They did not know the Lord, nor did they honor Him in any way—and that was the way they led the people. Samuel would be used to bring the people back to the Lord and His ways.

Every year Elkanah and Hannah traveled to Shiloh for the feasts and sacrifices. There they saw their son and doubtless talked much with him. Hannah made him a new robe each year and brought it to him at the time of the sacrifice. She was able to watch him grow and mature. Apparently Eli appreciated the ministry of Samuel. It was such a contrast to the ministry of his sons. Each year when Elkanah and Hannah came, Eli would offer a blessing on them.

📖 What was that blessing on Hannah (2:20)?

_____

_____

_____

_____

It appears that Eli spoke this blessing more than once. He prayed the Lord would give Elkanah and Hannah many children for the gift she had given in the boy, Samuel. That gift was given to the Lord, and Eli recognized and acknowledged him as such.

📖 What did the Lord do in Hannah's life (v. 21)?

_____

_____

_____

_____

_____

Did You Know?
PROPHET, PRIEST, AND JUDGE

Because of his lineage in the family of Elkanah of the tribe of Levi, Samuel was a Levitical priest. He also served as a judge in Israel in place of a king and as a prophet to the nation.

Did You Know?
SAMSON AND SAMUEL

Both men were born during the period of the judges to mothers who had been barren. Both served as judges over Israel and dealt with the Philistines as the enemies of Israel. They also were both under a Nazarite vow from birth (Judges 13:5, 7; 1 Samuel 1:11).

The Lord honored Eli's blessing upon Hannah and gave her three sons and two daughters. Not only that, but she had the blessing of seeing Samuel every year and watching him grow not only physically but also spiritually. Verse 21 says he *"grew before the Lord,"* a phrase referring to a continually growing knowledge of who the Lord is and what it means to follow Him. Hannah certainly had a growing knowledge of what it means to follow the Lord. She continued to experience His faithfulness in her life and saw His faithfulness in the life and ministry of her son, Samuel, a priest, a judge in Israel, a prophet, and the one who would bring God's choice of king to Israel.

Hannah **DAY FIVE**

FOR ME TO FOLLOW GOD

When we first met Hannah, we saw a woman barren and growing increasingly bitter. But she did not stay that way. She began to see her Lord, her circumstances, and herself in a new light. This is what happens when we bring our burdens to the Lord. The difficult circumstances she faced brought her to a crossroads, and the questions of her husband pointed her in the right direction. She could choose to stay resentful, or she could humble herself under the mighty hand of the Lord of Hosts. She chose to humble herself, and in brokenness she took the road to blessing. There really are only two ways to turn when we experience barrenness—either we take the path to bitterness, or we take the path to brokenness, which ultimately leads to blessing.

Think for a moment of your own life. What types of barrenness have you experienced? Look through the list below and check the areas where you have known barrenness.

__ Children	__ Employment	__ Pleasure	__ Attention
__ Friendships	__ Finances	__ Appreciation	__ Affirmation
__ Love	__ Sales	__ Peace of Mind	__ Honor
__ Respect	__ Ministry	__ Health	
__ Other _____			

More important than the particular kind of barrenness we experience, is what we choose to do with our barrenness. Will we bring it to the Lord, or will we turn inward with bitterness and anger? What determines our choice at this all-too-important crossroad of barrenness? It is really as simple as pride versus humility. Pride prompts us to "demand our rights." It tells us we know better than God does what is best for our lives. Sometimes we feel we have a right to the same blessing that someone else has. Humility, on the other hand, admits that God knows best what we need and when we need it. Humility leaves to God the choice of what to give us and when He will give it. God will never abandon us to barrenness. It is simply a land He chooses to take us through for a season. It is our choices, however, that may determine how long we stay there. You will remember that Israel was taken through the wilderness on the way to the Promised Land of Canaan. It was a dry and barren place, but God never intended them to stay there. In fact, some scholars estimate that without the penalty for their sin, the trip could have been as short as three days, and some say the trip could have taken as long as eleven days. The message is clear—**it didn't have to take forty years!**

> *There really are only two ways to turn when we experience barrenness—either we take the path to bitterness, or we take the path to brokenness, which ultimately leads to blessing.*

APPLY What is your normal response (or most recent response) to barrenness? Find yourself on the scale below.

Bitterness ◄ 1 2 3 4 5 6 7 8 9 10 ► Brokenness

At what crossroad are you? You can turn left to bitterness, or you can turn right to the blessing of surrender, and discover a life marked by the very atmosphere of heaven. It is there that the Lord Himself lives and walks everyday. Pause now and spend some time talking to the Lord. He will give you the grace to choose the right direction, if you will humble yourself before Him.

When God allows us to be "barren"—in relationships, in finances, in ministry, in whatever—it is never to harm us. He always does what is best for us. Psalm 119:68 says, *"Thou art good, and doest good."* That is always true for all people.

One of the things that helped Hannah was her seeing **who the Lord is**. She recognized Him as the LORD of Hosts. The turning point in her life came when she saw her circumstances as orchestrated by Him, and prayed to Him according to His nature and power as sovereign Lord.

How do we bring our barrenness to the Lord? I know that some of you are saying, "I am trying but it isn't working!" Most of us have little experience in really praying honestly. Many of us have been taught how to pray "spiritual sounding" prayers, but we have never learned how to really bare our hearts to the Lord. Yet if we look at the Psalms we find David doing this over and over. Peter tells us that we should be, *"casting all [our] anxiety upon Him, because He cares for [us]"* (1 Peter 5:7). In the book of Philippians the apostle Paul lays out guidelines for doing just that.

📖 Take a moment to read Philippians 4:6–7 and then identify the steps Paul lays out for bringing our barrenness to the Lord.

_____

_____

_____

_____

What are we commanded not to do?

_____

_____

_____

What does the fact that we are commanded tell us about anxiety?

_____

_____

_____

_____

_____

"Thou art good, and doest good; teach me Thy statutes."
Psalm 119:68

What boundaries does Paul establish for what we can pray about?

_____

_____

_____

_____

The first step is that we must choose to lay aside our anxiety. Anxiety should always be viewed as a red flag alerting us to the need to pray. Worry can be a direct result of our trusting in ourselves and our own resources instead of trusting in God. The emotions of anxiety are not sin, but allowing ourselves to be dominated by them, or letting them dictate our response to God is sin. We would not be commanded to *"be anxious for nothing"* if we were not able to lay that aside. Next, we are told the boundaries of our praying: *"in everything."* Isn't that comforting! Nothing is off-limits in our prayers. The word Paul uses here is significant. He uses the word *"supplication,"* referring to bringing God specific requests. Without specific prayer we have no way of recognizing the answers. What is to accompany our supplication? Why?

_____

_____

_____

_____

_____

Once those conditions are met, what are we to bring to the Lord?

_____

_____

_____

What promise do we have regarding the outcome of our requests (v. 7)?

_____

_____

_____

> **"Be anxious for nothing, but in everything by prayer and supplication with thanksgiving let your requests be made known to God. And the peace of God, which surpasses all comprehension, shall guard your hearts and your minds in Christ Jesus."**
> **Philippians 4:6–7**

Next, we are told to accompany these requests with *"thanksgiving."* In other words, we are to remind ourselves of all God has already done for us. Once these conditions are met, we are free to let our *"requests"* be made known to God. That means we can ask Him for anything! Notice that although Philippians 4:6–7 tells us what to do with our worries, it does not promise that God will give us whatever we ask for. Sound unfair? Actually, what God promises is even better. Instead of promising to honor our requests, regardless of whether they are beneficial to us, God promises to guard our hearts with His peace. How does He do that? When we follow this very specific formula, we are, in essence, laying our requests at God's feet. Once we've done that, we can have confidence that He hears us (Psalm 4:3). We can know that if our requests are within His will, He'll give them to us. If not, He'll say no. Either way we can have peace because our requests have now been filtered through God's will for us, which is *"good, and acceptable and perfect"* (Romans 12:2).

Hannah not only discovered the power of God, but she also found His peace. She discovered that He is a God of purpose. He never acts haphazardly. He always acts according to His loving purposes and plans. When she surrendered to Him, she found that she was also surrendered to His good purposes and plans.

But what if God's will is not what you want? Ask yourself this: "Do I really want what my all-loving, all-knowing heavenly Father says is not best for me?" Are you willing to settle for something less than God's will? Are you willing to humble yourself before the Lord and give Him your life, your plans, your failures and frustrations—even the provocations you have received over the years.

Spend some time with the Lord in prayer.

 Lord, I thank You that You care for me just like you cared for Hannah. Thank You for the humbling circumstances You have either allowed or authored in my life. I admit many of them have hurt me. I can see some of the good that has come from them, but I admit I don't see all the good yet. I thank You for what I can see, and I choose to trust You for what I can't see. What is most important is that **You see.** That's what matters. I Thank You that You see me— my circumstances, my "barrenness," my relationships, and my longings. Teach me to pray, to surrender, and to live in the blessings You give. I pray this in the name of Jesus Christ, my Lord. Amen.

Write a prayer to the Lord expressing your heart. You may want to use Philippians 4:6–7 as a model.

_____

_____

_____

_____

_____

_____

_____

_____

_____

_____

_____

God always acts according to His loving purposes and plans. When Hannah surrendered to Him, she found that she was also surrendered to His good purposes and plans.

Notes

Esther

USEABLE TO GOD WHEREVER HE PLACES US

The book of Esther is one of the most powerful dramas of the Old Testament. In it we see a young woman rising to position from humble beginnings, we see faithfulness, hardship, treachery, intrigue, desperation, disaster, miraculous rescue, and most significantly, the hand of God. Although He is never mentioned by name in the entire book, Jehovah appears in every scene and alongside every actor. Most of us will not have as far-reaching an influence as this beautiful orphan girl, nor can we hope to attain royalty. But knowing the sovereign hand of God, we can each have confidence that wherever He has placed us, we have been raised up *"for such a time as this"* (Esther 4:14). Esther's character was shaped in the crucible of adversity, yet when fully developed, it shined as pure gold. Instead of being a blessing, her beauty added to her hardship, for through her beauty she was selected to be used by the king as an object of pleasure. Yet because of her trust in God, her cruel position became a platform for ministry and a place of deliverance for her people. Through her example we can trust the hand of providence by learning practical lessons about how God can use us wherever He places us, no matter how difficult the circumstances may be. We observe in her story that, *"whoever believes in Him will not be disappointed"* (Romans 10:11).

> **Esther's character was shaped in the crucible of adversity, yet when fully developed, it shined as pure gold.**

WHERE DOES SHE FIT?

2200BC	1950	1700	1450	1200	950	700	450	100
SARAH 2155–2028		MIRIAM 1533?–1405				Daniel 619–534?		MARY and MARTHA 10BC?–60AD?
			DEBORAH 1300?–1200?	Solomon 991–931		ESTHER 504?–450?		
			Judges Rule 1385–1051	David 1041–971				
						Nehemiah 480?–400?		MARY, Mother of Jesus 20BC–60AD?
Jacob 2005–1858		Joshua 1495–1385	RUTH 1135?–1050?					
Isaac 2065–1885		Moses 1525–1405	HANNAH 1135?–1050?	VIRTUOUS . WOMAN Prov. 31				
Abraham 2165–1990		RAHAB 1445?–1385?	Samuel 1105–1022					Jesus Christ 4BC?–30AD?

THE POSITIONING OF THE PLAYERS

Containing all the elements of high drama, the book of Esther reads like a finely crafted play. The curtain rises at a difficult time in Israel's history. The nation no longer exists. It has been overrun and the people absorbed by the dominant world power, Persia. In the eyes of the world, the most important person on the whole planet is Ahasuerus, who reigns, from his capitol Susa, over an empire that stretched *"from India to Ethiopia over 127 provinces."* No one in those days took notice of a little orphan girl named Esther who was probably ten or eleven years old when Ahasuerus took the throne. Our story opens in the third year of Ahasuerus' reign (Esther 1:3). For six months he had been displaying the wealth and splendor of his kingdom, and now, he throws the biggest party in town (or the whole world for that matter). At the peak of this drunken gathering, King Ahasuerus called for his beautiful wife, Vashti, to be brought out so he can show off her beauty. Some scholars have suggested that she was to be paraded naked before his intoxicated guests. In any case, Vashti refused to be put on display like one of the king's linen hangings or couches of gold and silver. In a fit of inebriated rage, he foolishly heeded the advice of his counselors and had the queen deposed. It was a decision he would eventually come to regret. After a serious military failure he had some time to reflect and he started longing for his queen. But since the laws of the Medes and Persians could not be revoked, the only solution was to find a new queen. Enter Esther from stage left.

📖 Take a few moments to read Esther 2:2–4 and write what you learn about the details of the plans to find a new queen.

_____

_____

_____

_____

_____

The king's attendants observed his depressed state and decided that the easiest way to rid his mind of the old queen was to help him find a new one. So they suggested a "Miss Persia" pageant of sorts. The idea was to gather the most beautiful girls from each of the 127 provinces and bring them to the king's harem where he could make a new queen out of one of them. The Jewish historian Josephus indicates that there were as many as four hundred women included in the selection process of the new queen.

📖 Now, let's take a minute to see what details we can glean about this woman Esther, and how she came to be in the running for "Miss Persia."

Looking at Esther 2:5–6, write what you learn about Esther's guardian, Mordecai.

_____

_____

_____

_____

Did You Know?

THE LAWS OF THE MEDES AND PERSIANS

It was a unique feature of Medo-Persian culture that once a law was written, it could not be revoked. Not only do we see this in Esther, but in Daniel as well. It was this very fact that enabled king Darius to be tricked into a law that resulted in Daniel, his favorite advisor, being thrown into the lion's den.

Now look at verse 7. Why was Mordecai raising Esther?

_____

_____

_____

What are we told of her appearance?

_____

_____

_____

_____

We learn here that Mordecai was a Benjamite who lived in Susa, the capitol city of Persia. He was a descendent of one of the Jews taken into captivity by Nebuchadnezzar. The fact that he belonged to the tribe of Benjamin links him with the more conservative and spiritually sensitive nation of Judah. It was Judah's relative faithfulness to God that allowed that nation to exist more than a century after Israel (the Northern Kingdom) was conquered. Mordecai has raised his younger cousin Esther because both of her parents were dead. We are told that Esther was _"beautiful of form (her figure) and face"_ (her looks).

Because of her outward beauty, Esther was included among the women placed in the custody of Hegai, a eunuch in charge of the king's harem. The irony of this detail is that while most women would have been clamoring for a chance to be selected, Esther 2:8 tells us she _"was taken."_ This wording is in the Hebrew passive, suggesting that she was "taken by force." She didn't pick this job assignment. It was selected for her. Yet nowhere do we read of Esther complaining about her situation.

📖 Look at Esther 2:9 and write what you observe about how Esther is viewed by Hegai, the king's eunuch.

_____

_____

_____

_____

Esther, _"pleased him and found favor with him,"_ we are told. Much is revealed of Hegai's attitude in a few key words. First, we are told that he _"quickly"_ provided her with cosmetics and food. All of the women were given these things (2:12), but somehow she was prioritized. Second, we see that Hegai gave her seven _"choice"_ maids. We have no indication of whether other candidates were given maids, but we do know that even if they were, Esther's were "choice," the cream of the crop. Finally, we see that Hegai transferred her to the _"best place"_ in the harem. She had won him over!

Hegai wasn't the only person taken with this teenage beauty. We are told in Esther 2:15 that, _"Esther found favor in the eyes of all who saw her."_ While we might be tempted to interpret this as merely a reflection of her external beauty, we must recognize the hand of God in this as well. It was one thing to be one of the prettiest girls in the city. It was yet another to stand out when placed beside all the prettiest girls of the known world. Initially she was

Did You Know?
ESTHER'S NAME

Although we know her as Esther, this is her Persian name. It is from _"Aster"_ and means "a star," figuratively associated in that culture with good fortune. We are told in Esther 2:7 that her Hebrew name was _"Hadassah"_ which means "myrtle." The myrtle plant is an evergreen shrub native to the Middle East, with delicate and beautiful white flowers and fragrant leaves.

selected for her external beauty, but ultimately it was the internal beauty of her character that set her apart from the rest of the beautiful women. Let's look at some of the character qualities hidden in these brief verses.

Gracious—Esther's graciousness is seen first of all in her lack of complaint in what many would consider a cruel and unfair situation. She was being groomed to be a concubine of the king. Esther 2:9 tells us that Hegai, the man in charge of the harem, was pleased by her (*"Now the young lady pleased him and found favor with him"*). The Hebrew text literally reads, "She lifted up grace before his face." There was no sourness in her attitude.

Teachable—When it came to be each girl's turn to visit the king, she was allowed to have *"anything that she desired. . ."* (v. 13). Yet when it was Esther's turn, instead of selfishly asking for anything and everything, *"she did not request anything except what Hegai, the king's eunuch who was in charge of the women, advised"* (v. 15). She had a teachable heart and listened to advice.

Submissive—As an orphan, Esther was under the authority of her cousin, Mordecai. When she was selected for the king's harem, Mordecai instructed her that she should not let it be known that she was a Jew (Esther 2:10). She obeyed Mordecai's command. Even more telling is a statement that was made after she had already been crowned queen. In verse 20 we read, *"Esther had not yet made known her kindred or her people, even as Mordecai had commanded her, for Esther did what Mordecai told her* **as she had done** *when under his care"* [emphasis mine]. This is an excellent example of how we should submit to God-given authority.

📖 Read Esther 2:16–17 and list what is recorded about how the king received Esther.

_____

_____

_____

_____

Esther was taken to the king in the month of Tebeth, which would have been sometime in December. Each woman was given only one chance to impress the king (2:14), yet for Esther one visit was enough. We are told that the king, *"loved Esther more than all the women, and she found favor and kindness with him more than all the virgins. . . ."* Here was a man who could have had any woman he wanted, and was regularly given the most beautiful women to be found anywhere—yet Esther captured his heart. As a result, she was made queen in Vashti's place.

📖 One of the first evidences of God's providence in making Esther queen is found in how God used her to allow Mordecai to help the king. Read Esther 2:21–23 and answer the questions that follow.

What does Mordecai discover (v. 21)?

_____

_____

_____

_____

> *Ultimately, it was the internal beauty of Esther's character that set her apart.*

✏ **Did You Know?**

? **AHASUERUS**

Ahasuerus was the Hebrew name for Xerxes, who reigned over Persia from 485 to 465 BC. Secular history records that about this time, Xerxes led an ill-fated attempt to conquer Greece, and was defeated at Salamis. It was a dismal failure, and it was probably after he returned to Susa from this campaign, that in a state of depression he began to brood over his foolish choice to banish Vashti. Herodotus tells us he sought consolation in his harem. Four years pass from the time of Vashti's dismissal until Esther is brought to the king (see Esther 2:16).

How does he warn the king (v. 22)?

_____

_____

What is the result (v. 23)?

_____

_____

In his job as a guard at the king's gate, Mordecai uncovered a plot by two of the king's officials, Bigthan and Teresh. Their plan would bring harm to King Ahasuerus. Mordecai relayed the news to the king through his cousin, Queen Esther. The plot was investigated and found to be true. Through Mordecai's loyalty to Ahasuerus and the providential positioning of Esther, the king was protected from harm. It didn't take God long to use Esther in her position as Queen of Persia.

THE PRESENTATION OF THE PROBLEM

How did Esther, a humble orphan girl, overcome prejudice against her race, poverty and social position to climb to the top of the ladder of success as Queen of the most powerful nation on earth? Skeptics would look at her story and say she was incredibly lucky. Others might suggest that it was her effort, perseverance, and physical attractiveness that propelled her. But the believer must acknowledge that she was placed in such a position of prominence only through the providential hand of God. It was God who knitted her in her mother's womb and gave her that beauty. It was walking with God that developed the inner beauty of her character. Rightly does Mordecai suggest that she attained royalty for the purposes of God. Her position, where God had placed her, was not merely for her own pleasure or benefit. What He desires to do for others **through** us plays a part in every position He gives us. Today will be introduced to a man named Haman. In him we will begin to see some of the reasons God had placed Esther as Queen.

📖 The execution of two officials from King Ahasuerus' court paved the way for the introduction of another character into our drama. Look at Esther 3:1 and write what position was filled and what you learn about the man who fills it.

_____

_____

_____

_____

After the failed attempt of Bigthan and Teresh to take over the government, the king promoted a man named Haman. We are told that he was the son of Hammedatha the Agagite. Haman's promotion placed him in authority over all of the princes. Since princes normally ruled directly under the king, this suggests that he may have been the number two man in command, second only to King Ahasuerus.

HAMAN, THE AGAGITE

The name Agag featured prominently in the history of Israel. It was he who reigned as king of the Amalekites when God instructed Saul to utterly destroy them. The Amalekites had been placed "under the ban" because of the evil way they attacked Israel in the wilderness—from the rear, killing innocent children and the elderly first. Yet Saul was not fully obedient to God's injunction, and tried to keep Agag alive as a trophy of his military victory. It was actually Samuel who hewed Agag to pieces in execution of God's judgment. Apparently Haman was a descendent of Agag and perhaps had nursed a family grievance against the Jews all of his life.

📖 Now take a look at Esther 3:2–6 and answer the questions that follow.

What does Mordecai do that offends Haman (v. 2)?

_____

_____

_____

What reason did Mordecai give for refusing to bow (v. 4)?

_____

_____

What was Haman's response (v. 5)?

_____

_____

_____

What became his objective (v. 6)?

_____

_____

_____

As second in command, Haman was to be bowed before and paid homage. Mordecai, who was a servant of the king working at his gate, refused to bow. When asked by his co-workers why he refused to bow, Mordecai claimed that his religious beliefs (*"he had told them that he was a Jew"* [Esther 3:4]) did not allow him to bow before any man. Deuteronomy 6:13 states, *"You shall fear only the Lord your God; and you shall worship Him."* Jews took this verse to mean that they could give no form of worship to human rulers. Haman was enraged at Mordecai's disregard for Persian customs, but since the reason was his faith, Haman realized that killing him alone would not solve the problem. Therefore, he sought to destroy **all** the Jews.

📖 Look at Esther 3:7–9.

What was Haman's proposal to the king (v. 9)?

_____

_____

_____

What reason did he give for destroying the Jews (v. 8)?

_____

_____

_____

How did he determine the best time to execute his plan (v. 7)?

_____

_____

Haman's solution was to bribe the king to institute destruction on the Jews. Haman twisted Mordecai's actions to sound like rebellion against the king based on religion. To determine the most opportune day to put his plan into effect, the superstitious Haman cast lots (an ancient practice used to determine the luckiest day for an event or action). King Ahasuerus was unwittingly lured into the idea, and Haman's plan was authorized. The king didn't even accept his bribe. He simply gave Haman his signet ring with which he could exercise the necessary authority. Haman sent word to all the leaders throughout the kingdom, *"to destroy, to kill, and to annihilate all the Jews, both young and old, women and children,"* on the appointed day he selected by casting lots. The result was mass confusion. A dark day loomed on the horizon for Esther's people, the Jews.

The Performance of the Plan

Adolf Hitler was not the first person that attempted to destroy all the Jews, nor will he be the last. Throughout history, nations have taken their stand against God and His people. Human reasons may differ, but behind all the different schemes and strategies is the enemy of the Lord, Satan. Using pliable, godless men, he tries one stratagem after another. Satan's reason is not simply rooted in war against God, but in the reality that from the Jews would come the *"seed"* promised to Eve that would one day crush his head (see Genesis 3:15). If Satan were successful in destroying the Jews, he could thwart God's plan for his own demise. But Satan is no match for the sovereign Lord. Often we are deceived into the erroneous view that somehow Satan is the complimentary opposite of God as the two wage war to see which will reign supreme. But God has no equals, and He has no opposites. He alone is omnipotent, omniscient, and omnipresent. Satan is a created being with all the limitations of any other angel. If Satan is the opposite of anyone it would be the archangel, Michael. He is no match for God! Every time Satan comes up with a new strategem, God is way ahead of him. Before Haman even came up with the idea of wiping out the Jews, God had already put Esther in place. What Satan meant for evil, God turns around and uses to bring blessing to His people. The perfect example of this principle is taught in God's dealings with the cross. Satan thought that through killing the Messiah he would be victorious. Yet God turned his plan around and used it to seal both Satan's defeat and our salvation. That is the power of providence. Today we will look at how Haman's plan materialized, and how God used Esther to turn it into His good.

📖 Read Esther 4:1–3 and write down how Mordecai and the rest of the Jews responded once they received word of Haman's evil decree.

_____

_____

_____

_____

_____

When Mordecai discovered Haman's evil plot, he tore his clothes and put on sackcloth and ashes (outward signs of mourning in Middle Eastern culture).

He went through the city wailing loudly and bitterly. The response was concurrent throughout the provinces as Jews learned of their legally-sealed fate. Many fasted and sought God's divine intervention.

When Esther received news of Mordecai's mourning, she sent word to learn the reason, and Mordecai gave her a copy of the king's edict. Through a messenger, he asked her to go to the king and beg his mercy for her people. Certainly as queen she should be able to exert some influence, but law presented a problem. Even though Esther was queen, she was not allowed to visit the king without an invitation. Unless the king interceded, the penalty for such an unannounced visit would be death. Fearing death, Esther sent word to Mordecai and basically said, "I can't help."

📖 Read Esther 4:13–14 and write down the reasons why Mordecai thought it was imperative that Esther take so great a risk as an uninvited visit to the king.

_____

_____

_____

_____

Mordecai gives three reasons (all very persuasive) why Esther should risk her life to intercede for the Jews. First, he reminded her that she, too, was a Jew, and so the king's edict applied to her just as much as it did to every other Jew in the kingdom. Second, he exhibited great trust in God's sovereignty in reminding her that one way or another, God would deliver His people. He did not say, "If you remain silent, God's people are doomed." He stated, *"If you remain silent at this time, relief and deliverance will arise for the Jews from another place and you and your father's house will perish."* In other words, Mordecai implies to Esther that God would still deliver the Jews, but unless she interceded on the Jews behalf, she would not get to be a part of it. What a powerful lesson for us today! God wants to accomplish His purposes through us, but if we do not cooperate, His plan will still be carried out. He will simply use someone else to do it. As Job 42:2 relates, *"I know that Thou canst do all things, and that no purpose of Thine can be thwarted."* Even when we are faithless in our God-given tasks He remains faithful. Mordecai's final argument to Esther (v. 14) is to suggest that perhaps this Jewish dilemma was the very reason God had appointed her as queen. O, that we would have such a view about wherever God has placed us!

📖 Look at Esther 4:15–17.

What was Esther's decision concerning Mordecai's request for her to intervene?

_____

_____

_____

For what kind of help did she ask (v. 16)?

_____

_____

_____

"I know that Thou canst do all things, and that no purpose of Thine can be thwarted."

Job 42:2

Doctrine
FASTING

Although the text doesn't specifically mention that Esther's fast was for the purpose of prayer, Scripture clearly links the two together. In Oriental culture fasting was one of many ways a person expressed mourning. Although Scripture does not command fasting, it does mention it in a way that strongly stresses its importance. In the Sermon on the Mount, Jesus does not say, "If you fast . . . ," but "When you fast. . . ." Scriptural fasts can last for part or all of a day, several days, or even as long as forty days, and can mean doing without all food and water, food only, or abstaining from certain foods for a time (as in the Nazarite vow).

After hearing Mordecai's arguments Esther agreed to intercede with the king. What a powerful resolve is reflected in the statement, *"I will go in to the king. . . . If I perish, I perish"*! She had decided this was the right thing to do, and so the risks really did not matter. God never promises us that doing the right thing will be easy, but we cannot expect His strong support if we are not willing to do what is right, regardless of the cost. Esther asked the Jews of Susa to support her with prayer and fasting for three days, as she prepared to take so great a risk. She also committed to fasting so that she would be positioned to hear from God about what she should say and how she should say it.

Fasting does not twist the arm of God to get Him to do what we would like. It simply helps us to make seeking Him our highest priority. When our seeking of God is more important to us than even our daily needs, we are in a position of sensitivity to Him so that we can hear what He wants to say to us. The pains of hunger in a fast are regular reminders to return to prayer and seek the face of God. As we will see very soon, a lot of consequential things occured during this three-day delay. We must be ever watchful of running ahead of God and the work He desires to do on our behalf.

THE PRODUCT OF PROVIDENCE

 Esther **DAY FOUR**

One can only imagine the emotions Esther felt once she had committed to intercede with the king. Even if the king spared her, she placed her relationship with the king and her position as queen in serious jeopardy. Up until this point, she had told no one that she was a Jew. Once she resolved to follow Mordecai's advice, there is no indication of her wavering. Yet she did not go off "half-cocked." She waited on God for three days. Then, prompted by God, she waited another day to fully implement her plan. On the third day, she went to see the king. With composure and poise uncommon for a woman her age, she went quietly to the inner court of his palace and stood, waiting for his response.

📖 Read Esther 5:1–3 and write your observations concerning the king's response to Esther.

_____

_____

_____

_____

> *"The king's heart is like channels of water in the hand of the LORD; He turns it wherever He wishes."*
> **Proverbs 21:1**

When the king saw Esther standing in the court of his palace, the text tells us, *"she obtained favor in his sight."* He extended the golden scepter to her and invited her in. Obviously King Ahasuerus realized that Esther's visit was not undertaken lightly, for his first question is *"What is troubling you, Queen Esther?"* He is so moved with compassion for whatever would prompt her to take so great a risk that he promised to honor her request even it meant giving her half the kingdom. What a powerful answer to prayer!

Esther didn't come right out and say to the king what was on her mind. Instead, she invited Ahasuerus and Haman to a banquet she had prepared.

THE GALLOWS

The "gallows" spoken of here is not the kind of hanging platform we picture from the old American West. It didn't involve a noose around the neck, but rather was a large stake upon which the victim would be impaled. It was a gruesome and torturous death that left the victim on the edge of death for hours as the weight of their body forced them to slide further down the stake. This method of capitol punishment was the precursor to the Roman practice of crucifixion.

Coincidence is simply when God chooses to remain anonymous.

Although it may appear that she was getting cold feet, notice the phrase, *"had prepared."* The initial delay was part of her plan, not some last minute idea to buy time. When the meal was finished, the king again asked, *"What is your request?"* But Esther changed the subject and invited both men to a second banquet. Cold feet may have been an issue this time. Yet God had His hand in this delay. Let's look at what happened during the next twenty-four hours.

📖 Take a moment to look over Esther 5:9–14 and answer the questions that follow.

How did Haman view himself after the banquet with the king and queen (v. 9)?

_____

_____

_____

_____

How did seeing Mordecai affect his mood (v. 9)?

_____

_____

_____

What is the point of his bragging in verses 10–13?

_____

_____

_____

What solution was offered to Haman (v. 14)?

_____

_____

_____

_____

Haman left the banquet in good spirits. Yet as soon as he saw Mordecai at the gate, refusing to bow before him or pay homage, all of his joy was replaced by anger. When he gathered his wife and friends, he ran through the list of all the reasons he should be happy, and then confessed that he would never be satisfied as long as Mordecai continued to spurn him. What a powerful illustration of the truth that our flesh is never satisfied. With all he had, Haman could not find happiness, merely because he didn't have the respect and honor from a Jewish man that he didn't even like. The fleshly counsel of his wife and friends, instead of showing Haman how foolish it was to worry about Mordecai, encouraged him to get rid of Mordecai. "Build a gallows and hang him on it!" they advise. Revenge has so consumed Haman that this was the only suggestion that could encourage him.

Meanwhile, another important event occurred during this second delay that would have a powerful effect on the outcome of our story.

📖 Read Esther 6:1–14 and answer the questions that follow.

What occurred during the night after Esther's first banquet (vs. 1–3)?

_____

_____

_____

What was king Ahasuerus' plan to honor Mordecai, and how did he come up with it (vv. 4–9)?

_____

_____

_____

_____

What must Haman do (v. 11)?

_____

_____

_____

_____

Word Study
PROVIDENCE

Our word providence is made up of two Latin words, *pro* and *video*, and carries the meaning "to see beforehand and provide what is needed." The word provide also comes from those same two words. The Hebrew word translated "Provide" is *ra'ah* and means "to see"—same idea. The providence of God is clearly seen in the lives of Mordecai, Esther, and the Jews of Persia.

After the first banquet, king Ahasuerus was unable to sleep, so he requested someone to read to him from the book of records. Normally that would have been as exciting as reading a phone directory, so one could see how it could help with insomnia. Yet as the king listened to the monotonous droning of boring details, something caught his attention. He was reminded of how Mordecai had saved his life from an assassination attempt. When he realized that nothing had been done to honor Mordecai for his kindness, the king began looking for a fitting reward for the gate guard. He called out for an advisor, and who should happen to be there but Haman. Without giving the details, the king asked for a good plan to honor someone. Haman, in his arrogance, wrongly assumed the honor was meant for him, so he really "poured it on thick" so to speak! How his countenance must have fallen when he learned that Mordecai was the one to be honored—and that he would have to carry it out. What the unbeliever sees as a series of amazing coincidences, the believer must recognize as the hand of God's providence. It was God who troubled the king's sleep, and God who had the servant read of Mordecai's help. Most of all, we see God working in the timing of Haman's arrival. Coincidence is simply when God chooses to remain anonymous.

Our story is nearing its climax. The final pieces are about to fall in place.

📖 Look at Esther 7:1–10.

What is Esther's request of the king (vs. 3–4)?

_____

_____

_____

_____

The future of God's chosen people turned on a sleepless night and a paragraph from the chronicles of the king. How awesome is our providential God!

What does the king do to Haman (vs. 9–10)?

_____

_____

_____

> ## "The nations have sunk down in the pit which they have made; In the net which they hid, their own foot has been caught."
>
> ### Psalm 9:15

Finally, Esther answered the king and disclosed Haman's wicked plot. Notice that she included herself in Haman's edict (*"we have been sold, I and my people. . ."*). When the king realized how he had been duped, Haman's doom was sealed. As soon as the king is informed of the gallows Haman had built for Mordecai, he ordered that Haman be put to death on it. What a powerful reminder to all who would set their course for revenge!

Although the king could not revoke the edict of Haman, he gave Esther and Mordecai the freedom to add to it an edict of their own. Quickly word is sent in the king's name and sealed with his signet ring authorizing permission for the Jews to defend themselves and to take the possessions of any who oppose them. Only God's providence could turn the prospect of defeat into so glorious a victory! An interesting footnote is found in Esther 8:17, where we are told that, *"many of the peoples of the land became Jews."* In other words, many unbelievers saw what God had done for His people, and what He had done to Haman, who opposed them, and turned from their idols to serve the living God.

Esther DAY FIVE

FOR ME TO FOLLOW GOD

The memorable storybook phrase, "And they all lived happily ever after . . ." seems a fitting end to this tale. Mordecai was promoted to second in command. The Jews rid themselves of 75,000 of their enemies. The whole situation not only became a national celebration for the Jews, but for all of Persia as well. God's justice, as we see in this story, is not always immediate, but it is always ultimate.

Today we want to begin looking at how we can apply these lessons from Esther to our own walk with God. There is much we can learn, not only from Esther, but also from each character in this powerful drama.

One of the most important applications we can learn from Esther is that one person, walking in the providence of God, really can make a difference. You may not believe that. You may think that you are inconsequential to God's plan. You may think that being used as Esther was is reserved either for those rare saints with a faith greater than yours, or is just a random, happenstance occurrence, but think about it for a moment.

Why do you think God picked Esther?

_____

_____

_____

_____

May I suggest something? I believe that such inclusion in the workings of God is far less coincidental than we might believe. Second Chronicles 16:9 states, *"the eyes of the LORD move to and fro throughout the earth that He may strongly support those whose heart is completely His."* You see, God is constantly looking for someone whose heart is completely His, so that He can strongly support them. I believe He found such a person in Esther, and I believe it was her surrender and obedience to God (regardless of the risks to her life) that made her useable in His plan.

 Where has God placed you? Write where God has placed you specifically in each of the areas listed.

In your home—

_____

At work—

_____

In your church—

_____

In your country—

_____

God has placed you where you are in each of these areas, as well as in every other facet of your life, *"For such a time as this"* (Esther 4:14). How are you doing at being faithful to where He has placed you? (Identify where you fit on the scale below.)

Unfaithful ◄━━ 1 2 3 4 5 6 7 8 9 10 ━━► **Faithful**

Until we risk, we cannot make a difference. Are there any risks you need to take to be faithful to God where He has placed you?

_____

_____

_____

_____

One of the sources of Esther's courage was the godly example of her cousin and guardian, Mordecai. When faced with giving honor and worship to godless Haman, Mordecai had the courage to refuse to bow. Esther had plenty of time to reflect on this courageous conviction that she had probably witnessed in countless other situations growing up with Mordecai.

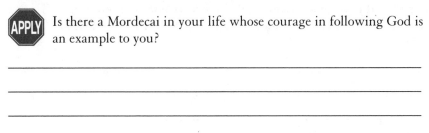 Is there a Mordecai in your life whose courage in following God is an example to you?

_____

_____

_____

_____

> *God is constantly looking for someone whose heart is completely His, so that He can strongly support them.*

Did You Know?
THE FEAST OF PURIM

The feast of Purim, celebrated each year in Israel, was instituted by Mordecai. It's name, Purim, refers to the casting of lots by Haman to pick the day of the Jews' destruction. *"Purim"* is the plural form of *"Pur,"* the Assyrian word meaning "lot." What a study in contrasts that this holiday, named for the random casting of lots, is really a celebration of the providence of God. Truly nothing is accidental with the Lord!

Are you a Mordecai to anyone else in the arena where God has placed you?

_____

_____

_____

From this godly man, Mordecai, we also learn the important lesson that doing right doesn't always make life easier. Years ago I heard a pastor recount a story from the early days of our nation. Henry Clay, one of our founding fathers, was preparing to introduce a bill into Congress. One of his political colleagues cautioned him that if he did so, it might ruin his chances to be President. Clay asked, "But is it right?"—to which his friend gave an affirmative reply. "Then I'd rather be right than be President," Clay vowed. And although he ran for the office several times, he was never elected to the highest office in America. Do you have a greater desire to be right than to be popular, or successful? Decisions like that take courage.

Another valuable lesson to be learned from Mordecai is that God can get your good deeds noticed whenever He wants. He even woke Ahasuerus up in the middle of the night to remind him. I'm sure that in moments of humanness Mordecai may have thought his good deed had been forgotten by all. But we can trust God to honor us in His own time as He sees fit.

Is there any good you have done that seems to have gone unnoticed?

_____

_____

_____

_____

Maybe you need to surrender the results of that deed to God.

Mordecai's example and Haman's malice lead us into some very practical applications. We see in these two men that our devotion to God will often offend the ungodly.

APPLY Can you think of any examples of this in your own life?

_____

_____

_____

_____

We also see in Haman some powerful words of warning. His life tells us that we should never underestimate the destructive impact of revenge. Look at Proverbs 26:27 and write your thoughts on how this is evident in Haman's life.

_____

_____

_____

_____

Romans 12:19–21 tells us, "Never take your own revenge, beloved, but leave room for the wrath of God, for it is written, 'Vengeance is mine, I will repay,' says the Lord. 'But if your enemy is hungry, feed him, and if he is thirsty, give him a drink; for in so doing you will heap burning coals upon your head.' Do not be overcome by evil, but overcome evil with good." When we take vengeance into our own hands we will never balance it with mercy as the Lord does.

APPLY Is there any evidence of revenge taking place in your life?

_____

_____

_____

_____

What do you need to do about it?

_____

_____

_____

Another valuable lesson to be learned from Haman is that we should never overestimate our own importance. Haman couldn't handle his own prosperity, and in the end pride was his undoing.

APPLY Are there any places in your life where pride is a problem?

_____

_____

_____

_____

How can you protect yourself?

_____

_____

_____

_____

Pride says, "I deserve . . . I earned . . . I have a right to. . . ." Humility says, "Lord, thank You for what You give, for Your hand of grace at work in my life."

A story is told of Charles Spurgeon, who at age 18 became senior pastor of a church of 5,000. It is said that at the end of every sermon, after enduring the compliments and ego strokes of the congregation, he would retire to his home and kneel down by his bed. He would go through the motions of physically removing an imaginary crown from his head, and then he would pray, "Lord, all of the glory I have received today, I give to You, for You alone are worthy."

Let's spend some time in prayer with the Lord right now.

 Lord, thank you for this powerful reminder of Your providence. Nothing in my life is accidental or escapes Your notice. Help me to trust where You have placed me, that You have raised me up for *such a time as this*. Help me to have the courage to do the right thing regardless of what it costs me, and to not be surprised if the ungodly are offended by my stand. Guard me from taking my own revenge – help me to leave that in Your hands. I may never be noticed or promoted as Esther and Mordecai were, but help me to be ever diligent toward those things that seek advancement of Your kingdom. Amen.

Prayer of Application . . .

As we close our lesson this week, take to heart any areas the Lord has singled out to you and express them in prayer to Him.

_____

_____

_____

_____

_____

_____

_____

_____

_____

_____

You have come to His Kingdom "for such a time as this" (Esther 4:14).

Notes

Notes

The Virtuous Woman

LIFE LESSONS FROM PROVERBS 31

Although Scripture gives no clear identity to the "virtuous woman" (as she is called in the KJV) in Proverbs 31, it is impossible to rightly consider the women of the Bible without addressing the truths found there. The phrase, "*a virtuous woman*" is first used in Boaz' description of Ruth's reputation (Ruth 3:11). It is used again by Solomon in Proverbs 12:4, where we read, "*A virtuous woman is a crown to her husband*" (KJV). To our female readers, I ask the following questions: When were you first "introduced" to this Proverbs 31 woman? How did you feel? Were you overwhelmed with all that she does, angry that you thought God expected all this of you, determined that you would be this woman for God? For some, this listing of character qualities is a source of guilt, laying out a phantom "perfect woman" a level that no woman could

The virtuous woman is not the yardstick by which all women are measured, but the goal toward which all women should be moving.

WHERE DOES SHE FIT?

2200BC	1950	1700	1450	1200	950	700	450	100
SARAH 2155–2028		MIRIAM 1533?–1405				Daniel 619–534?		MARY and MARTHA 10BC?–60AD?
			DEBORAH 1300?–1200?	Solomon 991–931		ESTHER 504?–450?		
			Judges Rule 1385–1051	David 1041–971				
						Nehemiah 480?–400?		MARY, Mother of Jesus 20BC–60AD?
Jacob 2005–1858		Joshua 1495–1385	RUTH 1135?–1050?					
Isaac 2065–1885		Moses 1525–1405	HANNAH 1135?–1050?	VIRTUOUS WOMAN Prov. 31				
Abraham 2165–1990		RAHAB 1445?–1385?	Samuel 1105–1022					Jesus Christ 4BC?–30AD?

ever hope to attain. It constantly reminds them of what they are **not**. For others, it becomes a source of pride as they focus on the DOING of Proverbs 31, but miss the BEING that it points to ultimately.

To our male readers, I ask these questions: Are the things God prizes most highly in a woman the things you prize most highly? Does the way you follow God help or hinder the woman in your life in her process toward becoming a virtuous woman? When you read these verses, do you find yourself praising God for the virtues in her, or looking at them as a yardstick to find places where she doesn't "measure up"? Do you find that you are bitter and scornful when she doesn't meet the high standard of Proverbs 31, or are you caring and loving, driven to prayer on her behalf?

If you are beaten down by this "perfect" woman, take heart. I have good news for you. She is the **ideal** woman. She is not the yardstick by which all women are measured, but the goal toward which all women should be moving. She is the ideal woman God wants to develop all women to be as they follow Him. Did you catch that? GOD is the one working the transformation. He who began this good work in you, will be perfecting it until the day of Christ Jesus (see Philippians 1:6). Seeing what you can become (by His grace and work) should be a catalyst, not a condemnation. Studying these truths will take you deeper into following Him. If you are a perfectionist, a right understanding of truth will set you free from "trying" to be or do **for** Him, so that you might walk with Him, and allow Him to make you the woman He wants you to be. If you have become comfortable and satisfied with less than God desires, then these passages will be a divine "nudge" out of complacency and into growth. When all is said and done, the most important message to glean when we reach verse 31 is that **He**, not she, is to be our focus.

STUDYING THE BOOK OF PROVERBS

Unlike the epistles of the New Testament that most of us are more familiar with, Proverbs does not lay out its truth in a legal flow of logic. Rather, each verse is often grouped in thematic sections, or designed to stand on its own. Therefore, initially taking the time to group the verses according to sub-themes may give the reader more clarity than a simple verse-by-verse study.

GETTING A HANDLE ON PROVERBS

As you can already see, this is going to be a different sort of lesson. It is kind of hard to get intimately acquainted with someone who does not exist. Although this passage does not fit the pattern we have followed in previous studies, one can quickly see how it cannot be neglected when considering the women of Scripture. This chapter is also unique in that, due to the nature of this portion of Scripture, it is directed more definitively toward our female readers. However, men should not think that there is nothing relevant in this chapter for them. Men will be made more aware of their own struggle to a virtuous ideal and challenged anew, if they are married, to "love your wife as Christ loved the Church."

To fully appreciate Proverbs 31, you need to have some understanding of the purpose of the Proverbs in general. Proverbs is a collection of wisdom. It sets forth truth with direct statements, contrasts, and comparisons. It is part of that section of our Old Testament known as the "Wisdom Books" that incorporate Job, Proverbs, Ecclesiastes, and some of the Psalms. The Proverbs deal with applying God's wisdom to specific situations and decisions of our lives. King Solomon, David's son, wrote most of the Proverbs, but there are some sections, including the one we are studying in this lesson that were most likely written by others. Later on we'll look at some ideas on who may have written Proverbs 31, but today we want to focus on getting in the flow of the thirty chapters of Scripture that precede it.

📖 Take a minute to read Proverbs 1:2–4 and write down what you learn.

What is the purpose of the book of Proverbs?

_____

_____

_____

_____

_____

How do we access what it has to offer? (Look at the action words.)

_____

_____

_____

_____

The ultimate goal of Proverbs is to give us *"prudence"* (this word has the idea of "shrewdness"), *"knowledge"* (the information we need), and *"discretion"* (Hebr.—the idea of "a plan," or taking the information and putting it into application). Solomon wants us to have wisdom and allow it to govern our lives. The way this powerful collection of wise sayings accomplishes its goal is seen in the action words of verses 2 and 3. We are called to "know," to "discern," and to "receive." In other words, you have to study and have a teachable heart to benefit from what is written here. Proverbs 1:7 tells us, *"fools despise wisdom and instruction."* The word "instruction," used here and in 1:2–3, is from a Hebrew root (*yasar*) meaning "to chastise, or correct by discipline and admonition." A "fool" ultimately is one who is unteachable.

📖 Looking at Proverbs 2:1–4, what things must we do if we are to acquire the wisdom offered in this book? (Notice, there are 8 verbs or actions to take.)

_____

_____

_____

_____

Solomon addresses this treatise to his son. In this father/son interaction, we are allowed to enter into his private counsel. We are admonished to do the following:

a) Receive his sayings

b) Treasure them

c) Make our ear attentive to them

d) Incline our hearts to understanding them

e) Cry for discernment

f) To lift our voice for understanding

g) To seek wisdom as silver

h) Search for wisdom as if it were hidden treasure

Did You Know?
HEBREW POETRY

Hebrew poetry is very different than the kind of poetry most of us are used to, which is based on rhyming words and meter. Instead, Hebrew poetry is based more on rhythm and the rhyming of **ideas**. This style of poetry is known as parallelism. In it, the author states an idea, then supports it in the next line or lines. Most often, a simple rephrasing of the premise in the second line supports the initial idea. Another version of Hebrew Parallelism presents the opposite idea in the second line, contrasting it with the first. Still, a third form is to take the initial idea and build on it in succeeding lines. Parallelism transcends normal word-rhyming poetry because it is a poetic form that is easily translated into all other languages.

Each of these action words communicates a sense of longing desperation, a sense of value. If we are to have wisdom, we must really want it.

📖 Once we obey God's instructions and seek Him with all our hearts, what does Proverbs 2:5 tell us will result?

_____

_____

_____

_____

_____

Put Yourself In Their Shoes
THE GOOD SOIL

In Matthew 13 Jesus teaches the "Parable of the Sower." In this parable the seed represents the Word of God, and the soil represents the heart of man. The main point of this parable is that it is not the quality of the seed that determines the harvest, but the preparedness of the soil. In explaining the parable to the disciples, Jesus says that the seed sown in good soil represents a person who meets three criteria: **1)** One who hears the Word, **2)** One who understands the Word, and **3)** One who bears fruit.

In seeking true wisdom, we will find the Lord. At the root of all wisdom is a reverence for Him. In Proverbs 1:7 we are told, *"The fear of the Lord is the beginning of knowledge."* The word "fear" does not mean to be afraid of Him, but rather, to so revere Him as to fear displeasing Him in how we live our lives. The flip side of this truth is seen in Psalm 14:1 which reads, *"The fool has said in his heart, 'There is no God.'"* There are two fundamental realities of life that sooner or later each person must reckon with: **1)** There is a God, and **2)** You are not Him.

What does all of this have to do with Proverbs 31? Plenty! To fully appreciate what Proverbs 31 is saying, we must understand how to study it and glean from it what it has to offer. An important distinction to make when you are studying Proverbs is that these sayings of wisdom are not so much promises as they are probabilities. They are not focusing as much on immediate results as they are on ultimate ones.

📖 Now let's move ahead to Proverbs 31:28 and 31. What are the rewards of this pursuit? What outcome can we hope for if we apply the wisdom that this chapter has to offer and move toward being the virtuous woman described here?

_____

_____

_____

_____

_____

The virtuous woman has the praise of her children and her husband. Those who know her best will praise her most. What a tremendous hope! Someone has said that our reputation is what others **think** we are, but our character is what our family **knows** we are. Look at what the husband says here, *"Many daughters have done nobly, but you excel them all."* In the eyes of her mate, she is the greatest! How sad it is that so often we are on our best behavior with strangers, and show our worst, careless words and deeds, to our family. The outcome of godliness is that the better we are known, the more we are praised. Notice that the virtuous woman is praised, not by her own lips, but by her family, and by her deeds (*"let her works praise her in the gates"*).

📖 There is a secret to attaining the kind of character Proverbs 31 exalts. Look at Proverbs 31:30 and identify what it is.

_____

_____

_____

There is no makeup that will make you look better than godliness. There is no hairstyle that can hold a candle to holiness. There is no etiquette that earns respect and honor like righteousness. Peter admonishes us, *"let not your adornment be merely external—braiding the hair, and wearing gold jewelry, or putting on dresses; but let it be the hidden person of the heart, with the imperishable quality of a gentle and quiet spirit, which is precious in the sight of God"* (1 Peter 3:3–4). That should be the most important thing to all of us.

THE CHARACTER OF A VIRTUOUS WOMAN

I hope you are already beginning to value the wisdom this book of Proverbs has to offer. When Solomon began to reign, he asked God for wisdom, and the Lord honored his request. God said to Solomon, *"Behold, I have given you a wise and discerning heart, so that there has been no one like you before you, nor shall one like you arise after you"* (1 Kings 3:12, [emphasis mine]). No one has ever had more wisdom than Solomon had. Now you may be saying, "But I thought Proverbs 31 was written by King Lemuel?" Many (if not most) scholars believe that King Lemuel and Solomon are the same person. I also hold this opinion. In any case, Proverbs 31 is included in Solomon's collection of divinely inspired wisdom we call the book of Proverbs. As we dive into this treasure of wisdom, we will look at everything admirable in a woman and a wife. Remember, she is not the yardstick by which all women are measured, but the goal women should be moving toward. She is the woman God leads others to be as they follow Him.

Take a look at Proverbs 31:10 and read it reflectively.

Who is this verse supposed to be speaking to (see also 31:1)?

_____

_____

What is the main message?

_____

_____

_____

What is its application toward women?

_____

_____

_____

🔍 Did You Know?

❓ WHO IS KING LEMUEL?

"Lemuel" is not a formal name, but is more of a nickname. It means, "belonging to God." By the general consent of both Jewish and early Christian writers it has traditionally been seen as one of many titles referring to Solomon. Proverbs 1:1 lists him as the sole author of the book. If this is true, "Lemuel" may have been a pet name used of him by his mother, Bathsheba. He was also known as "Jedidiah" (beloved of the Lord), and many view the "Agar" of Proverbs 30 as referring to him as well, though Scripture nowhere confirms this.

As we begin looking at this passage, its introductory verse (and all that follows) is directed first of all to King Lemuel. The point is significant. While there are tremendous applications to women on who they should be becoming, it is first and foremost, written to tell a man what kind of woman he should seek as a wife. It is a two-part message that begins with a rhetorical question, *"An excellent wife, who can find?"*—making it clear that a wife like this will be hard to find. She is rare! This is not because God is unable to make many women like this, but because few stay consistently yielded to Him as to attain this level of excellence. To the man who finds such a woman, she will prove to be the greatest treasure. When the verse says, *". . . her worth is far above jewels,"* the Hebrew term for "far above" literally means "remote." In other words, the comparison is not even close!

As we look at the woman of Proverbs 31, we will be grouping its verses by themes. We want to begin by looking at the character of this virtuous woman.

📖 Take a look at Proverbs 31:25 and write down your observations about what this verse has to say of her character.

What do you think it means that she "clothes" herself with strength and dignity?

_____

_____

_____

_____

_____

What does the phrase *"smiles at the future"* say about her?

_____

_____

_____

_____

_____

We know from verse 22 that the virtuous woman does not neglect her outer appearance, but this verse makes clear that her adornment is not merely external. Most women I know would never be seen in public in their bathrobe and curlers. Yet are we so careful about the character clothing we wear in public? This woman "clothes" herself with strength and dignity. What a balancing pair of qualities! The word strength is sometimes translated "force" or "boldness." She is strong and confident, a beautiful quality when balanced with dignity. But where does this balance come from? Confidence that is rooted in self makes one proud and is not usually expressed with dignity, but confidence that is rooted in a right understanding of God and who He has made you to be is always tempered with humility. This right understanding of God, I believe, is what enables her to "[smile] *at the future.*" One who knows how to trust God does not spend her days in anxiety and worry. The believer is not immune to such emotions, but is never to be controlled by them (see Philippians 4:6–7).

Did You Know?

THE STRUCTURE OF PROVERBS 31

Proverbs 31, if it is to be viewed as part of the "oracle" taught to King Lemuel by his mother, was probably a poem he learned as a child. The uniqueness of its structure is lost on those who cannot read Hebrew. The structure is based on an "alphabetic acrostic." The author took each letter of the Hebrew alphabet (22 total), and beginning with verse 10, wrote one verse for each letter extolling the virtues of the *"excellent wife."* Psalm 119 is another example of the alphabetic acrostic, where the author devotes eight verses to each letter of the Hebrew alphabet to sing praises of the Word of God.

In Matthew 12:34 Jesus said, *". . . the mouth speaks out of that which fills the heart."* Our words have much to say about our character. Look at verse 26 and see what her words are saying about her heart.

What comes out when she opens her mouth?

_____

_____

What flavors her teaching?

_____

_____

How do these two balance each other?

_____

_____

_____

"She opens her mouth in wisdom." Don't you wish that came out every time you opened your mouth? Remember that wisdom is not simply knowledge, but is knowledge made practical—it is application-focused truth. Not only that, but her teaching is flavored with kindness. What a beautiful balance is seen here! Wisdom given without kindness can hurt more than help. Wisdom without kindness becomes the "I told you so" chorus. But this woman's wisdom is shared with a kind heart, making it much easier to swallow.

We already saw from our study of verse 28 in the first day of our lesson, that one of the products of a virtuous character is the praise of those VIP's who know her the best. What mother doesn't long to have her children and her husband speak well of her? But such praise that is not earned by character is simply hollow flattery. God does not want women to be "men pleasers," enslaved to a popularity contest with their families. What He wants is for each woman to seek to be the kind of woman deserving of praise whether it is ever given or not. The text does not make it clear that these blessings are given **to** her, but rather they seem to be **about** her. While we would all love to hear such words, praise given about us to another is worth even more than praise given to us.

Where does such praise come from? Ladies, what must happen for these beautiful words to be spoken about you? What must you do?

Look at verse 30 and write your observations.

What actions does the world employ to earn praise?

_____

_____

_____

_____

_____

> In Matthew 12:34 Jesus said, ". . . the mouth speaks out of that which fills the heart." Our words have much to say about our character.

How is charm "deceitful?"

_____

_____

The word "vain" means "empty or hollow, transitory, unsatisfactory." How is this applicable to beauty?

_____

_____

_____

What does the last half of the verse list as the key to becoming deserving of true praise?

_____

_____

_____

> **"Charm is deceitful and beauty is vain, But a woman who fears the Lord, she shall be praised."**
> **Proverbs 31:30**

The world delights in praise, and the worldly are so foolish as to be satisfied with it, even if it is undeserved. In fact, many a worldly person is enslaved in trying to achieve the praise of others. The word "charm" here could equally be translated "favor." To be deceitful it must be the favor of men, for God is not fickle with His favor, nor deceptive. Man, though, often uses charm and flattery to portray something that isn't true of the heart. Flattery has well been described as "saying things you don't mean to people you don't care for." Beauty, likewise, is equally fickle. Outer beauty is vain or empty because it can hide an ugly heart, and is of no consequence in eternity. Man focuses on the outward appearance, but God always looks at the heart (see 1 Samuel 16:7). The woman who truly is praiseworthy is the one who fears the Lord. To her, His is the only opinion that matters, yet it is this very heart that makes her so attractive to others.

The Virtuous Woman | **DAY THREE**

THE LABOR OF A VIRTUOUS WOMAN

Are you a "working woman?" Personally, I have never met a woman who wasn't. My wife does not have a job outside the home, but when anyone asks her, "Do you work?" she is quick to reply, "Every hour of the day!" She is the first one up, and usually the last one to bed. Is she the Biblical ideal? Is she a better mom and wife because she stays at home? Is the woman with a job outside the home less godly, less committed to her family? I grew up in a single-parent home with my mom as the breadwinner. I can appreciate the difficulties of juggling work and family. Opinions abound on this touchy subject. But before we try to answer it, let me make an important point. God has placed the truths of Scripture in a cultural frame. To rightly understand and apply the Bible, we have to be able to separate the two. We cannot make a biblical mandate out of something that was cultural, any more than we can dismiss as culture things about which Scripture is clear and emphatic. As we will see today, the virtuous woman of Proverbs 31 is both a homemaker and a businesswoman. The two do not have to be at odds with each other, as long as they are both surrendered to God.

As you look at the labor of the virtuous woman, you get a glimpse of her priorities. While she earns an income outside the home, that does not come at the expense of her home and family. If you look at the subject matter dealt with in this chapter, more verses are devoted to her family than any other single area. Clearly that is her number one priority. Yet she is able to reach beyond that priority to accomplish other things as well. She cares for herself and her needs, she has a cottage industry that provides income, and as we will see in tomorrow's lesson, she is able to reach out in ministry. A good summary of her heart for her home is found in verse 27, *"She looks well to the ways of her household, and does not eat the bread of idleness."*

📖 Look at these verses and write down your observations on the virtuous woman's provision for her family.

v. 14—

_____

_____

_____

v. 15—

_____

_____

_____

v. 19—

_____

_____

_____

v. 21—

_____

_____

_____

v. 22—

_____

_____

_____

When you look at these verses together, a pattern begins to emerge. Truly, *"She looks well to the ways of her household, and does not eat the bread of idleness."* To fully appreciate how she is like a merchant ship, you have to understand the workings of their culture. A merchant ship would load itself down with goods from its own country, then travel to various ports bartering those goods for valuables that could not be found at home. In the same way, the virtuous woman trades her own products to provide good things for the family. They are all better off for her labor. That she rises while it is still night speaks of labor obviously, but it also speaks of preparedness. She arises early enough to be prepared to meet needs. The principle goes beyond merely fixing a

> "She looks well to the ways of her household, and does not eat the bread of idleness."
> Proverbs 31:27

meal. In verse 19 we are told that she stretches out her hand to the "distaff." While this has sewing and weaving in view, it really means "she reaches for profitable work." She is finding useful things to do. Because of her diligence, she doesn't fear what the weather (or the days) may bring. Her family has what it needs. But in all of this labor, she doesn't sacrifice herself. She *"makes coverings for herself"* (literally, "tapestries," probably referring to home décor instead of clothing), and is well-clothed (fine linen and purple were not common clothing—they were costly, indicating a value to herself and her appearance). Because she does not eat the bread of idleness, her labor meets the needs of her family and herself as well.

Not only does the virtuous woman look well to the ways of her household, she also is an economic asset to the family. Our modern debate on whether a woman should work outside the home or stay at home and keep house was a moot point in the days of Solomon. Every home was a business, and every business was a home. Not only was it abnormal for the woman to leave home at nine to work an eight hour shift, it was abnormal for the man as well. As we will see in the verses that follow, the virtuous woman was part of one of the home/businesses that made up the industry base of Palestine. She organized her time so that there was time left over once the household work was done. Certainly work and homemaking were easier to juggle when everyone worked out of their homes.

📖 Look up the Proverbs 31 verses that are listed in the excercises throughout the remainder of Day Three, and write down your observations on the virtuous woman's income-producing work.

v. 13—

_____

_____

_____

In verse 13 we see that she *"looks for wool and flax."* Is this for her own family, or her cottage industry? We can't say for sure, but it was probably for both. These two materials were used primarily in clothing—wool as a winter material and flax as a summer material. We see in other verses that she made both clothing for her family and clothing to sell. Does this mean that the virtuous woman has to be able to sew? Sewing is only the example. We must keep our focus on the principle of work rather than making a doctrine from the type of work. This is where the last half of the verse focuses: *". . . And works with her hands in delight."* This not only reveals what she does (*"works"*) but how she does it (*"in delight"*).

v. 16—

_____

_____

_____

Verse 16 not only shows that she purchased a piece of land, but includes two revealing components. First, she "considers" a field. She is an evaluator. She weighs the costs and benefits of things. Second, she buys it from her earnings. This is a two-income family. Something that she does earns an income. Now this doesn't devalue the woman who has no "earnings," for the verse

Did You Know?

WHAT IS FLAX?

Flax is a plant that has been cultivated from the earliest periods of the world's history. It has a meter-long fibrous stem which, when beaten, was used for making rope or for dyeing and weaving. Joshua 2:6 indicates that Rahab hid the spies in the stalks of flax which she had laid out on her roof, presumably for the purpose of drying them out. The material made from flax was very light and breathable, making it well suited for the hot summers of Palestine.

literally reads, "from the fruit of her palms." The fruit of her palms may be earning a profit from sales, or it could be saving money by managing part of the family budget.

v. 17—

_____

_____

_____

_____

v. 24—

_____

_____

_____

_____

What does it mean that she *"girds herself with strength, and makes her arms strong?"* It doesn't necessarily mean regular visits to the health spa. It means she keeps herself capable for her God-given tasks. She sells linen garments and belts. The point is not what she sells, but that she makes something for which there is a market. It could be a product like baked goods, crafts, or decorations. It could possibly be a service such as cleaning or childcare, or it could be a skill such as artwork, writing, or bookkeeping. Every person has unique skills, abilities and talents, and since a laborer is worthy of one's wages, anyone can earn a profit somewhere. It really hinges on the time available after the family needs are met. Season of life and individual circumstances may define when and how much one can do. Small children at home will definitely limit opportunities for profit-making, while having grown kids or no kids might enhance such opportunities.

v. 31—

_____

_____

_____

_____

Verse 31 closes this chapter with an interesting point worth noting: *"Give her the product of her hands. . . ."* It is not wrong for the woman to share in the fruits of her labor. Balance is key here. There are those in our generation who neglect their families to work, not because of need but so they can pursue material goals. We cannot sacrifice our families on the altars of selfish materialism. A second point to be seen is in the statement, *". . . let her works praise her. . . ."* Whether any income results from a woman's labor is not as important as the value of knowing her labor is important. Her contribution is valuable. In every life there is the need for our works to bring praise to us. What can we say of the virtuous woman? Truly *"She looks well to the ways of her household, and does not eat the bread of idleness."*

Doctrine
IS WORK A RESULT OF SIN?

Work is a good thing. It was part of God's plan before the fall. Sweat may find its origin in sin, but not work. Jesus once made the statement, *"My food is to do the will of Him who sent Me, and to accomplish His work"* (John 4:34). He compared work to food. Think about the purposes of food. It has nutrition to sustain us, and flavor to satisfy us. Work is supposed to be that way too. It is supposed to sustain us (meet our needs) and satisfy us (give us fulfillment). Whatever work God gives us to do—whether parenting or production, homemaking or hardware—it should sustain and satisfy.

THE RELATIONSHIPS OF A VIRTUOUS WOMAN

> **"It is better to live in a corner of a roof, Than in a house shared with a contentious woman."**
>
> **Proverbs 21:9**

God created us for relationship. He gave us the gift of communication to enable us to "commune." God's will for our lives is ultimately defined by relationships. His Law is fulfilled through relationships. Jesus was asked, *"Teacher, which is the great commandment in the Law?"* His answer was two-fold: Love God with all your heart, soul and mind, and love your neighbor as yourself. *"On these two commandments,"* He replied, *"depend the whole Law and the Prophets"* (Matthew 22:40). In other words, if you take care of relationships, all other things will take care of themselves. The virtuous woman is one who has her relationships in perspective. She knows how to manage her relationship with her husband, her family, and her neighbor, because she manages her relationship with God. Notice, Jesus placed loving God at the top of the list. Proverbs makes it clear that a woman can master the tasks listed here and still be a failure if she can't manage the relationships. Proverbs 15:17 says, *"Better is a dish of vegetables where love is, Than a fattened ox and hatred with it."* In Proverbs 21:9 we are told, *"It is better to live in a corner of a roof, Than in a house shared with a contentious woman."* And again, in Proverbs 21:19 we read, *"It is better to live in a desert land, Than with a contentious and vexing woman."* This value on relationship is just one more way Proverbs 31 makes clear the order of our priorities in life. Today we want to see how those priorities are lived out in relationships.

📖 Take a look at Proverbs 31:11–12.

In verse 11 we are told that, *"The heart of her husband trusts in her."* What are some specific things that build trust in a husband?

_____

_____

_____

What things destroy it?

_____

_____

_____

With all you have seen so far in Proverbs 31, what comes to mind with the phrase, *"he will have no lack of gain"*?

_____

_____

_____

What impact does verse 12 have on "trust" and "gain"?

_____

_____

_____

_____

In 2 Corinthians 7:16 Paul says, *"I rejoice that in everything I have confidence in you."* That confidence was even sweeter because of all the problems that he had worked through in his first letter to them. Trust had been built. You can see that this aspect of the virtuous woman takes time. That ought to be a goal in every significant relationship we have. It speaks volumes about any relationship that the heart can trust, but how much more it speaks of the closest of human relationships—marriage. What builds trust? Transparency, communicating, keeping your word, building up your mate (or your friend)—these are the bricks and mortar that make for a relationship of trust. On the other side, dishonesty, aloofness, not talking, constant criticism—these are the things that destroy trust. If our homes have safe and satisfying relationships, we are already a success. We have the most important gain life has to offer. A track record of doing good **and** not doing evil brings us to the place where the heart of our VIP's trust in us. Notice the phrase, *"all the days of her life."* This kind of relationship is not the result of a sprint. It is a distance run—it takes consistency.

📖 What does Proverbs 31:23 show as a result to the husband of having a virtuous woman for his wife?

_____

_____

_____

What a powerful thought that **he** is known because of **her**! Many of us do not realize how much impact we have on those around us. I heard of a godly man in one church who was turned down as a possible elder, not because of his own walk, but because his wife was known as a gossip. God's design is that a man is better off because he has a wife. Proverbs 18:22 *"He who finds a wife finds a good thing, And obtains favor from the LORD."* That is His desire, His design. He wants the man to be bettered by his wife. She should be such a strong support that he is well thought of because of her.

Not only does the virtuous woman manage her home relationships well, but she reaches out beyond that circle to those God brings into her world. In Proverbs 31:18 we are told, *"She senses that her gain is good."* In other words, she is satisfied with the way things are. Then we are told, *"Her lamp does not go out at night."* At a casual glance we may think that means she is staying up late working. We already see that she arises early. Maybe she is burning the candle at both ends. But if we understand the culture, a different picture emerges. First of all, in that culture you couldn't go down to Wal-Mart and buy a box of matches. An efficient home always kept a lamp burning as a source of fire. But more to the point, a hospitable home kept a lamp burning in the window, inviting visitors. In those days an inn was hard to come by, and motels didn't exist. Travelers were usually at the mercy of local hospitality. Whether a family member, a neighbor, or a passing stranger was in need of help, the virtuous woman was ready to serve at any time.

📖 Look at Proverbs 31:20 and write what you see about her ministry heart.

_____

_____

_____

_____

She *"stretches out her hands"* to the needy. In the preceding verse (19) we saw that she is one who *"stretches out her hands to the distaff"*—she reaches for work. Here we see that she also reaches for ministry. The wording pictures more than random acts of kindness. To "extend" or "stretch" communicates intentional ministry, going out of one's way. She has a heart to look for needs and meet them

The more detailed our examination of this powerful chapter becomes, the more danger we have of being overwhelmed. The author closes out in verse 30 by reminding us of the most important relationship the virtuous woman has. Look at this verse and then paraphrase it in your own words.

_____

_____

_____

_____

_____

Charm, beauty, these are the things in which women of the world place their trust. Yet they are not the building blocks of meaningful relationships. In fact, if you think about it, those things work against being real, connecting with the heart. The foundation of all horizontal relationships is the vertical relationship—our relationship with God gives us the security to be real and vulnerable. It is walking in God's grace that makes us agents of grace to others. Even our ability to grant forgiveness and ask for forgiveness is tied to our relationship with God. We cannot make ourselves into a virtuous woman. But if we walk with God day after day, yielding our lives to His control, He will keep making us more like Jesus until He returns.

The Virtuous Woman **DAY FIVE**

FOR ME TO FOLLOW GOD

In Luke 2:52 we see an interesting glimpse into the early life of our Lord. There we are told, *"And Jesus kept increasing in wisdom and stature, and in favor with God and men."* There is an encouraging message to be found in this verse. First, we see here the four main areas of life. Wisdom denotes the intellectual side of life, and stature denotes the physical. Favor with God clearly points to the spiritual, and favor with men points to the social. God wants us to grow and develop in each of these areas. But isn't it amazing to think of Jesus **in process!** He *"kept increasing"* in each of these areas. Wherever we are, there is always room to grow. If we look at the Proverbs 31 woman and say, "no woman could ever be like that" then we have already defeated ourselves. But if we understand that this is what God wants women to develop into, and that development involves process, then we will find the grace to start the journey. We should look at this list of character qualities, tasks, and relationships as a way to see what fresh areas of our lives need to be yielded to the Lord. Remember, victory is not me overcoming sin, it is Jesus overcoming me. Today, as we bring this lesson to a close, we want to look at the applications God has for us right now at this place in the journey to becoming a virtuous woman.

Your reputation is what those who don't know you well **think** you are—your character is what those who know you well **know** you are. One of the first steps in coming to a place of growth is the willingness to admit that you need to grow. As you consider the three main areas we saw addressed in Proverbs 31, which of the three would you say needs the most work in you?

____ Development of your own character
____ Your labor/work
____ Your relationships

Remember, the virtuous woman of Proverbs 31 is not a standard or yardstick to measure up to, but the goal toward which women should be moving. She is the woman God is developing women to be today as they follow Him. The first step for women to change is not gritting their teeth and trying harder to be the perfect woman. It is surrender. You see, the most important word in the Christian life is not commitment, but **surrender.** We can be committed in the flesh, but surrender is admitting what we cannot do in our own strength. It is running up the white flag in our hearts and saying, "I surrender, You can be Jesus in me."

Look up the following verses and make notes to remind you who (and Whose) you are. As you do, ask yourself how does each verse help free you from trying in your own efforts to be like the woman described in Proverbs 31:10–31.

Romans 3:24, 28

_____
_____
_____

Romans 5:1–2

_____
_____
_____

Romans 8:2, 10

_____
_____
_____

Romans 11:16

_____
_____
_____

Galatians 2:20

_____
_____

"And Jesus kept increasing in wisdom and stature, and in favor with God and men."

Luke 2:52

Ephesians 1:3

_____

_____

_____

Colossians 3:3

_____

_____

_____

1 Thessalonians 5:24

_____

_____

_____

2 Peter 1:3

_____

_____

_____

*Remember, God does not want women to "be like" the virtuous woman, He wants women today to **become** that woman. He doesn't want their best imitation of her.*

Remember, God does not want women to "be like" the virtuous woman, He wants women today to **become** that woman. He doesn't want their best imitation of her.

APPLY As you consider your labor, is there any area the Lord has pointed out to you this week that needs to change?

In your priorities?

_____

_____

_____

In your effort?

_____

_____

Is there anything you need to surrender afresh?

_____

_____

APPLY What about your relationships? Consider your relationship with your husband and children (if you have them).

Is there anything for which you need to ask forgiveness?

_____

_____

Is there anything you need to begin doing?

_____

_____

What about ministry? Are there any things you need to do to "reach out" your hand to the needy?

_____

_____

Most importantly, it is the woman who fears the Lord who shall be praised. No woman will ever become like the woman Proverbs 31 speaks of apart from God's working in her life. One of the most important tools He uses to do that is His Word. Make sure you are making time in your week to study God's Word. As the great evangelist D. L. Moody used to say, "The only way to keep a broken vessel full is to keep the faucet running."

For God to do that molding work He desires to do in our lives, we need to remain on the potter's wheel. Romans 12:1 says, *"I urge you therefore, brethren, by the mercies of God, to present your bodies a living and holy sacrifice, acceptable to God, which is your spiritual service of worship."* There is no worship of God apart from surrender. Why not take a moment right now to make the prayer below your own as you yield your life to Him in a fresh way.

Spend some time in prayer with your merciful Father right now.

Lord, I look at the woman in Proverbs 31, and I see many areas in my life where I desperately fail. All my efforts to change myself have fallen short. Others may be fooled, but You know what I am, and what I am not. Thank You for showing me what I can be by Your grace. Take control of the throne of my heart—make me into the person You want me to be. I repent of trying to be that on my own. By faith, I thank You for what I will become. I praise You that You began this work in me when You saved me, and that You will keep on perfecting it until the day I meet you face to face. Help me to be patient. Amen.

As we close our lesson this week, take to heart any areas the Lord has singled out to you and express them in prayer to Him.

_____

_____

_____

_____

_____

_____

_____

_____

_____

Notes

Mary and Martha

SEEING WHAT IS ETERNAL

M ary and Martha, two sisters from the town of Bethany, are known primarily as the sisters of Lazarus. Others remember the statement of Jesus, *"Martha, Martha"* (Luke 10:41), and think of someone scurrying about in busy, even worrisome, activity. But, there is so much more to be seen in the lives of these two followers of Jesus. While they can teach us some things about anxious activity, even activity intended for the Lord's use, there is much more we can learn from them about growing in our relationship with Jesus, about truly listening to His Word, and then living out that Word in active belief.

They can teach us much about what has eternal significance and what is eternally insignificant.

WHERE DOES SHE FIT?

2200BC	1950	1700	1450	1200	950	700	450	100
SARAH 2155–2028		MIRIAM 1533?–1405				Daniel 619–534?		MARY and MARTHA 10BC?–60AD?
			DEBORAH 1300?–1200?	Solomon 991–931		ESTHER 504?–450?		
			Judges Rule 1385–1051	David 1041–971				
	Jacob 2005–1858	Joshua 1495–1385	RUTH 1135?–1050?			Nehemiah 480?–400?		MARY, Mother of Jesus 20BC–60AD?
	Isaac 2065–1885	Moses 1525–1405	HANNAH 1135?–1050?	VIRTUOUS WOMAN Prov. 31				
Abraham 2165–1990		RAHAB 1445?–1385?	Samuel 1105–1022					Jesus Christ 4BC?–30AD?

These women can also teach us the difference between what has eternal significance, and what is eternally insignificant. They can show us much about the patience of the Lord with His disciples and about how He enacts the fullness of His plans. They can show us some things about the difference between time and timing. As Mary and Martha came to know, Jesus is the master of perfect timing. These two followers of Jesus also show us much about pure worship, the kind of worship in which Jesus takes delight.

LEARNING TO LISTEN TO THE WORD OF THE LORD

W e are introduced to Mary and Martha in the final six to seven months of Jesus' earthly ministry. During the first part of October (Israel's month *Tishri 15–21*), probably in 29 AD, Jesus and His disciples were in Jerusalem for the Feast of Tabernacles. John tells us Jesus and the disciples ministered there, and that Jesus used the occasion to proclaim His promise of Living Water to all who came to Him. He then declared *"I AM the Light of the world"* and focused their attention on His relationship to the Father (John 7:37–52; 8:12–30). He also proclaimed His Word to be truth that sets one free, if one abides in that Word. He is the Son who sets people "free indeed" (John 8:31–36). Finally, He spoke of the relationship between Himself, the Father, and Abraham. The Jews claimed Abraham as their father, while Jesus said the devil was their father. He then declared, *"Before Abraham was, I AM,"* thus making Himself equal with God. They sought to stone Him, but He miraculously escaped (John 8:39–59).

Within a few weeks of these incidents at the Feast, Jesus and His disciples were journeying from Samaria to Judea and came to the village of Bethany, two miles east of Jerusalem. It was located on the east side of the Mount of Olives. They were invited into the home of Mary, Martha, and Lazarus, apparently a family of some means who could host such a group. Perhaps these three were among those who heard Jesus and believed in Him at the Feast of Tabernacles. It would have been quite natural for them to invite Jesus to their home. This probably occurred within the month of October or early November of 29 AD.

📖 Read Luke 10:38–39. We are introduced to Martha and Mary. What is your first impression of Mary? How does Mary act toward Jesus (10:39)?

_____

_____

_____

_____

_____

_____

"If any man is thirsty, let Him come to Me and drink. He who believes in Me as the Scripture said, 'From his innermost being shall flow rivers of living water.'"

John 7:37–38

Mary had a heart that was hungry to learn. She willingly sat at Jesus' feet to hear Him as He taught and explained the Scriptures. Her listening heart reflects the attitude Jesus had spoken about in Jerusalem at the Feast in October. It is quite possible, even probable, that Mary, Martha, and Lazarus attended the Feast of Tabernacles. They were only a two-mile walk from the Temple area, and this feast was one of the three required for Jewish men. It is very probable that they heard Jesus' teachings recorded in John 7 and 8. There Jesus said that those who abide in His word would be free. When Jesus came to their house, Mary chose to sit and listen carefully to Jesus' words. The verb tense of *akouo* (translated "heard" or "listening") used in Luke 10:39 refers to one who is **continually** hearing or listening—a lifestyle of listening to His word. Whether or not these three heard Jesus in Jerusalem, one thing is certain, Mary was a disciple who longed to abide in Jesus' word, to know the truth, and to walk in the freedom He promised.

📖 What do you see about Martha in Luke 10:38, 40?

_____

_____

_____

_____

Martha welcomed Jesus and His disciples into her home. The word translated "received" or "welcomed" carries the idea of welcoming as a guest. She gladly received them, but then Martha became very distracted with preparing and trying to serve a meal. The word translated "cumbered" or "distracted" literally means being dragged here and there, or being pulled in many different directions. The verb tense means to be continually distracted. Her continual focus was on the details of serving. She had not yet made listening to the Lord's word a priority. For her, serving (even if it meant being fretful in serving) was first on her priority list.

How did Martha act toward Jesus (10:40)?

_____

_____

_____

_____

Martha actually tried to rebuke both Mary and Jesus with her statement in verse 40. First of all, Martha questioned Jesus' care for her and her many preparations. She wanted to know why Mary could get by with not helping her prepare the meal. She then promptly entreated the Lord to tell Mary to get up and help her. This is a very different picture of a disciple than the picture we see in Mary. Martha's agenda of preparing an elaborate meal (perhaps pridefully wanting to impress Jesus) robbed her of the joy of fellowship with Him.

📖 Jesus had a response to Martha's actions and her questions. What did He tell Martha in Luke 10:41? Write a brief summary of Jesus' description of Martha. You may want to research some of the words Jesus used in verse 41 (especially in a Greek-English New Testament Dictionary).

> *"If you abide in My word, then you are truly disciples of Mine; and you shall know the truth, and the truth shall make you free."*
> *John 8:31–32*

When Jesus first came to the home of Mary and Martha, we see two very different pictures of a disciple.

_____

_____

_____

_____

_____

_____

_____

Doctrine
ONLY ONE

Theologians have debated whether the "only one" thing Jesus speaks of in Luke 10:42 refers to Mary's choice to sit at His feet, or the food Martha was preparing (meaning "only a few dishes are necessary, really only one"). In either case, there can be no doubt of His affirming Mary's choice to make time for His words. He was more concerned with His opportunity to feed their souls than their opportunity to feed His body.

Jesus spoke to Martha very clearly. He claimed that she was worried and bothered about too many things. The word translated "worried" or "careful" refers to a divided mind. Martha's mind was trying to look in two (or more) directions at once, and she was unable to devote adequate time for any particular direction. The word translated "troubled" or "bothered" refers to someone disturbed by circumstances around him or her. It is used of a noisy crowd or riotous mob. Jesus did not want Martha to be troubled with all her serving.

📖 What did Jesus say concerning Mary?

_____

_____

_____

_____

_____

First of all, Jesus saw that Mary had made **a choice** (*"Mary has chosen. . ."*). She was seated at His feet listening to His word. This was a good choice. The Greek word translated "good" refers to that which is most beneficial and helpful, or that which is most pleasing and satisfying, like something that fits just right. She made the right choice and could enjoy that now and forever, for what she chose would not be taken away from her. In Jesus' mind only one thing was necessary. That one thing was what Mary had chosen to do—to stop what she was doing in order to sit at His feet, to concentrate on what He was saying, and to continually listen to His word with a heart ready to obey. This is the heart of a disciple—one who listens in order to learn a lifestyle. This is who Jesus calls to follow Him, disciples who would obey all He said.

 Are you listening to the Lord's word with a heart like Mary? Or are you busy, busy, busy trying to serve the Lord or the church or your family or even yourself? Is the Lord speaking to you through the example of one of these ladies? Stop and pray. Talk to the Lord. Evaluate where you are in your walk with the Lord. Listen to His word. That is the good choice. If we do not take time to listen to the Lord, things that really aren't important to Him will distract us.

What else did Mary and Martha learn from Jesus? He was not through teaching and instructing them in what it meant to follow Him. The next recorded incident in their lives will help us see that very clearly.

LEARNING TO WAIT ON THE WORKS OF THE LORD

According to John 10:22, Jesus and His disciples were in Jerusalem again, this time for the Feast of Dedication. This began on *Kislev* 25 and lasted eight days (our mid-December). This feast is also known as the Feast of Lights or Hanukkah. During that time, Jesus healed a man born blind and later spoke to many about Himself being the Good Shepherd and about being one with the Father (John 9:1–39; 10:1–39). This teaching increased opposition from the Jewish leaders, and because of this opposition, He and His disciples probably went to Perea east of the Jordan River and ministered there (John 10:40–42). Most likely, this was in January of 30 AD, about three months before His crucifixion.

📖 While Jesus was ministering across the Jordan, Lazarus became very ill. What did Mary and Martha do, according to John 11:3?

_____

_____

_____

_____

_____

Why did they do this? What do you think they expected?

_____

_____

_____

_____

_____

> *Time is an important ingredient in the workings of the Lord. Timing is more important.*

Mary and Martha had seen Jesus' works of healing. They knew that Jesus loved (*agape*) them (11:5). He was committed to doing all that was best for them. Verse 3 uses the word *phileo*, which tells us that they knew Jesus loved Lazarus like a brother or a best friend. They also knew Jesus could heal him; therefore, they sent to inform Him of Lazarus' serious illness. They were certain Jesus would want to come in light of the circumstances. They expected Him to come immediately.

📖 What did Jesus do according to John 11:4–6?

_____

_____

_____

_____

_____

Jesus truly loved Mary, Martha, and Lazarus. When the messenger brought news of Lazarus' serious condition, Jesus confidently declared that this sickness was not unto death (ultimately), but was for the glory of God, so that the Son of God would be glorified through it. That message was carried back to Mary and Martha. The disciples thought all was well. Jesus then stayed where He was two more days. Mary and Martha would have to wait.

Why did Jesus wait two more days? What determined His schedule? As we look at the life of Jesus, we see a consistent pattern. In the fall of 27 AD, in His first year of ministry, we find Him in Samaria at Jacob's well. After talking to the woman of Sychar He began talking to His disciples about His purpose in life.

📖 What do you see about Jesus in John 4:34?

_____

_____

_____

_____

📖 About a year later, in the late summer of 28 AD, Jesus was in Jerusalem where He healed a lame man on the Sabbath. Some began openly questioning and opposing Him. What was His response about His works according to John 5:19–21, 30, 36?

_____

_____

_____

_____

_____

_____

📖 A few months later (January of 29 AD), Jesus again faced opposition— this time it was in the region of Galilee. What did He reveal about His ways there? Read John 8:28–29 and record your answer.

_____

_____

_____

_____

📖 The incident with Mary and Martha occurred about a year later (January of 30 AD). How do the truths found in John 4, 5, and 8 relate to Jesus' ways with Mary and Martha?

_____

_____

_____

_____

_____

Word Study
WAITING ON GOD

Waiting on God is one of the foundation stones of learning to follow Him. In the Old Testament we are often told to "wait on the Lord." In Psalm 27:14 the Hebrew word for "wait" (*qavah*) means "to bind together (by twisting)," like the threads that make up a piece of fabric. We can paint a picture with this word, a picture of the Lord binding strands of thread together with which He then begins making a beautiful tapestry. Often we have to wait while He is working His threads into place. As we wait in faith, our waiting becomes active trust. Abraham, Joseph, Moses, Joshua, David and many others experienced this tapestry work of the Lord. Mary and Martha experienced it as well.

Jesus did nothing on His own initiative. The Father instructed Him in what to say and what to do. Even the timing of Christ's works were determined by the Father. In this incident with Mary and Martha, we find a clear example of Christ waiting on the works of the Lord. What He did, and what He still does, is marked by the Father's timing. They had to wait, but it was a purposeful wait. God was preparing to display His glory, His perfection, and power. Martha and Mary would eventually learn to wait on the works of the Lord.

Time was not the crucial factor that Mary and Martha may have thought that it was. **Timing** was the important factor here. In the Father's timing, He sent Jesus to raise Lazarus and reveal Himself in greater ways. They wanted their brother healed, and even the Father wanted to raise Lazarus from the dead. This would be a preview of the reign of the one who is the Resurrection and the Life. His Kingdom would be marked by life, not death, and the proof was about to be seen. In the meantime, Mary and Martha were learning to wait on the Lord.

APPLY Are you dealing with some **time** versus **timing** issues in your life? Are you having to wait on the works of the Lord? Stop and talk to the Lord about these things. Write down your thoughts, make a journal entry, or write a letter to the Lord.

_____

_____

_____

_____

_____

_____

LEARNING TO BELIEVE JESUS' WORD– TRUSTING THE FATHER'S WILL

After a two-day wait, Jesus was ready to go to Judea to Lazarus' house (John 11:7). He always acted in oneness with the will of His Father. He wanted His disciples to do the same and He wanted Mary and Martha to do so as well. Jesus knew the full extent of Lazarus' illness and what would happen in His absence. When Jesus informed His disciples that it was time to go to Judea to the home of Lazarus, the disciples, somewhat alarmed at the prospect of returning to the place where many wanted to stone them, questioned His decision to leave where they were. Verse 8 says *"Rabbi . . . are You* [note, not "are we"] *going there again?"* They did not want to return to imminent danger.

Here Jesus began speaking to them about why He did what He did. In John 11:9–10, He made it clear that as long as He and they were walking in the light of day no one would stumble—no harm would come. He knew that as long as He was doing the Father's will, He was protected and so were the

"Jesus Christ is the same yesterday and today, yes and forever."

Hebrews 13:8

Jesus had a work to do while it was "day." It would not be cut short as long as He was following the Father's will.

disciples. His (and their) enemies would not cut short the day's work that the Father had given Him to do.

📖 Jesus knew Lazarus had died and He knew it was the Father's will to awaken him from the "sleep" of death (11:11). Jesus was glad for the disciples' sakes that He was not there when Lazarus was sick. Why would Jesus say that? What did He want for His disciples?

_____

_____

_____

_____

_____

Jesus anticipated that His disciples were about to move to a new level of understanding of who He was and a deeper level of trust in Him. He wanted them to believe in Him in some new ways, with new revelation and fresh understanding. The timing was perfect. They would see His power over death in a new light. It was time to go to Bethany. Jesus and the disciples traveled the day's journey to Bethany, and when they arrived they learned that Lazarus had been in the tomb four days.

📖 Martha was the first to meet Jesus. What was her response to Jesus' coming according to John 11:21–22?

_____

_____

_____

_____

Martha responded as many of us would—"If only. . . ." She knew that if Jesus had been there, He would have been fully capable of healing Lazarus. She had seen and heard of His many works. Just a month before, He had healed the blind man in Jerusalem—a fact many of the Jews from Jerusalem and Bethany remembered even later. She was confident that if Jesus had been there He could have asked of God and the Father would have granted His request, but not now and not here. It was too late. Or was it?

Where did Jesus focus her attention (John 11:23)?

_____

_____

_____

_____

On what did Martha focus (John 11:24)?

_____

_____

_____

_____

Doctrine

THE SEVEN "I AM" STATEMENTS OF JESUS

Jesus said I AM:

• the Bread of Life (John 6:35)

• the Light of the World (John 8:12)

• the Door of the Sheep (John 10:7, 9)

• the Good Shepherd (John 10:11, 14)

• the Resurrection and the Life (John 11:25–26)

• the Way, the Truth, and the Life (John 14:6)

• the True Vine (John 15:1, 5)

What did Jesus emphasize (John 11:25–26)?

_____

_____

_____

_____

Jesus focused Martha's attention on life, not death. He stated first that Lazarus would rise again. Martha then focused on the resurrection at the end of the age. She believed he would rise on the last day. In the midst of her mourning the death of her brother, Jesus drew her attention to Himself as the Resurrection and the Life (v. 25). Belief in Him meant life even in the face of death. It meant never truly dying. He was bringing Martha to a new level of trust in who He was and what it meant to follow Him. The resurrection of Lazarus is a preview of His life-giving resurrecting power.

In this declaration, Jesus proclaimed _"I AM,"_ emphasizing His ever-true nature as death-destroyer and life giver. This could be translated "I am always . . ." or "I have been, I am now, and I will ever be the Resurrection and the Life—the Conqueror of Death and the Giver of Life. Jesus used the Greek word _zoe ("life")_, referring to the essence and fullness of life—life at its deepest level. That is the Life He IS and the Life He gives.

What did Martha say to Jesus (John 11:27–28)?

_____

_____

_____

_____

_____

Martha declared her statement of faith. She emphasized what she believed. In essence, she said, "Yes, Lord, I have believed and still believe." She said "Yes" to His being "the Resurrection and the Life" and she fully believed He was the Christ, the Messiah, the Coming One often promised in the Scriptures. She knew He was the Son of God, the Teacher, but had not yet fully experienced Him as the Resurrection and the Life. Jesus was about to expand her understanding of Himself and lead her to a deeper level of worship and trust.

📖 Martha went to call Mary, who immediately came to Jesus. What was Mary's first response to Jesus in John 11:32, and how did Jesus respond in return according to John 11:32–33?

_____

_____

_____

_____

_____

_____

Jesus focused Martha's attention on life, not death.

To paraphrase John 11:25, Jesus essentially said, "I have been, I am now, and I will ever be the Resurrection and the Life— the Conqueror of Death and the Giver of Life."

In His timing, Jesus was bringing them to a new level of comprehension of Himself, of His power, and of His word.

Mary came to Jesus weeping, falling at His feet. Her words sounded like a repeat of Martha's "if only You had been here." When Jesus saw her weeping, He groaned in spirit and was troubled. Some translate this "He was indignant in spirit," and He shook or shuddered as He looked around Him—as He saw all the results of sin and death. Jesus wanted to go straight to the tomb, and as He went He wept. The Greek word for "wept" in John 11:35 indicates a quiet expression of tears—not a loud mournful sob. Those around Him took this as an expression of His love for Lazarus. At the tomb, He again groaned in His spirit, evidently moved by the sorrow of Martha and Mary, but also troubled by all He saw. Jesus then called for the removal of the stone at the entrance to the tomb. At Martha's objections, He again posed the question of true belief in Him—belief that would see the glory of God, the fuller expression of His nature and power. Christ was leading them to a deeper level of trust, surrender, and worship.

📖 Read John 11:40–42. What did Jesus emphasize once more?

_____

_____

_____

_____

Why did Jesus pray aloud?

_____

_____

_____

_____

What did He want the people to believe?

_____

_____

_____

_____

Did You Know?

⊘ **CONSOLING MARY AND MARTHA**

The statement in John 11:18–19 that *"many of the Jews"* had come to console Mary and Martha is a probable indication that these were prominent Jews from Jerusalem. It is also an indication that this family was a family of some means, very prominent in the community.

Jesus made it clear to Martha that through belief in Him she would see the glory of God. That is what He said when word of Lazarus' sickness first reached Him (11:4), and when she met Him coming into town (11:26). She would see God at work. Jesus prayed, confident in His relationship with the Father, and confident in answered prayer. Jesus and the Father were always one in their desires and choices. It was the Father who **sent** Jesus to earth for the salvation of man. It was the Father who **sent** Him in daily ministry—**where** He went and **when** He went. In this instance, the four days in the tomb were orchestrated by the Father. God the Father sent Jesus across the Jordan, and led Him to stay there two more days after news of Lazarus arrived. The Father sent the Son to Bethany so that He arrived on the fourth day. Jesus also wanted them to see that the Father sent Him into the world as the Resurrection and the Life, the Conqueror of Death, and the Giver of Everlasting Life.

For Mary and Martha as well as the disciples and many of the Jews there that day, a new era had dawned. Through what they saw they would gain a new vision of Jesus and the Father. They saw His glory manifested! Through this miracle of resurrection they would form an opinion about Jesus, and many would mix that with faith. The Greek word for faith, *pistis,* is rooted in a word that implies being persuaded to the point of whole-hearted trust. Many were persuaded that day. They learned to believe the Word of Jesus and to trust the will of the Father.

LEARNING TO WORSHIP THE LORD WITH A WHOLE HEART

After Jesus raised Lazarus from the dead, the Jewish officials heard the reports of the miracle and began intensifying their opposition. They began plotting the deaths of Jesus and Lazarus. Jesus and His disciples withdrew from Bethany (and Jerusalem) to Ephraim, a town just north of Bethel. From there they traveled through Samaria and Galilee before coming back to Perea. Then Jesus began His final journey to Jerusalem, going through Jericho and on to Bethany arriving six days before Passover.

Did You Know?

JESUS IS PROPHET, PRIEST, AND KING

In the Old Testament kings were anointed on the head. This was also true of the High Priest and sometimes of a prophet. In anointing Jesus on the head, which Jesus proclaimed was His anointing for burial, perhaps Mary was honoring Jesus as king. The Scripture shows us that He is all three—the Prophet, the King, and our High Priest.

📖 What happened after they arrived in Bethany according to John 12:1–2 and Mark 14:3?

_____

_____

_____

_____

Lazarus' sisters made a supper for Jesus apparently at the home of Simon the Leper. It is likely that Simon was once healed by Jesus. John tells us that Martha was serving them. Note that this was not a fretful service but rather a time of fellowship. This shows us that it was not Martha's serving that Jesus had rebuked a few months before, but her serving to excess that had distracted her from something more important.

📖 What did Mary do according to John 12:3, Matthew 26:7, and Mark 14:3? Each writer contributes some unique details of what Mary did.

_____

_____

_____

_____

_____

While they were reclining for supper (the normal way they ate in Jewish homes), Mary came to Jesus with an alabaster vial full of pure nard, a very precious oil, highly valued for its fragrant quality. Mary broke the vial and

Did You Know?

THE POUND OF NARD

The pound of nard mentioned in the gospels was probably a Roman pound equal to twelve ounces. The ointment in the vial was pure nard, not mixed or diluted. This ointment was red in color and had a sweet aroma and a pleasant flavor. It was derived from an aromatic herb grown in the high pasture land of the Himalayas between Tibet and India. This treasure was carried from this remote region on camel back through many mountain passes to the trade routes and into Israel. It was very expensive to buy and was considered a great treasure to inherit or to be given.

Word Study

WASTE

The disciples followed Judas and asked Jesus *"why this waste?"* (Matthew 26:8) using the Greek word *apoleia* often translated "destruction." Judas is called the *"son of perdition (apoleias)"* in John 17:12. Judas was a "son of waste" who wasted his life on self, selfish pursuits, and self-centered living even to the point of betraying the Son of God to get thirty pieces of silver. His vision was so blinded that he saw worship of Jesus as a waste, gifts to Jesus as a waste, and, as shown in his betrayal, he saw Jesus Himself as a waste.

poured the oil on the head of Jesus, filling the entire room with a sweet-smelling aroma. Then she poured some on His feet and stayed there wiping his feet with her hair.

According to John 12:4–6, what was the reaction of Judas?

_____

_____

_____

_____

_____

Why did Judas respond this way?

_____

_____

_____

_____

Judas was apparently the first one to speak. When he saw this valued treasure being poured out, he calculated the value of the perfume to be three hundred denarii, a year's wages for a common laborer. Since Judas kept the money box, and had been stealing some of the funds belonging to Jesus and the disciples for ministry, his eye was on the money he could gain through the sale of this precious perfume. His thieving heart cared nothing for the poor.

How did the other disciples respond? Read Matthew 26:8–9 and Mark 14:4–5 and record your findings.

_____

_____

_____

_____

_____

The disciples were indignant, the Greek word carrying the idea of an unwillingness for something to occur, of being pained or angry. They called Mary's gift a waste. They followed the counsel of Judas and offered their suggestion that the money could have been given to the poor. Not only that, they were scolding Mary, taking a stand of disgust and displeasure at this "waste."

How did Jesus respond according to Mark 14:6?

_____

_____

_____

_____

What was Jesus' response in Mark 14:7?

_____

_____

_____

_____

_____

Jesus responded with a clear statement about the value of her deed. While they were talking about wasting perfume and giving to the poor, He brought them to a true evaluation of what they were thinking. He commanded them to leave her alone, to stop bothering her. She had done a good deed, an appropriate and fitting deed, which was delicately beautiful in His eyes. Jesus further explained that there would always be opportunities to give to the poor, but that they would not always have Him there as He was that day—alluding to His impending death. Here was God incarnate in their midst and Mary worshiped Him as such. He was of supreme value and her gift was fitting for who He was. He was about to be crucified and buried. Jesus considered her anointing of Him as preparation for the day of His burial now less than a week away.

How did Jesus further honor her according to Matthew 26:13?

_____

_____

_____

_____

Her deed had the mark of eternity on it. Her ministry to Jesus would be memorialized throughout the world wherever the gospel was proclaimed. It would forever be a part of the sacred record of Scripture and a continual example and exhortation to pure worship. Again in Mary's life, what others considered insignificant, Jesus considered eternally significant. What others called a waste, Jesus considered an act of worship.

FOR ME TO FOLLOW GOD

 DAY FIVE

From that eventful night Jesus faced His final week of ministry. On the next day (Sunday), He made His triumphal entry into Jerusalem. The King of Israel, the Messiah, the Son of God, the Savior of the world was to reveal His greatest work yet, first on the Cross and then in the Resurrection. Mary, Martha, and Lazarus were most likely very much a part of that week. Jesus and His disciples stayed in Bethany each night, probably at the home of Mary and Martha. On the day of His crucifixion, they were there. Surely, He revealed Himself to them as part of that group of believers who witnessed some of His resurrection appearances over the next forty days.

After Jesus ascended (from Bethany [Luke 24:50]), Mary, Martha, and Lazarus were part of the 120 who gathered for prayer for ten days. Then on the Day of Pentecost they were part of that wondrous outpouring of the

Put Yourself In Their Shoes
WHY THIS WASTE?

When missionaries, Jim Elliot and Nate Saint, as well as Peter Fleming, T. Edward McCully, and Roger Youderian were brutally massacred in the jungles of Ecuador, the headlines of the leading newspaper in the capital city read "Why This Waste?" These missionaries left behind their wives and children. They gave their lives trying to reach a tribe of Indians that numbered about 50. Without the vantage point of eternity, the world always views such sacrifice as a waste. It is of great worth to remember Jim Elliot's words, "He is no fool who gives up what he cannot keep to gain what he cannot lose."

promised Holy Spirit. Doubtless, they became an integral part of the early church and often spoke of what the Lord taught them about listening to His word, about learning to wait on Him and His works, about believing His word and trusting His will, and about the meaning of true worship. We have the record of what they shared so that we might also learn to walk as they walked following Jesus.

 What about you? Are you daily listening to His Word like Mary, or are you wrapped up in insignificant things? Are you being nourished in your heart, or are you spiritually malnourished? Maybe you need a "Spiritual" examination. It's like a physical examination, only it's an evaluation of your "heart." A good place to start is by looking at how you spend your time, because how you spend your time is how you spend your life. Stop and evaluate. How much time each week do you spend in the following activities?

Bible reading _____

Meditation in Scripture _____

Prayer _____

Television (each day) _____

Small groups
for encouragement
and accountability
(men, women, youth) _____

Video rentals _____

Sports activities _____

Church activities _____

Video games _____

Community clubs _____

Civic organizations_____

You may want to take a time inventory and see where your time goes. Make a list of seven days and record what you do in 15-minute intervals from the time you wake up to bedtime. This list is likely to be a real eye-opener.

 Can you relate to Mary and Martha having to wait on the Lord? Are you in God's "waiting room" and uncertain when you will be moving to another room? Is it one of those "tight places?" Look at Psalm 46. Verse 1 can literally be translated "God is our Refuge and strength, abundantly available for help in tight places." Could that be a word of comfort or reassurance to you? Verse 10 says, *"Be still, and know that I am God"* (KJV). The words *"Be still"* can also be translated, *"Cease striving"* (NASB) or "Let go, relax, and know that I am God" or "experience Me as God" in your life. Reread Psalm 46, and meditate on it. It will make your time in the "Waiting Room" much more profitable. Listen to His Word to you and obey what He says. It would be good to write some of your insights or applications in the space below.

_____

_____

_____

_____

_____

_____

Is there an area where you are having difficulty **believing** God right now? Is there a need or an area that He must fill with His Life? The saints in the Old and New Testaments often prayed to the Lord, using one of His many names because that particular name fit the situation—*Jehovah-Jireh* meaning the Lord our Provider, *Jehovah-Shalom* meaning the Lord our Peace, or The Comforter, The Mighty God, etc. Come to Him for Who He is just as Mary and Martha did. Talk to Him. Ask Him to fill the void you are facing right now.

Is there something that you know is **God's will,** but you are struggling over it? Are you afraid to step out in faith? Has the Father revealed His will, but not His timing? Talk to Him and take the next step. He will give enough light for at least one step, and then when we take that step by faith, He will give enough light for another step. Trust Him. Perhaps it would help to stop and write Him a letter.

Dear Father,

_____

_____

_____

_____

_____

_____

_____

_____

_____

 How is your **worship** of the Lord? Is your relationship with Him the most valued relationship you have? Do you spend time with Him? How is your giving to Him? Are you gracious in your giving, or are you greedy? What about your devotion to studying the Scriptures or your prayer time? Do you ever give your time to help someone in need? Are you sharing your God-given talents in any way?

Spend some time with the Lord in prayer.

 Lord, so many times I get caught up in the temporary and the insignificant. Too often I become stirred up over things that won't matter a second in eternity. I waste time, money, and effort. Give me sight to see what is eternal. Give me wisdom as I read and listen to Your Word. Teach me to recognize what is a waste and what is worthwhile. May my worship of You be marked by unselfish, no-strings-attached giving. I'm seeing more and more that this life is like *"a vapor that appears for a little while and then vanishes away"* (James 4:14). *"Teach* [me] *to number* [my] *days, That* [I] *may present to Thee a heart of wisdom"* (Psalm 90:12). And Lord, Teach me to trust Your timing while I spend my time on this earth. Teach me to trust how You work, where You work, and when You work. May I lay aside all my agendas in surrender to You and Your eternal ways.

Lord, give me sight to see what is eternal.

Prayer of Application . . .

Write a prayer to the Lord in light of all you have learned this week.

_____

_____

_____

_____

_____

_____

_____

_____

_____

_____

_____

A Chronology of the Activities and Events of Mary and Martha

DATE	EVENTS	SCRIPTURE
Tishri 15–21 (October), 29 AD	Jesus and the disciples ministered during the Feast of Tabernacles.	John 7:2–39; 8:12–20 (JERUSALEM)
Fall (Oct. or Nov.), 29 AD	Jesus and the disciples visited the home of Mary and Martha (BETHANY, 2 miles east of Jerusalem).	Luke 10:38–42
Kislev 25, lasting 8 days 29 AD	Jesus and the disciples ministered during the Feast of Dedication, also known as Hanukkah or the Feast of Lights. (JERUSALEM)	John 10:22; 9:1—10:39
January, 30 AD	Jesus and the disciples traveled "beyond Jordan" and ministered. This was most likely the area known as Perea (east of the Jordan and due east of Jerusalem. (PEREA)	John 10:40–42
January, 30 AD	Lazarus, the brother of Mary and Martha, became very sick. (BETHANY)	John 11:1–2
DAY 1 (Scenario if Jesus was in Perea)	Mary and Martha sent word to Jesus about Lazarus' sickness (one day's travel time from Jerusalem to Perea) (BETHANY—PEREA).	John 11:3
DAY 1	Lazarus died that same day and was placed in a tomb.	John 11:6, 14, 17, 38
DAY 2–3	Jesus stayed in PEREA two more days.	John 11:6
DAY 4	Jesus and the disciples traveled to BETHANY. When He arrived, they told Him He had been in the tomb for four days.	John 11:17
	Martha ran to meet Jesus before He reached Bethany. They talked about Lazarus' death. Jesus proclaimed Himself as the Resurrection and the Life.	John 11:20–27
	Martha went to get Mary, who then came to Jesus and they talked.	John 11:28–33
	Jesus was asked to go to the TOMB. He prayed to His Father for all to hear. Jesus then called Lazarus from the dead and he arose and came forth.	John 11:34–44
	As a result of this miracle, many Jews believed in Jesus. Some reported these things to the Pharisees, who then convened the Sanhedrin. They began to plot Jesus' death. (BETHANY, JERUSALEM)	John 11:45–53
Jan. to Apr., 30 AD	Jesus withdrew to EPHRAIM, north of Bethel (about 14 miles north of Jerusalem). From there He and the disciples went into SAMARIA, GALILEE and back to PEREA, finally coming to JERICHO before His entry into JERUSALEM.	Matthew 19:1–30 20:1–34 Mark 10:1–52; Luke 17:11–37; 18—19:1–28
Friday, *Nisan 7*, 30 AD	Jesus and His disciples arrived in BETHANY six days before the Passover.	John 12:1
Saturday Evening *Nisan 8*, 30 AD	Martha, Mary, and Lazarus made Jesus a supper at the HOME of Simon the Leper (BETHANY)	Matthew 26:6 Mark 14:3 John 12:2
	Mary came, broke a valued alabaster vial, and anointed the head and feet of Jesus with the costly fragrant oil.	Matthew 26:7–13 Mark 14:3–9 John 12:3–8
	Many Jews came to see Jesus and Lazarus there in BETHANY. The chief priests were plotting to put Lazarus and Jesus to death.	John 12:9–11
Sunday, *Nisan 9*, 30 AD	Jesus made His triumphal entry into JERUSALEM as the multitudes cried out to Him, *"Hosanna! Blessed is He who comes in the name of the Lord! The King of Israel!"* Many sought Him because He had raised Lazarus from the dead.	Daniel 9:24–26; Matthew 21:1–11; Mark 11:1–10; Luke 19:29–38; John 12:12–22
	During this week, it is likely that Jesus spent each night at the home of Lazarus, Mary, and Martha in BETHANY.	Matthew 21:17 Mark 11:11, 19 John 12:1

DATE	EVENTS	SCRIPTURE
Monday, *Nisan* 10 through Sunday, *Nisan* 16, 30 AD	On Monday, Jesus cleansed the Temple of those buying and selling, of the moneychangers, and of those selling doves. Jesus taught His disciples during this final week, and He faced the antagonism of His enemies. He was crucified, buried, and then rose on Sunday. It is likely that Mary, Martha, and Lazarus were present for much of this week's activities. (JERUSALEM)	Daniel 9:24–26 Matthew 21:12–13; 22—27 Mark 11:15–33; 12–15 Luke 19:45–48; 20—23; John 12:12–50; 13—19
Sunday, *Nisan* 16, 30 AD	On Sunday, Jesus arose from the dead.	Matthew 28:1–8 Mark 16:1–8 Luke 24:1–12 John 20:1–10
For Forty Days	Jesus began appearing over a period of forty days. He appeared to His disciples, several of the women who followed Him, and to over 500 at one time. (JERUSALEM, GALILEE, and in other parts of ISRAEL) He ascended from BETHANY on the fortieth day. Most likely Mary, Martha, and Lazarus were a part of those that saw Him during some of these appearances.	Matthew 28:9–20 Mark 16:9–20 Luke 24:13–51 John 20:11–18; 21:1–25 Acts 1:1–11
For Ten Days	After He ascended, the disciples gathered for prayer to await the coming of the promised Holy Spirit. Again, Mary, Martha, and Lazarus would have likely been a part of that.	Luke 24:52–53 Acts 1:12–14
Pentecost Sunday	The Holy Spirit came giving birth to the Church and sending witnesses into Jerusalem, Judea, Samaria, and the uttermost parts of the world. Mary, Martha, and Lazarus were some of those witnesses of Jesus.	Acts 2—28

Palestine in the Time of Jesus

- Extent of Herod's kingdom
- ■ Herodian fortress city
- ○ Decapolis city (time of Herod)
- ● Other city
- ▲ Mountain

ABILENE
Abila
ITUREA
Abana R.
Damascus
Sidon
SYRIA
▲ Mt. Hermon
Pharpar R.
Caesarea-Philippi
PHOENICIA
Leontes R.
Tyre
TRACHONITIS
Raphana
L. Hula
Hazor
J. Jarmuk
GALILEE
Chorazin
Ptolemais (Acco)
Capernaum
Gennesaret
Bethsaida
Gergesa
GAULANITIS
TETRARCHY OF PHILIP
BATANEA
Mt. Carmel ▲
Kishon R.
Cana
Magdala
Tiberias
Sea of Galilee
Hippos
Jarmuk R.
AURANITIS
Nazareth
Mt. Tabor ▲
Gadara
Abila
Nain
Bethany beyond Jordan
Mediterranean Sea
Dor
Caesarea (Strato's Tower)
Megiddo
Scythopolis
Pella
Dion
SAMARIA
Salim?
DECAPOLIS
Sebaste (Samaria)
Mt. Ebal ▲
Amathus
Gerasa
Mt. Gerizim ▲ Sychar
Jordan R.
Jabbok R.
Me Jarkon
Antipatris (Aphek)
Alexandrium
PEREA
Philadelphia (Amman)
Joppa
(SEMI-INDEPENDENT MUNICIPALITY)
Jamnia
Esbus (Heshbon)
Azotus (Ashdod)
Emmaus
Cyprus
Jericho
Mt. Olivet ▲
Bethany
Medeba
Jerusalem
Bethlehem
Hyrcania
Ashkelon
JUDEA
Herodium
Machaerus
Hebron
Adora
Gaza
Dead Sea
Arnon R.
IDUMEA
Masada
Arad
Beersheba
Malatha
Besor Br.
NABATEA
Zered Br.

0 10 20 30 miles
0 10 20 30 kilometers

© 1999 MapQuest.com, Inc

Notes

Mary Mother of Jesus

THE JOURNEY OF A BONDSERVANT

Mary stands as one of the most, if not the most honored women of all time. Her life is a reflection of someone who truly loved and followed the Lord God of Israel with all her heart, mind, soul, and strength from her childhood all the way to her death. She called herself the bondservant of the Lord, a fitting description of both her heart attitude and her whole-hearted actions. A bondservant was one who willingly followed her master out of love and a surrendered will. As we walk through the life of this bondservant, we will discover what she learned about the meaning of surrender. We will see that Mary knew much about the Lord, for she knew the Scriptures well. She was marked by a worshiping heart, and she had a humble, teachable heart. She was always pondering things in her mind, turning them over to understand what the Lord was saying. She did not always understand the Lord or His ways. On her earthly journey with

The journey of a bondservant, where he goes, when he goes, why he goes, and how he goes, is ever tied to his or her master.

WHERE DOES SHE FIT?

2200BC	1950	1700	1450	1200	950	700	450	100
SARAH 2155–2028		MIRIAM 1533?–1405				Daniel 619–534?		MARY and MARTHA 10BC?–60AD?
		DEBORAH 1300?–1200?		Solomon 991–931		ESTHER 504?–450?		
			Judges Rule 1385–1051	David 1041–971				
						Nehemiah 480?–400?		MARY, Mother of Jesus 20BC–60AD?
	Jacob 2005–1858	Joshua 1495–1385	RUTH 1135?–1050?					
	Isaac 2065–1885	Moses 1525–1405	HANNAH 1135?–1050?	VIRTUOUS WOMAN Prov. 31				
Abraham 2165–1990		RAHAB 1445?–1385?	Samuel 1105–1022					Jesus Christ 4BC?–30AD?

Jesus as her son, she did not always comprehend what He was saying, what He was doing, or why He was doing it. She was growing in her faith one step at a time. That is where she can help us. We can learn from her questions, from her perplexing moments, and from the ways of God the Father in raising His Son in her home. We can also learn from the ways of Jesus Himself as He grew, as He began His ministry, and as He fulfilled His Father's will. Let's learn more about Mary, this bondservant of the Lord.

Mary Mother of Jesus

DAY ONE

A BONDSERVANT TRUSTING THE PROMISES OF HER LORD

God never gave up His plans for a people who would love Him, obey Him, and follow Him.

God is the only true "promise-keeper." Every promise He makes, he fulfills. Mary would be an eyewitness, as a myriad of promises from all of God's prophets through the ages found their fulfillment in her son, Jesus. We are first introduced to her in the Gospel of Luke, but that is not where this story begins. To find the actual beginning we must go to the book of beginnings, the book of Genesis. There we find the creation of man and woman and their placement in the beautiful Garden of Eden, where God provided everything they needed. There He also gave them a choice about **how** they would live life, represented in two trees, the first one being the Tree of Life and the other being the Tree of the Knowledge of Good and Evil. He gave them freedom to eat of the Tree of Life and warned them of the deadly consequences of choosing the other tree. In that Garden the serpent came tempting Eve to eat from the forbidden tree and she chose to follow the lie he spoke. Adam also ate, and sin entered this world and with it came death. However, God was not finished with Adam and Eve nor with their children. He still had plans for a people who would choose to follow Him, love Him, and obey Him. With those purposes in mind, He came walking in the Garden seeking Adam and Eve. There He met with them and began to unfold His plans and promises.

📖 What is God's promise in Genesis 3:15?

_____

_____

_____

_____

_____

I WILL ESTABLISH YOUR THRONE FOREVER

"When your days are fulfilled and you rest with your fathers, I will set up your seed after you, who will come from your body, and I will establish his kingdom . . . I will establish the throne of his kingdom forever . . . And your house and your kingdom shall be established forever before you. Your throne shall be established forever."
2 Samuel 7:12, 13, 16 (NKJV)

God promised that He would put enmity between the serpent and the woman and between the seed of the serpent (all those who are children of the devil—John 8:44) and the Seed of the woman ("He" is Jesus Christ). He promised that the Seed of the woman would crush the head of the serpent while the serpent would bruise the heel of the man (see Genesis 3:15). This Seed would have a nature that would hate evil and would deal with it on earth. That's why He would crush the serpent's head. We find later in Genesis 22:17–18 that God promised Abraham a "seed" [*singular*] who would rule and bless the nations of the earth. In the midst of David's reign

God promised David a "seed," [*singular*] and He promised to establish the kingdom of that seed of David forever (2 Samuel 7:12, 16).

These promises to Eve, Abraham, and David were matched with hundreds of other promises about a Messiah to come, the Anointed One of God. Every Jewish home thought that perhaps He would be born to them. In fact, the single thread passing through every book of the Old Testament, tying all of them together is the ever-unfolding promise of God that a Savior is coming. The prophecies continued and the years passed, but there was no Messiah. When we come to the story of Mary it has been about 400 years since Malachi prophesied. Israel was still waiting, praying, and expecting a Messiah to come.

Around 7 or 6 BC, the angel Gabriel appeared to a priest named Zacharias as he ministered in the Temple in Jerusalem. Gabriel promised Zacharias that he and his wife Elizabeth were going to have a son who would be the forerunner of the Messiah (Luke 1:5–25). Six months later this same angel appeared to a young lady named Mary in the small town of Nazareth, about 70 miles north of Jerusalem.

📖 Read Luke 1:26–27. What details do you find about Mary?

_____

_____

_____

_____

Mary lived in Nazareth. She was a virgin engaged or betrothed to a man named Joseph, a descendant of David. Luke traces Mary's genealogy back to show that she also was a descendant of David through his son, Nathan (Luke 3:23, 31). It is likely that Mary was about 15 or 16 years old at this time since Jewish girls often married at that age.

📖 What was the angel's announcement and promise (Luke 1:31–33)? List the facts one by one.

_____

_____

_____

_____

_____

📖 What was Mary's concern and question (Luke 1:34)?

_____

_____

_____

_____

_____

_____

Did You Know?
WHO WAS GABRIEL?

It appears that Gabriel is one of the leading angels in the heavenly order of angels. He along with Michael ministered in significant ways in the giving of and fulfillment of prophecy. Gabriel ministered to Daniel around 538 BC (Daniel 8:16; 9:21) as well as to Zacharias and Mary prior to the births of John the Baptist and Jesus (Luke 1:19, 26).

THE PROMISE TO MARY

"And behold, you will conceive in your womb and bring forth a Son, and shall call His name JESUS. He will be great, and will be called the Son of the Highest; and the Lord God will give Him the throne of His father David. And He will reign over the house of Jacob forever, and of His kingdom there will be no end." Luke 1:31–33 (NKJV)

Every word God speaks has power, power enough to come to pass.

The angel explained that Mary would conceive in her womb and bear a son named Jesus. He would be great and would be in fact the Son of the Most High. One day He would reign over the throne of His father David, over the house of Jacob forever, and over His endless kingdom. Mary could not understand how this could be since she was a virgin. How could she bear a son?

How did the angel respond to her question (Luke 1:35)?

_____

_____

_____

_____

What assurances did he give her (Luke 1:36–37)?

_____

_____

_____

Gabriel explained that the Holy Spirit would come upon her, and the power of the Most High would work in such a way that the Child she would then carry and bear would be called the Son of God. God Himself would be this Child's Father. After explaining this mystery, Gabriel gave Mary assurance by pointing out that another miracle (similar but certainly not the same) had occurred with her relative, Elizabeth. Though Elizabeth had been barren all her life and was now far past the logical childbearing age, she was in her sixth month—just three months until she would give birth to her child! The angel concluded with the promise, *"Nothing will be impossible with God."* Literally, he said, "not any word from God is without power." In other words, every word, every promise God speaks has **power**, enough power behind it to bring it to pass.

How did Mary respond to the angel's words (Luke 1:38)? You may also want to read Elizabeth's testimony (which God somehow revealed to her about Mary' response) for a more detailed picture of Mary's response.

_____

_____

_____

_____

Did You Know?
A BONDSERVANT'S HEART

A bondservant served his or her master because of the love the master showed and because of the love he or she had for the master. The bondservant gladly lived in the resources, the schedule, and the property of the master since he or she had none of their own (Deuteronomy 15:12–17).

Mary replied first by acknowledging that she was simply the bondslave of the Lord. The Greek word *doulos* can also be translated "bondservant." Her first response was a submissive, obedient heart. Whatever you say, I will obey. Then she said *"be it done to me according to your word."* I believe you. She trusted the promises of God.

The angel departed and Mary traveled to her relative's house in the hills of Judah, about 50 miles south of Nazareth. There she rejoiced with Elizabeth over what God was doing by bringing her a child so late in life. Even in Mary's greeting, Elizabeth and the baby in her womb were filled with the

Holy Spirit and joy. Then Elizabeth rejoiced in Mary's response of trust. She knew that Mary *"believed that there would be a fulfillment of what had been spoken to her by the Lord."* (Luke 1:45)

What do you see about Mary in her Song of Praise in Luke 1:46–55?

_____

_____

_____

_____

_____

Mary, knowing she needed a Savior, praised God as "my Savior." She knew His word, the Scriptures. She knew of the mercy of God in fulfilling His promises to Israel. As a bondservant of the Lord, she experienced the fulfillment of the promises made to Abraham himself. The strains of her praise looked prophetically to the total fulfillment of all His promises in the reign of the Messiah. Luke 1:55 notes that God's promises were to Abraham "and his seed" (*singular*), referring to the Messiah, the seed of the woman and the seed of David. The Lord had promised His help, His salvation. By the revelation of the Lord, Mary recognized that now He was bringing that to pass. Four thousand years of promises going all the way back to Adam and Eve were all intersecting in the womb of this simple teenage girl. He was at work fulfilling those promises through her, a humble bondservant. What would this bondservant discover about the Lord and His ways? What would it mean to know the Messiah as your very own son? We will begin to see that in Day Two.

A BONDSERVANT TRUSTING HER LORD IN THE PLACES HE LEADS

Mary Mother of Jesus

DAY TWO

Hearing the news about Elizabeth, Mary probably went to her house specifically to help her during the last three months before she delivered her child. Mary stayed with Elizabeth for those three months and then went back to Nazareth. It appears that when Mary returned to Nazareth, Joseph discovered that she was with child. Thinking that wrongdoing had been committed against him, he planned to quietly dissolve the betrothal. Then an angel spoke to Joseph in a dream revealing that this Child was of the Holy Spirit. This Child was actually a fulfillment of a promise made long ago—a virgin would conceive and bear a son named Immanuel, meaning, "God with us." (Isaiah 7:14). With that understanding, by faith Joseph married Mary, but kept her a virgin until she brought forth her firstborn son Jesus.

Mary's journey to Elizabeth's house was the first of many journeys she would take as a bondservant of the Lord. The Lord had a design for His Son that meant she and Joseph would not live ordinary lives. When any of us follow

"Behold a virgin will be with child and bear a son, and she will call His name Immanuel."

Isaiah 7:14

Word Study

GOD

The Greek word for God is *theos*. It is rooted in the word *theo* meaning "to put in place," the idea being that whoever puts things in place is by definition God. God is "The Placer" not only in the lives of Mary, Joseph, and Jesus, but in our lives as well.

Did You Know?

SHEPHERDS IN THE BETHLEHEM FIELDS

The Shepherds in the Bethlehem Fields were keepers of the flocks used in the Temple in Jerusalem just five miles away. One could almost read between the lines and hear the angels declare, "The Lamb that takes away the sin of the world has been born tonight in Bethlehem. These flocks will soon not be needed."

Word Study

BETHLEHEM

Jesus was born in Bethlehem just as the prophet Micah foretold. The name "Bethlehem" in Hebrew means "house of bread." Jesus, the "Bread of Life" was born in the "house of bread" and placed in a manger (a feeding trough).

God as faithful bondservants, our lives are never again the same. We enter into the plans and places of our Master. In the next few months that truth would dawn on Joseph and Mary in ways they never thought. As a married couple about to give birth to the Messiah, they began on a journey that took them to destinations they never dreamed of.

What do you discover about these new places on the journey in Luke 2:1–7?

_____

_____

_____

_____

_____

The first new direction came as a result of a government-ordered census. Everyone was required to register based on his or her tribal ancestry. Because Joseph was a descendant of David of the tribe of Judah, they had to travel to Bethlehem, the city of David, to register. After the 70–75 mile journey they arrived in Bethlehem and found there was no place to spend the night. Probably because of others returning to register, the inn was full. There was no room in the inn—Luke 2:7 says literally, "there was no **place** (*topos*) in the inn." They had to lodge temporarily in a stable. Shortly thereafter, Mary gave birth to her son, the Lord Jesus. This, too, was a fulfillment of prophecy, the prophet Micah having stated that Israel's Ruler would be born in Bethlehem (Micah 5:2). That night an angel proclaimed that same message to the shepherds in the fields nearby. *"Christ* [Messiah] *the Lord* [Ruler and King] *is born in the city of David."* The shepherds ran to see this Child and to report all the angels said (Luke 2:8–20). What a strange place for the birth of the King! But it was God's place.

What was Mary's response to the words of these shepherds (Luke 2:19)?

_____

_____

_____

_____

Mary listened carefully to all that the shepherds said. Luke 2:19 says she was continually keeping all these things in her heart, the picture being of her carefully guarding and keeping them together in her mind as in a treasure chest. That same verse adds that as she was doing this she kept **pondering** them. That word in the Greek, *sumballo*, in this context means she brought them together and joined them with other thoughts so she could carefully compare and reflect on all they mean. She must have had the words of Elizabeth running through her mind. Added to that were the conversations she and Joseph had over the things the angel Gabriel had told her, over his dream, and over the required journey to Bethlehem. In all this Mary was learning what it meant to be a bondservant of the Lord.

Eight days after His birth when Jesus was circumcised, Joseph and Mary officially gave Him the name Jesus as the angel Gabriel had instructed them. According to the Mosaic Law, on the fortieth day after His birth, Joseph and Mary came to the Temple to present Jesus to the Lord as the firstborn. With this presentation they offered the required sacrifices, in their case the sacrifices of the poor, two turtledoves or two young pigeons. Before they were able to reach the place of sacrifice, they were met by Simeon, a righteous and devout man, one who walked with God, longing intently for the appearance of His Messiah. At that moment, the Temple became a place of prophecy.

📖 What do we learn from this man? Read Luke 2:25–35 noting the grandeur of this godly man, Simeon. How did Joseph and Mary respond to Simeon's words?

_____

_____

_____

_____

What specific message did Simeon have for Mary (2:34–35)?

_____

_____

_____

_____

Did You Know?
❓ PERIOD OF PURIFICATION

The Mosaic Law set a period of forty days for purification of a mother who had born a son, eighty days for one who bore a daughter (Leviticus 12:1–8).

Joseph and Mary marveled at the actions and the words of Simeon. They saw the awesome moving of the Spirit of God before their very eyes. What other wonders would their eyes behold? What they had already seen and experienced was incomprehensible. Then Simeon had a word specifically for Mary. His message would not be all wonder and awe, for he warned that days of soul-piercing pain would come. This baby would cause many to fall and many to rise. Many would speak against Him, would oppose Him and His message, and, eventually these opponents would persecute Him to death. But that is not all—for Mary herself would feel the pain of others rejecting her son, but she would also feel the pains of His convicting voice in her own soul like the sharp two-edged sword that reveals the thoughts and intentions of the heart (Hebrews 4:12–13). Mary was a bondservant whose Master was teaching her His ways as she brought up His Son. She had a teachable heart and was listening carefully.

After this Joseph and Mary and the infant Jesus moved into a house in the small town of Bethlehem. Joseph worked as a carpenter, perhaps on one of the many building projects Herod had going at the time. Bethlehem would be only a temporary residence for this family. The next time we hear of them is at least eighteen months, possibly two years later. Joseph and Mary were about to travel to yet another place with this Child.

📖 What do you discover in Matthew 2:1–14? [Note the words **house** and **Child** in verse 11.]

_____

_____

_____

_____

_____

_____

Did You Know?
❓ JOSEPH AT WORK IN BETHLEHEM

Among his many building projects, Herod had been working on the Temple and Temple Mount since 20 BC. His massive palace near Bethlehem known as the Herodion covered 56 acres.

What was the determining factor in what they should do and where they should go?

_____

_____

_____

_____

The magi from the east had seen the Star of Bethlehem about two years before their arrival in Jerusalem. They began their journey sometime during this period seeking for the King announced by the stars. When they arrived in Jerusalem, the religious leaders knew from the Scriptures that the Ruler of Israel would come out of Bethlehem. They informed Herod and the magi of the location, and he sent the Magi to Bethlehem. These wise men found the Child Jesus with Mary in the house in Bethlehem and presented Him their gifts as their hearts worshiped Him. The Lord warned the Magi in a dream to stay away from Herod so they departed for their country, taking a different route away from Judea. Apparently that same night God warned Joseph to take this young Child with Mary and flee to Egypt and stay until he received further word. Joseph promptly obeyed and they fled at night, escaping certain death for this Child Herod jealously hated. While they were in Egypt, Herod ordered the killing of all male children two years old and younger in the area of Bethlehem. Joseph, Mary, and the baby Jesus' journey to Egypt was another new path for these bondservants of the Lord, a path marked by the protective care of a heavenly Father.

 *Did You Know?*

THE WISE MEN

Some believe these Magi had read the prophecies of Daniel and perhaps others handed down from the time of the Babylonian captivity (605–536 BC). Daniel specifically spoke of a king to arise in Israel (Daniel 8:25; 9:24–26).

📖 Where did Joseph and Mary go from Egypt (Matthew 2:15, 19–23)?

_____

_____

_____

_____

What was the determining factor in where they moved?

_____

_____

_____

_____

Joseph and Mary stayed in Egypt until the death of Herod (most likely in 4 BC). Their sojourn in Egypt probably lasted no more than three or four months, possibly less. There in Egypt the Lord again spoke to Joseph in a dream, telling him to come back to Israel. When they arrived in Israel they found Herod's son Archelaus reigning in Judea. Joseph feared for the Child's life and God again warned him in a dream to stay away from Judea. Joseph and the family traveled back to Nazareth where they settled in and stayed for many years. Again it was a fulfillment of the promises of God and part of the path God had them on as His bondservants.

Being a bondservant means being flexible in all the places God takes us, in all the ways God changes those places, and in the time and the timing by which He works in those places. It means trusting the paths God chooses for us. With this as in all God's ways, God had a sovereign purpose motivating His actions. Mary would find out more about that in the years to come. She had seen His promises to her fulfilled, and her faith was growing. Now she was learning to trust Him in the places He chose for her.

A Bondservant Trusting the Purposes of Her Lord

Not only did Mary have to trust the promises of God and then trust Him in the places He chose for her, she was going to have to trust the purposes He had for her and for her son. We hear nothing over the next ten years. Most likely several of the children Joseph and Mary had were born during this time. We know of at least four other sons and at least two daughters born to Mary and Joseph. The sons would have been learning the trade of their father and studying the Law of the Lord on a regular basis. The next incident in the life of Mary centers on the week of Passover (and Unleavened Bread) when Jesus was twelve years old.

Luke 2:41–46 records that after attending the Passover Feast (which included the Feast of Unleavened Bread), Joseph and Mary and the caravan of friends and relatives from Galilee began the journey back to Nazareth. After the first day's travel, they began looking for Jesus. Perhaps each thought Jesus was with the other as they journeyed. That could have easily happened with the men and boys often traveling and talking together separate from the women. After looking throughout the caravan and talking to friends and relatives, they could not find Him. The next day they traveled back to Jerusalem and began the search, apparently looking for the better part of a day. On the third day they found Him in the Temple area with the teachers of the Law listening and asking questions of him.

Did You Know?

ATTENDING THE PASSOVER

A Jewish lad was expected to attend the Passover Feast at the age of 12. In all they did, Joseph and Mary sought to follow the Lord and His Law—both the spirit and the letter of the Law.

📖 How did Mary respond when at last they found Jesus (2:46–48)?

_____

_____

_____

_____

_____

📖 What was Jesus' response to Mary (2:49)?

_____

_____

_____

_____

_____

Joseph and Mary were amazed to see Him sitting among the teachers in the Temple. They could not comprehend what He was doing there. Mary was the first to speak out in what appears to be a mild motherly rebuke. They had searched and searched and their anxiety had grown and grown. She certainly could not understand what had gotten into Him. Jesus was surprised at their surprise. Why would they have to wonder where He was? He was enveloped in the things of His Father, the things related to knowing and living the truth, the matters that centered in the Temple. It was the most natural place to be in His mind. Mary was beginning to be confronted with a new and different understanding of God's purposes for her son.

How did Mary and Joseph face His answer (2:50)?

_____

_____

_____

_____

Again they failed to understand all that was going on, what Jesus was thinking, or why He would do such a thing. The Greek word for "understand" (*suniemi*) means literally "to send together." In other words, they could not put together all the pieces of the puzzle of this twelve-year-old Child. Their perception was not matching their observation. Of course, we can't blame them. How can we comprehend the God-man? Here we can sympathize with their need for a fuller understanding of the ways of the Father, of the purposes of God, of how God was fulfilling His promises about the Messiah. That understanding would come, but it would come slowly.

APPLY How do you respond when God's purposes for your life differ from your own? Are you teachable and moldable to His purposes, or do you struggle?

Jesus readily traveled back to Nazareth with Joseph and Mary and there He submitted to their leadership. What was Mary's continued thought during these days (2:51)?

_____

_____

_____

_____

Mary kept thinking on all that Jesus had said and all that had occurred. The Greek word for "kept" *(diatereo)*, paints a beautiful picture of continually guarding something knowing that it is valuable and wanting to get the full value out of it. In this case Mary continued to think through these matters to get to their full meaning. She added these things to the treasure store of what she had already heard and seen as she sought to follow her Lord as a faithful bondservant.

The next time we see Mary, about eighteen years have passed (December of 26 AD). Jesus was about thirty years of age and Mary about forty-six. There is no mention of Joseph and many believe he may have died during this eighteen-year period. Most likely, Mary was a widow cared for by her sons. Jesus has left home traveling as a Rabbi and has begun to gather some disciples around Him. In John chapter one, we find five disciples spending time with Him. In John 2 we find Mary, Jesus and His disciples all invited to a wedding in Cana just a few miles from Nazareth. Since all of them attended, this was very likely some relative of the family. Here we will see another opportunity to discover the purposes of the Lord Jesus.

📖 Read John 2:1–12. What did Mary say (John 2:3)? Why do you think she said this?

_____

_____

_____

_____

📖 How did Jesus respond to her statement (John 2:4)?

_____

_____

_____

_____

A wedding feast could last as long as seven days, and as this wedding feast continued Mary noticed that the wine was running out. It is possible that she was a relative of the groom and, knowing that it was the groom's responsibility to provide everything needed at the feast, she sought to help with the potentially embarrassing situation. She immediately told Jesus of the need. Surely He would understand the situation and He could do something.

At this point Jesus clearly made a distinction between how He fit in with Mary, His mother, and the matters at hand. He said to her, *"Woman,"* indicating something of a new relationship with her. He said to her, *"What do I have to do with you? My hour has not yet come."* In this is a Hebrew idiom, "What to Me and to you" implying "what does the matter at hand have to do with Me or you?" With this statement in Cana, Jesus established the trademark of all He did throughout His entire ministry—anything He did was done at the initiative of His Father (John 5:19, 30; 8:28–29; 14:10; Acts 2:22). All He did, He did based on the Father's timetable. He was always *"about His Father's business,"* and Mary needed to know that. Jesus showed no disrespect to Mary. She would always be His mother, but more importantly, He would always be her Lord, and His purposes must become hers as well.

📖 What was Mary's response (John 2:5)?

_____

_____

_____

_____

She responded as a bondservant would with a submissive heart. It is possible that she was a helper at the wedding and so told the servants, *"Whatever He says to you, do"*—they too could act as bondservants. That is good advice for any of us. Whatever Jesus says to us, we should do!

Did You Know?

THE HOME OF JESUS

Jesus made His home in Capernaum probably with Peter. That became His residence and the place to which He continually returned during most of His ministry.

"Whatever He says to you, do" (John 2:5)— Wise counsel for any one at any time.

Jesus instructed the servants to fill six stone waterpots with water. Each could hold between 17 and 25 gallons, so there would have been between 100 and 150 gallons of water available. Jesus instructed them to take some to the manager of the feast. When they did they saw that He had turned the water into the best grade of wine, giving this couple a lavish wedding gift, revealing His glory to the five disciples with Him, and showing His mother His greater purposes, the purposes of His Father. He was on a schedule set by His Father, and the time for each word and each deed would become clearer as His hour approached.

There is one other incident that involved Mary and Jesus in which she had to learn once again to trust His purposes and His ways. It occurred in the town of Capernaum on what is known as the "busy day" of Jesus ministry (in the fall of AD 28 after about two full years of ministry). Jesus' ministry had drawn great crowds and a measure of controversy. Mark 3:19–21 says He went into a house (most likely His home in Capernaum) and while He was there great crowds again gathered. His family in Nazareth (*"His own people,"*) hearing of all that was going on *"went out"* (from Nazareth to Capernaum) seeking *"to lay hold of Him, for they said, 'He is out of His mind'"* (NKJV). We don't know how Mary saw all this, but it is probable that her sons persuaded her to come along.

📖 What happened when they *"arrived"* (Mark 3:31)? Read the parallel passage in Matthew 12:46–50. On what does Jesus focus?

_____

_____

_____

_____

What does this tell us about His purposes?

_____

_____

_____

_____

What do you think Mary was thinking in all this?

_____

_____

_____

_____

When Mary and her sons arrived they went to Jesus' house and tried to get in. They wanted to talk to Jesus, to try and reason with Him and bring Him to His senses. Someone in the house reported to Jesus that His mother and brothers were outside "seeking" Him and wanting to speak with Him. Jesus questioned the man, "Who is My mother and who are My brothers?" Jesus then motioned toward His disciples and said these were His mother and brothers! Why would Jesus say that? Christ was not rejecting His family, yet His focus was not on a blood relationship—but on a relationship of faith and obedience.

> **Doing the Father's will was the mark of a bondservant and Mary, through her Son, was learning what that meant.**

Jesus wanted to make it abundantly clear that only those who do the will of His Father in heaven are in a true relationship with the Son. This is not a statement about salvation by good works, but rather a statement about those whose lifestyle is one of following the Father, of listening and obeying out of a faith relationship. Jesus' purpose was to establish that relationship with the lost—He came *"to seek and to save"* the lost (Luke 19:10), to save them **out of** a wrong relationship with God in which they were facing His wrath and **into** a right relationship in which they would experience His mercy and grace (Matthew 1:21; 18:11; Luke 9:56). How could Mary be so mistaken and confused about Jesus and God's purposes for Him? She was human. It only makes more sense to us because we have the whole picture laid before us.

This was another very important point in Mary's journey, and in her growth as a bondservant. She, too, must submit to the Son's purposes because they were the purposes of the Father. Doing the Father's will was the mark of a bondservant, and Mary, through her Son, was learning what that meant. Just as she had learned to trust the promises of God and the places he chose for her, now she was learning to trust His purposes.

A Bondservant Trusting the Power of Her Lord

Mary Mother of Jesus

Mary was gradually learning to trust God. Like all of us, hers was a growing faith. As she put her faith in God, she found Him faithful—faithful to fulfill all He promised, faithful in every place He chose for her, faithful in His purposes. Throughout the ministry of Jesus there is another truth that Mary learned: she must trust His **power** to fulfill His promises and His purposes. This was most evident in her own home. How would her children understand who Jesus was? How could she help them comprehend the promises she and Joseph had been given? How could they accept the ways of Jesus in their own lives? She would have to trust the power of her Lord and Son.

We see this conflict in a general way in Jesus' first visit to Nazareth after His ministry had begun (Luke 4:16–31—around January of 28 AD). After expounding on the Scripture in Isaiah about His coming, the people of Nazareth were ready to throw Him off the brow of the hill on which Nazareth stood, but He escaped that particular attempt on His life. Doubtless Mary and her children were in Nazareth at the time, but we do not know anything about their responses to this situation. We do, however know something from His final visit to Nazareth which occurred about nine months later.

📖 Just a few weeks, perhaps a month or so after the incident in Capernaum, Jesus came to Nazareth (fall of AD 28). Read the account in Mark 6:1–4. Who is there?

_____

_____

_____

What happened? What did Jesus do?

_____

_____

_____

What was the response of the crowd?

_____

_____

_____

Put Yourself In Their Shoes
OFFENDED AT JESUS

"Blessed is he who keeps from stumbling over Me," or "who is not offended because of Me" (Luke 7:23, NKJV). It is possible to be offended or stumble over Jesus— over what He says, over how He does something, over His timing, or over His ways. It is not a foregone conclusion that we will stumble, but it is possible. Many in Nazareth did so.

Jesus came to Nazareth and on the Sabbath went into the synagogue as was His custom. The townspeople there included at least two sisters and perhaps also Mary and His four brothers. (There is no mention of Joseph at this time.) Jesus taught and may have performed some miracles since those are mentioned in verse 2. Regardless of the wisdom of His teaching and the power of His miracles, the crowd took offense at Him.

What did Jesus say concerning the whole incident?

_____

_____

What does this tell you about the family situation, at least among His brothers and sisters?

_____

_____

_____

Jesus spoke forthrightly. He said that a prophet has no honor **1)** in his home town, **2)** among his own relatives, and **3)** in his own household. That covered the whole crowd, **including** His family. They had not believed in Him as the Messiah, and they were offended at what He taught. There is no indication in the text that Mary was any different. Perhaps she also struggled with unbelief. Only the power of God could change their hearts. Jesus left Nazareth never to return. He would trust His Father to draw them to Himself. The next time we hear of Jesus' brothers is about a year later in the fall of AD 29 as they mockingly told Jesus to go up to the Feast of the Tabernacles and show Himself to His followers. Jesus told them His time had not yet fully come (John 7:1–9). Six months later His time had fully come and Jesus was on the way to the cross. There we see Mary once again.

📖 Read John 19:17–27. What do you find in verses 26–27?

_____

_____

_____

_____

_____

In light of Jesus being on the cross, what do you see in these statements?

_____

_____

_____

_____

_____

In the third of seven statements Jesus made from the cross, He spoke directly to His mother Mary, *"Woman, behold your son,"* referring to the Apostle John. As He had called her *"woman"* at His first miracle at the wedding in Cana, again He reiterated their relationship as one of Lord and Savior with a redeemed bondservant. He was caring for her as His mother, but also speaking as her Lord. To John He gave the responsibility of caring for Mary as an oldest son would. John too followed Jesus as Lord and obeyed Him with love. This very fact argues against Jesus' brothers being believers at this point. There, a few hours later, Mary watched as her Son died. She must have struggled terribly with wondering why He did not save Himself. She asked herself, "Was it that He couldn't save Himself?" But that was not the end of the story.

Jesus arose from the dead on the third day. That Sunday He appeared to some of His disciples and some of the women. Over the next forty days He appeared to several believers, and made one specific appearance to His brother, James. Then ten days before Pentecost, He met His disciples in Bethany on the Mount of Olives and instructed them to wait in Jerusalem until the coming of the promised Holy Spirit. Afterward He ascended into heaven.

📖 What was His promise in Acts 1:8?

_____

_____

_____

📖 What do you find in Acts 1:12–14?

_____

_____

_____

Who was included in this group?

_____

_____

_____

_____

What was their focused activity during these days?

_____

_____

_____

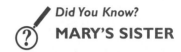

Did You Know?
MARY'S SISTER

It is probable that Mary's sister who stood with her at the cross (John 19:25) was Salome the wife of Zebedee and the mother of James and John. That would have made John a first cousin of Jesus (Matthew 27:56; Mark 15:40; 16:1).

What does this tell you about Mary?

_____

_____

_____

Jesus promised His disciples that they would receive power when the Holy Spirit came upon them. That would occur in a few days, and they were to wait in Jerusalem until the Holy Spirit had come. With that power of the Holy Spirit, they would be witnesses of Jesus, telling others all they had seen and heard. When they returned from the Mount of Olives, they went to the upper room where they had been staying and spent many hours there in prayer. They were one in heart and mind, continuing in prayer over the next ten days.

Mary and her sons were part of that group which included the eleven apostles and several of the women. Jesus' brothers had finally believed in Him as their Messiah, Lord and Savior. The power and love of Jesus demonstrated on the cross and in the resurrection had won the hearts of His brothers.

The promises of Scripture Mary had heard as a child, the promises from the angel Gabriel, and the promises Jesus had spoken dozens of times during His years of ministry, were all beginning to come to fulfillment. Mary was still learning what it meant to be a bondservant. In a few short days she would become one of those who experienced the coming of the Holy Spirit during Pentecost Sunday. From that day on she would be an empowered witness telling the story of her Lord and, yes, of her Son. In the days of the early Church, men like Matthew, Mark, Luke, and John would in all likelihood hear her testimony and record those things marked by the Holy Spirit so that today we also know the story. With that truth, we can better learn what it means to be a bondservant of the Lord Jesus Christ, and we can share all we are seeing and learning as His bondservants.

Jesus brought His followers together in oneness. So many who had so many opinions just a few days or weeks before were brought to a oneness by the resurrection power of the Lord Jesus.

Mary Mother of Jesus

DAY FIVE

FOR ME TO FOLLOW GOD

When the angel Gabriel came to Mary and told her she had been chosen to bear the Son of the Most High, the Son of God, she yielded to that call exclaiming, "Behold, the bondservant of the Lord; be it done to me according to your word." Over the years she learned the fuller meaning of what it meant to be a bondservant. She found that the promises of her Master were true, and He could be trusted. She discovered that His ways and His plans often call for His servants to be placed in unique situations and distant places. She also found out that His purposes are not always easy to discern. Sometimes He seems to be acting in a way that is unreasonable to us.

 What about you? Can you say you are a bondservant of the Lord? Perhaps it would be good to see the heart of a bondservant in the Scripture. Read Deuteronomy 15:12–17. According to verse 16, what is at the heart of the relationship between a master and a bondservant?

_____

_____

_____

_____

_____

Do you trust your Master because of the way He has treated you?

_____

_____

📖 What does Matthew 6:24 say about your love for your Master?

_____

_____

_____

In all His ways He is ever showing us, as He showed Mary, that His will, done His way, must be done with **His power.** Mary certainly saw that time and time again. We need to learn the same truths. That same Holy Spirit that indwelt her on the Day of Pentecost indwells all believers today to guide them into being the bondservants He wants.

(APPLY) Are you loving and holding to the One Master, Jesus Christ? Or is something else receiving your love and your steadfast attention? To what or to whom are you most loyal and devoted?

☐ Money   ☐ Position
☐ Personal pleasures ☐ Prestige
☐ Things   ☐ _____ (you fill in the blank)

Over time, Mary discovered the faithfulness of God in fulfilling His promises? Do you trust His promises in your life?

_____

_____

_____

Mary had to trust the Lord as He led her and Joseph from place to place. (It was all because of Jesus.) Are you trusting the Lord in where He is placing you? Are you trusting Him in your neighborhood, in your job, in your church or area of ministry? How about in your family? List those "places" in your life where you need to trust Him more and pray to the Lord about them.

_____

_____

_____

_____

_____

_____

Do you have a bond-servant's heart? Are you teachable, flexible in His Hands, and able to be directed in His will?

Mary had to learn that the purposes of the Lord were often different from what she expected. Are you facing struggles over how the Lord is doing something in your life or in the life of someone you love? Are you wondering what He is doing, or why He's doing what He's doing? Do you ever question His timing? Write down these struggles and pray for patience and for God's purposes to be accomplished in you.

_____

_____

_____

_____

_____

Are you trusting the "Placer" and the "Timer" in your life? Remember, He can be trusted!

Mary discovered that she had to depend on the Lord's power to change the hearts of her sons. She had to trust the Lord's purposes and His ultimate power in going to the cross to deal with sin (her sin included). She had to trust His power to witness effectively of all He had said and done in her life. List those areas of your life, your relationships, and your witness where you have been trusting your own power and pray for God to accomplish them by His strength and in His time.

_____

_____

_____

We know that Mary was cared for by the Apostle John for the rest of her life. She had lived as a bondservant and her Master made sure she was cared for. We too can trust our Master, the Lord Jesus Christ. Know assuredly He will care for you and will show you how to walk as a loving bondservant as He shows you who He is as your trusted and loving Master.

Why not pause right now and talk to Him about His care.

Lord, You were about Your Father's business all along. May I understand and walk in the things that You are about today. May I walk in the expectancy of Your promises, in the confidence that You are the "Placer" in my life, in the joy of knowing Your purposes are being worked out in my life, and in the power of Your Spirit for my everyday walk. May I be the kind of witness that is gladly available to tell all that I have seen and heard about You. Thank You for being such a loving and trustworthy Master. Thank You for Your patience with me, and for Your mercy and Your kindness. May I reflect the trusting, loving heart of a bondservant as I follow You. In the Name of Jesus, Amen.

Considering all you have seen and learned from this study of Mary, what applications or truths has the Lord emphasized in your life. Express those in a prayer to Him. You may want to do it in the form of a letter to Him.

_____

_____

_____

_____

_____

_____

_____

_____

_____

_____

_____

_____

The Life of Mary the Mother of Jesus

DATE*	EVENTS	SCRIPTURE
ca. 22–20 BC	Mary was born most likely in the region of Galilee, probably in Nazareth	
ca. 7–5 BC	Possibly around the ages of 14–16, Mary became engaged/betrothed to Joseph of Nazareth.	Matthew 1:18
ca. 7–5 BC	The angel Gabriel appeared to Zacharias inside the Temple at Jerusalem and told him that he and his wife Elizabeth would have a son named John. He would be the forerunner of the Messiah.	Luke 1:5–23
ca. 7–5 BC	The Lord fulfilled His promise through the angel and Elizabeth became pregnant.	Luke 1:24–25
ca. 7–5 BC Six months later	The angel Gabriel came to Nazareth and announced to her that as a virgin she would conceive by the Holy Spirit and bear a son, the Son of the Most High. His name would be Jesus. Mary believed the word of the angel.	Luke 1:26–38
	Mary traveled south to the hill country of Judah to the home of Zacharias and Elizabeth, her relatives. When she came into the house and greeted Elizabeth, the baby John leapt for joy in his mother's womb, and Elizabeth was filled with the Holy Spirit.	Luke 1:39–45
	Mary praised God, her Savior for all the things done for her, the bondservant of the Lord.	Luke 1:46–55
ca. 7–5 BC	Mary stayed with Elizabeth for three months and then went back to Nazareth.	Luke 1:56
ca. 6–4 BC	John the Baptist was born. Zacharias began to speak after nine months of silence. He offered praise for all the Lord was doing.	Luke 1:57–79
	Joseph found out that Mary was with child and planned to put her away secretly— to dissolve the marriage. A betrothal was as legally binding as the marriage itself and could only be broken by a divorce.	Matthew 1:18–19
	An angel of the Lord appeared to Joseph in a dream and explained that this child was of the Holy Spirit. This was a fulfillment of the prophecy of Isaiah—a virgin would conceive. His name would be Immanuel, God with us.	Matthew 1:20–23
	Joseph obeyed what the angel said and took Mary as his wife. They were married but he kept her a virgin until she gave birth to Jesus.	Matthew 1:24–25
ca. 6–4 BC	Probably in her ninth month, Mary and Joseph traveled from Nazareth to Bethlehem in order to register as part of the census decreed by Caesar Augustus.	Luke 2:1–5
	They arrived in Bethlehem and took up quarters in a stable, because there was no place for them in the inn in Bethlehem.	Luke 2:6–7
Birth— First Day	Mary gave birth to her firstborn son Jesus there in the stable in Bethlehem. She wrapped Him in cloths and laid Him in the feeding trough.	Luke 2:6–7; Micah 5:2
	The angels appeared to the shepherds keeping watch over the Temple flock near Jerusalem. (Bethlehem was 5 miles from Jerusalem). They told them that the Messiah had been born in Bethlehem.	Luke 2:8–14
	The shepherds went straight to Bethlehem to see the Child. They told Mary and Joseph and any others there all they had seen and heard.	Luke 2:15–17, 20 Luke 2:18–19
Eighth Day	Jesus was circumcised. Mary and Joseph named the baby, Jesus, just as they had been told to do.	Luke 2:21; Leviticus 12:1–3
Fortieth Day	Joseph and Mary took the baby into the Temple in Jerusalem to present Him to the Lord as the firstborn and to offer the required offerings.	Luke 2:22–24 Leviticus 12:1–3
	Simeon came into the Temple under the direction of the Holy Spirit and took the Child in his arms. He blessed the Lord and prophesied over Him. Then he prophesied to Mary about the mission of Jesus. Simeon prophesied that Christ was appointed for the rise and fall of many in Israel and that a sword would pierce even Mary's own soul.	Luke 2:25–35
	At that precise moment the prophetess, Anna came up and gave thanks to God and spoke of this Child to many in the Temple.	Luke 2:36–38
	Joseph and Mary presented the offering required for those who were poor— two turtledoves or two young pigeons.	Luke 2:24 Leviticus 12:6–8
ca. 6–4 BC	Joseph, Mary, and Jesus stayed in Bethlehem for the next several months. After about 18 months to two years, magi (wise men) from the east (Babylon or Persia) came looking for Him who was born King of the Jews. Herod called for them having heard they were seeking the Child. He ascertained from them the time the star appeared announcing the Child's birth (apparently about two years before—2:16). He sent them to Bethlehem based on the word of the prophet Micah.	Matthew 2:1–8, 16; Micah 5:2

DATE	EVENTS	SCRIPTURE
ca. 4 BC	The magi came into the **house** and saw the **Child** with Mary. They worshiped Him and presented Him their gifts. Then they left for their country, avoiding Herod.	Matthew 2:9–12
Same night	An angel of the Lord appeared to Joseph in a dream instructing him to escape to Egypt away from Herod. They arose and left that night for Egypt.	Matthew 2:13–14
	Herod ordered the killing of all the male children two years old and younger in the area of Bethlehem. This was based on the timing of the star of Bethlehem.	Matthew 2:16–18
ca 4 BC	Herod died in 4 BC. Joseph, Mary, and Jesus stayed in Egypt during the months until Herod died (that same year).	Matthew 2:15
ca. 4 BC	When Herod was dead an angel of the Lord appeared to Joseph in a dream and instructed him to return to Israel.	Matthew 2:19–20
	Joseph took Mary and Jesus and returned to Israel. He heard Herod's son Archelaus was reigning over Judea including Bethlehem), and God warned him in a dream about Archelaus. Therefore he went to Nazareth in the Galilee region.	Matthew 2:22–23
	Jesus grew in strength and wisdom in the home of Joseph and Mary.	Luke 2:40
	Joseph and Mary had at least four other sons and two or more daughters during their married life. Most likely these children were born during the first twelve years of Jesus' life before the trip to Jerusalem. This means Joseph and Mary had a home of five boys (including Jesus) and at least two girls (at least 7 children).	Matthew 13:55–56; Mark 6:3
Nisan, 8 or 9 AD	At the age of twelve Jesus traveled with Joseph and Mary to Jerusalem for the observance of Passover in the spring of 8 or 9 AD (the month *Nisan*). They stayed the full 8 days of Passover and Unleavened Bread and then began the journey back.	Luke 2:41–43
Travel Day 1	Joseph and Mary traveled a day's journey with their caravan of relatives and friends from Galilee. Jesus was not with them. He was in the Temple talking with the teachers of the Law.	Luke 2:43–44
Return Day 2	Joseph and Mary returned to Jerusalem.	Luke 2:45
Next Day Day 3	They found Jesus in the Temple talking with the teachers.	Luke 2:46–47
	Joseph and Mary were amazed. Mary questioned Jesus out of her anxious heart. Jesus was surprised that they were surprised. He was doing the business of His Father. Joseph and Mary did not understand what Jesus meant.	Luke 2:48–50
Trip Back to Nazareth	Jesus went back to Nazareth with them and was subject to Joseph and Mary. Mary kept all these things in her heart, never forgetting them, often pondering them.	Luke 2:51
	Jesus grew in wisdom, stature, and in favor with God and men.	Luke 2:52
	During some or most of the next 18 years Jesus worked with Joseph in his carpentry trade.	Matthew 13:55
ca 9–26 AD	Apparently sometime during those 18 years, Joseph died and Mary, became a widow. We hear nothing else of Joseph after the visit to Jerusalem when Jesus was 12. There is no mention of his presence during Jesus ministry.	
ca. October 26 AD	Jesus began His public ministry around the age of 30. He was baptized by John the Baptist and then was led about in the wilderness by the Spirit There He fasted 40 days while being tempted by the devil.	Matthew 3:13–17; 4:1–11; Luke 3:21–23; 4:1–13; Mark1:9–13
ca. December, 26 AD	Jesus attended a wedding in Cana in Galilee. With Mary His mother there, it is possible that it was the wedding of a relative. Mary spoke to Him about the host running out of wine. Jesus completed His first miracle by turning water into wine. Five disciples were there with Him.	John 2:1–11
January, 28 AD	Jesus made His first visit to Nazareth. Most likely, He saw Mary at this time. The people rejected Him and tried to throw Him off the brow of the hill but He escaped.	Luke 4:16–31
Fall of 28, "Busy Day"	Jesus' mother and brothers, having heard of all that was going on in Capernaum, traveled there in order to "take custody of Him" thinking that He had *"lost His senses."*	Mark 3:21
Fall of 28, "Busy Day"	Jesus was in Capernaum in a house when His family arrived and sought to *"lay hold of Him"* Apparently, because of all the confusion caused by the multitudes, some blamed Jesus for that confusion.	Mark 3:20–21, 31
Fall of 28, "Busy Day"	With all the seeming confusion, Jesus' mother and His brothers (half-brothers) sought to get into the house where He was teaching so that they might speak with Him, probably to stop all this confusion and talk of the multitudes. Jesus spoke of the most important relationship with Him— being those who obeyed His Father.	Matthew 12:46–50; Mark 3:31–35; Luke 8:19–21

DATE	EVENTS	SCRIPTURE
Fall of 28	Jesus made His final visit to Nazareth. The people of Nazareth mentioned Jesus' family being there including Mary. Jesus noted that a prophet receives no honor in his home town, among his own relatives, and in his own household.	Matthew 13:54–58; Mark 6:1–6 John 7:1–9
Fall of 29	Jesus' brothers mockingly urged Him to go to the Feast of Tabernacles so all could see Him.	
Nisan, 30 AD	The next time we hear of Mary is at the Cross when Jesus was being crucified. He looked at her and said, *"Woman, behold your son,"* referring to John. To John He said, *"Behold, your mother."* John took Mary into his care from that day forward. Mary would have been about 50 to 52 years old.	John 19:25–27
	Mary saw her son, Jesus, die on the Cross	John 19:28–30
	It is likely that Mary saw Jesus in one of His appearances during the 40 days from His resurrection to His ascension.	1 Corinthians 15:3–6
Ascension (Thurs.) to Pentecost (Sunday), 30 AD	Mary and her sons were some of the 120 who met in the Upper Room for prayer from the Day of Jesus' Ascension to the Day of Pentecost (10 Days). She participated in the events of the Day of Pentecost, and was a part of the early Church. She was cared for by the Apostle John.	Acts 1:13–14; 2:1–12, 41–46
ca 60? AD	Tradition says Mary moved to Ephesus with the Apostle John and his family and died there.	

* Dates are approximate since the Scriptures do not give the age of Mary or the exact years of the events of Jesus' life.

Notes

Notes

The Bride of Christ

WALKING IN THE BEAUTY OF HOLINESS

This is a different sort of lesson to find in a study on women of the Bible, but when God defined His relationship with the Church, He depicted her as a woman. He called the Church His bride. What is God saying through this? When we look at Biblical imagery, the pictures from the culture of the Old Testament and from the Jewish world of the first century can be very helpful in understanding the ways and will of God. The imagery of a bridegroom and a bride, of a husband and wife, gives us many pictures that help us understand our relationship to the Lord Jesus Christ. Just as we look at a wedding album to get a clear picture of a bride and groom, we can look at these pictures in Scripture to see Christ and His Bride, the Church. Some pictures we will readily recognize. Others may be a surprise, but all that we see will bring us to a new and better understanding of what it means to walk with and follow our Bridegroom. We will discover

> *The imagery of a bridegroom and a bride, of a husband and a wife, gives us many pictures that help us understand our relationship with the Lord Jesus Christ.*

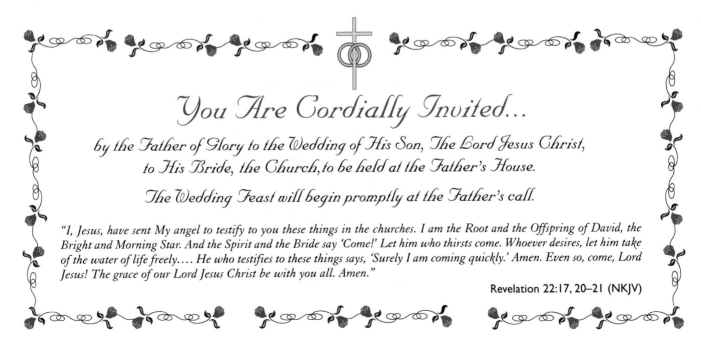

You Are Cordially Invited...

by the Father of Glory to the Wedding of His Son, The Lord Jesus Christ, to His Bride, the Church, to be held at the Father's House.

The Wedding Feast will begin promptly at the Father's call.

"I, Jesus, have sent My angel to testify to you these things in the churches. I am the Root and the Offspring of David, the Bright and Morning Star. And the Spirit and the Bride say 'Come!' Let him who thirsts come. Whoever desires, let him take of the water of life freely.... He who testifies to these things says, 'Surely I am coming quickly.' Amen. Even so, come, Lord Jesus! The grace of our Lord Jesus Christ be with you all. Amen."

Revelation 22:17, 20–21 (NKJV)

amazing love, tender mercy, strong leadership, and joyful fellowship. We will see our relationship with Him as it was meant to be. We will discover what it means to truly walk in the bonds of oneness and in the beauty of holiness. There's a Wedding about to take place, but all is not yet ready. The church is an engaged bride getting ready for her wedding. Now, lets discover what it means to be the Bride of Christ preparing for The Wedding and learn what it means to follow our Bridegroom until then.

The Bride of Christ **DAY ONE**

THE PROPOSAL OF THE BRIDEGROOM

In Ephesians 5:31–32 Paul states, *"For this cause a man shall leave his father and mother, and shall cleave to his wife; and the two shall become one flesh. This mystery is great; but I am speaking with reference to Christ and the church."* Why a bride and bridegroom? What is so important about this picture? God designed the husband and wife relationship to be a bond of oneness, and through that a deepening and growing relationship. He uses this relationship as a picture of the oneness with Him for which mankind was created. We know that oneness was shattered by sin as recorded in Genesis 3. However, God did not give up on His purpose, and plans for man to walk in oneness with Him again. He chose the imagery of a bride to convey what it was He wanted, a Bride for Himself. In the Old Testament we see Israel sometimes pictured as the bride or wife of Jehovah. In the New Testament we see that picture made clearer and sharper with the image of a Bride for the Messiah, the Lord Jesus. The Scriptures use that imagery to reveal the process of bringing man back to the Lord and to that oneness with Him we were created to enjoy forever.

📖 One of the most important discussions in Scripture about a bride and bridegroom is found in a conversation between John the Baptist and his followers. Read John 3:22–30 and identify who the **bride** is.

_____

_____

_____

_____

Who is the **bridegroom**?

_____

_____

_____

_____

Who is the friend of the bridegroom?

_____

_____

_____

_____

God designed the husband and wife to walk in oneness, a picture of the oneness He desires for Himself and His Bride.

This passage points to a very important truth. Some of the wedding imagery in Scripture is different from the way we think of a wedding today. What is the meaning of what John the Baptist said? Picture those who heard John. What did they think when he spoke of a bride, a bridegroom, or a friend of the bridegroom? To understand that, it is vitally important to see the process that a bridegroom and bride went through to become a wedded couple. The elements of a Jewish wedding will help us see that and will help us see how the Lord is at work with His Bride, the Church . . . and with you and me as part of that Bride.

When a young man wanted to marry, often he and his father, or a representative of his father, or a "friend of the bridegroom" would leave the home of the young man and travel to the home of the young maiden. They knew that a dowry, a ransom price, would have to be paid for this bride. Once at her home, they would discuss the price and make arrangements to pay it. That price was often very high, even as much as a year's wage or the price of a house. The price paid reflected both the value of the bride and the wealth of the bridegroom.

📖 We know that Jesus came to earth, sent by His Father *"to seek and to save that which was lost."* (Luke 19:10). He came to pay a price for His Bride. What do you discover about this in 1 Peter 1:18–19?

_____

_____

_____

_____

_____

What does this tell you about the value of the Bride and the wealth of the Bridegroom?

_____

_____

_____

_____

First Peter makes it clear that we were redeemed (or paid for), with the precious blood of Christ, not with the temporal riches of this earth, not with mere gold or silver. The price He paid indicates the value He places on His Church, His Bride, and reveals the value of the relationship in His eyes. He, the unblemished Lamb, paid His priceless blood that we might have an unblemished relationship with Him. What value can we place on the price He paid? Christ poured out the most valuable treasure of all time and eternity, His very life (see Acts 20:28).

In the arrangements for a Jewish wedding, when the price was agreed upon they held a somewhat formal, covenant ceremony. The young man would speak his vows offering himself to love and care for his bride in the bonds of marriage, and a piece of money would be given as a pledge. The young lady would give her consent to marry the young man and then the two would often sign a formal agreement and seal their vows with a drink from

Did You Know?

BETROTHAL AND MARRIAGE IN ABRAHAM'S DAY

In Genesis 24 we see Abraham sending his representative Eliezer, his oldest servant, to Mesopotamia to find a bride for Abraham's son Isaac. He traveled from their home to the city of Nahor over 400 miles away and there met Rebekah. He spoke of Isaac's wealth and Abraham's commitment to find a bride from his own people. He then arranged the wedding between Rebekah and Isaac giving her a dowry of many gifts, including gold and silver jewelry and gifts of clothing (Genesis 24:53).

a common cup of wine. This was the Jewish equivalent of our modern engagement process.

📖 What parallels do we see in our relationship to Jesus Christ? Read what Jesus said to His disciples in Matthew 26:26–29.

_____

_____

_____

_____

_____

_____

In His last meal with the disciples, Jesus took a piece of bread and a single cup to institute the Lord's Supper, a memorial of the new covenant that He was making with them. Both He and the disciples drank from that cup. He said it represented His life poured out for His Church, for the forgiveness of sins. He instructed them to partake of the bread and the fruit of the vine on a regular basis to remember Him until He joined them in His Father's kingdom. Paul spoke of this supper and said that one of the main purposes of this celebration was to *"proclaim the Lord's death* **until He comes**" (1 Corinthians 11:26). Here again we see an example for a waiting bride to follow. She recognizes the price His love has paid and lives her life in light of that, proclaiming to others how much she is loved and how much she desires to walk in purity for the sake of her covenant bridegroom.

In the formal engagement ceremony, a benediction would be spoken and sometimes gifts were given to the bride. This ceremony (or betrothal, as it was called), was then legally binding. The couple were treated as if they were married except that the marriage was not consummated, and they could not live together until they were actually married. It could only be dissolved by a legal divorce (like Joseph considered when he found that Mary was with child and thought she had done wrong, Matthew 1:18–20). After this ceremony the couple then focused on the time of preparation for their wedding celebration and their new life together. We will look at that in Day Two.

📖 One final thought on our "betrothal" to Christ—read Ephesians 1:13–14 and write down the parallels you see there between our belief and betrothal.

_____

_____

_____

_____

What phase of the Jewish wedding process is pictured in our initial belief (v.13)?

_____

_____

_____

Put Yourself In Their Shoes

WALKING IN PURITY

In 1 Corinthians 11:28, Paul urged the believers to use the memorial of the Lord's Supper as a time to examine their lives before the Lord until His coming for them. This serves as yet another picture of walking in purity as we await our Bridegroom.

A modern betrothal is formalized with an engagement ring. What equivalent to that do you see here (v.14)?

_____

_____

_____

At the moment we first believed, we were "sealed" with the Holy Spirit. The word used here pictures the ancient practice of sealing important legal documents with wax, bearing an impression of the person represented. It is a sign of formality, permanence, and security. The Holy Spirit comes into our lives when we are justified (forgiven), and begins the process of our salvation, much in the same way that engagement begins the process of marriage. It is important to realize that our salvation will be completed when we see the Bridegroom face to face. This is why Paul says, *". . . for now salvation is nearer to us than when we believed"* (Romans 13:11). Our salvation is sealed (guaranteed) by the Holy Spirit of God. For our salvation to fail, it is not we who must fail, but God. In Ephesians 1:14 we are told that the Holy Spirit is given to us as a "pledge" of our inheritance. That same Greek word is used in modern Greece to refer to an engagement ring. It means earnest money or a down payment, something given beforehand to confirm what is promised. The Holy Spirit in our lives is God's guarantee that He will come for His bride.

A TIME OF PREPARATION

 The Bride of Christ **DAY TWO.**

Jesus has chosen us to be His bride. We are to be "wedded" to Him. What a tremendous thought that He has selected us! One of the last things the bridegroom and the bride talked about at the betrothal was the groom's return for her. At this meeting the bridegroom promised to return for his bride **after** he had prepared a **place** for them to dwell, often a place on the family land. With that promise, the bridegroom left his bride and returned to his home to prepare the promised place. He would begin building a dwelling at the "father's house." At the same time, the bride would be preparing her wedding garments awaiting the bridegroom's return. She would not know the exact day but would know the season, since it was usually about twelve months or less.

In the Gospel of John, after Jesus had the supper with His disciples and promised to pour out His life for the forgiveness of sin, the disciples all pledged their loyalty to Him with Peter even vowing to go to the death for Him. After Jesus told him he would deny Him, He began to speak words of comfort and promise.

📖 Read John 14:1–3. What did Jesus say? Could this be like a bridegroom's promise to His bride?

_____

_____

_____

_____

"And if I go and prepare a place for you, I will come again, and receive you to Myself; that where I am, there you may be also."

John 14:3

Jesus promised to go to His Father's house to prepare a place for His disciples. In the culture of that day, a son would often build a house adjoining the father's house and those houses linked together would share a common courtyard. All the father's sons would raise their families together in that close-knit community. Though it was technically "next-door," that place to which the son brought his bride was known as the father's house. As the son built the house, the father oversaw the construction, and it was by his say-so that the house was considered finished. The father would tell the son when it was time to go and get his bride. Since the bride would not know the exact day, she had to be ready with her wedding garments, watching and waiting for the return of her bridegroom.

We know Jesus is preparing a place for us, but what is He doing to prepare us for that place? Ephesians 5 is one of the clearest passages on the relationship between Christ (our bridegroom) and us (His bride). This passage declares that we belong to Him and shows us the preparation process for the wedding to come.

> 📖 What do you see about the price Jesus paid for His Bride (Ephesians 5:25)?

_____

_____

_____

_____

This passage again reveals the great price Christ paid. He loved the Church so much that He gave up Himself for her. He delivered Himself over to death. In John 10:17–18, Jesus says, _"I lay down My life. . . .No one has taken it away from Me, but I lay it down on My own initiative. . . ."_ He did that for His Church, His Bride.

> 📖 As part of this "mystery" of Christ and the Church, what does Paul see about the Church in Ephesians 5:30–32?

_____

_____

_____

_____

God revealed to Paul that there is a parallel between the relationship of Christ to the Church and that of a husband to his wife (Genesis 2). Just as the husband and wife were designed to be one flesh, one body, so the Lord has designed that the Church be joined as one body with Christ.

> 📖 How does this relate to the prayer Jesus prayed the night before He went to the cross? Read John 17:13–26. What does Jesus repeat most often (verses 21, 22, 23)?

_____

_____

_____

_____

Jesus is preparing a place for us and He is preparing us for that place.

Jesus prayed to the Father that His disciples might be protected from the evil one (Satan), that they might be sanctified or set apart in His truth, His Word, and, above all, that they would be one, experiencing the same kind of oneness that Jesus experienced with His Father. He desired that all His disciples (including us) might intimately know and understand what it means to be one with the Father and Himself. The importance of this is clear in the fact that He repeats this desire in verses 21, 22, and 23.

📖 Because He desires this oneness to grow and deepen, we find Christ acting in a certain way toward the Church. What do you discover in Ephesians 5:28–30?

_____

_____

_____

_____

_____

Just as a man takes care of his body, so the Lord Jesus nourishes and cherishes His Bride, seeing her as a part of Himself. The word for nourish carries the idea of giving everything necessary to bring to full maturity just as we would with our children, making sure they get the right vitamins, minerals and other nutrients. The word for cherish (*thalpo*) properly means "to warm, keep warm" and is used in 1 Thessalonians 2:7 of a nursing mother tenderly caring for her child, a picture of security and protection. The Lord does the same for us. He is preparing us for our wedding day, feeding us, protecting us, and helping us grow in every way.

📖 Christ has a two-fold goal for His Bride. The first part of this goal is found in Ephesians 5:25–26. Summarize what you find there.

_____

_____

_____

_____

Christ loved His Bride and died for her. With His perfect sacrifice He provided full forgiveness and cleansing through His blood (1 John 1:7–9). He did this that He might sanctify her, make her holy and pure, set her apart as His own—in a class all by herself. The Bride is made holy before Him and for Him by His perfect cleansing work. Verse 26 says He "cleansed her by the washing of water with the word." In the reference to the washing of water with (or in) the word, some see a reference to the vows (the spoken words) made at the betrothal ceremony. By those words, the bridegroom set apart his bride as his own, and by her faith in those words she lived out that truth. She was his—spoken for and paid for. In John 17, when Jesus prayed for His own to be sanctified (or set apart), He spoke of them being sanctified in the truth (*"Thy word"*). What He speaks is truth which, when mixed with faith and obedience, sets us apart from all lies and deceptions unto Him and His will.

Did You Know?

A BRIDE'S PREPARATION

It is said of Esther that the days of her beautification in preparation for the king included *"six months with oil of myrrh and six months with spices and the cosmetics for women"* (Esther 2:12). Baths and anointing with oil were common in the Middle East in preparation for a future wedding day. In Ezekiel, the Lord speaks of bathing and anointing His bride Israel with oil. The Lord Himself has cleansed His Bride and continues to perform His work of beautifying her with the oil of His Spirit. He has provided all that is needed so that she will be prepared as a beautiful and pure Bride when she meets her Bridegroom.

GOD'S BRIDE CLOTHED IN SPLENDOR

"I also clothed you with embroidered cloth … and I wrapped you with fine linen and covered you with silk. And I adorned you with ornaments, put bracelets on your hands, and a necklace around your neck … and a beautiful crown on your head. Thus you were adorned with gold and silver and your dress was of fine linen, silk, and embroidered cloth."
Ezekiel 16:10–13

As His Bride we should keep a pure focus—always listening to His Word, choosing His will, and following His ways.

📖 The second aspect of the Bridegroom's goal for His Bride is found in Ephesians 5:27. What is Christ's goal there?

_____

_____

_____

_____

_____

Christ desires to present the Church to Himself in glory (*endoxos*), a word that can refer to radiant or shining clothing. She will be marked by great beauty without and within. The word "present" (*paristemi*) carries the idea of "standing beside" Him. He wants her standing by His side in glorious robes of splendor without spot, wrinkle, or any other blemish—all the effects of sin and the fall removed. The Bride will stand holy and blameless or "spotless." That is the goal He is fulfilling now as He prepares us, His Bride.

THE PURITY OF THE BRIDE

Can you remember the last wedding you attended? Can you picture the decorations, the dresses the bridesmaids wore, the bride as she came down the aisle? Psalm 29 is a hymn praising the might and sovereign rule of the LORD over all creation. Verse 2 says, *"Worship the LORD in the beauty of holiness."* Some translate *"the beauty of holiness"* as *"holy array."* In either case, the Lord is worthy for us to come before Him clothed in the splendor and majesty of holiness within and without. That is certainly what He wants for His Bride. The gleaming, white wedding gown portrays the bride's life of purity, set apart for her bridegroom. Let's see what more the Scripture says about the preparation of the Bride, particularly the purity of this Bride of Christ.

📖 How do we continue to prepare for the bridegroom's return? What do we do in cooperation with Him? What is the one thing the Church is to do in response to all Christ has done (Ephesians 5:24)?

_____

_____

_____

_____

The Church is to be continually submissive to Christ as the Head of the Church. This does not mean we just follow Him in "church matters." It means we are to have a pure focus on Him—a single eye, a set direction. It means that in all of life we follow Him. We adjust to Him, adapt to Him, and line up with Him. We arrange ourselves under Him and His leadership always listening to His Word, choosing His will, and following His ways. These are all characteristics of a Bride who walks in the beauty of holiness.

Often there were two attendants in the wedding process, a friend of the bridegroom and a friend of the bride. We have seen John the Baptist in the former role. Another passage of Scripture appears to refer to Paul in the task of the latter, the friend of the bride.

📖 Read 2 Corinthians 11:2–3 and record what you discover there.

_____

_____

_____

_____

_____

What was Paul's main concern?

_____

_____

_____

_____

Paul, as a friend of the Bride, betrothed the Corinthian believers to Christ and he was seeking to make sure that they remained "a pure virgin." He was guarding them with a godly jealousy so that these believers did not commit spiritual adultery in following after some false teachers or false teaching. He did not want them to be deceived and led astray from _"the simplicity and purity"_ of their devotion and love for Jesus Christ. The word "simplicity" pictures one with a single and pure focus, never looking away to any other. Paul knew that when the the Bridegroom returns for His Bride, it is vital that the Church be a pure Bride, not deceived, not lacking in devotion and love, but focused on pleasing their one husband and looking forward to rejoicing at the feast.

📖 What additional truths do you find in 1 John 3:1–3?

_____

_____

_____

_____

What does this passage tell us about what we are to do while we await the return of our Lord?

_____

_____

_____

_____

Did You Know?

A FRIEND OF THE BRIDE

Moses acted as a friend of the Bride bringing Israel to the Lord at Mount Sinai (Exodus 19:17). Exodus 19:10–16 speaks of the consecration and cleanliness required of the nation in preparation to come before the Lord. This meant preparation within and without in order to meet the Lord when He called for them.

THE FATHER'S LOVE

"See how great a love the Father has bestowed upon us, that we should be called children of God; and such we are. For this reason the world does not know us, because it did not know Him. Beloved, now we are children of God, and it has not appeared as yet what we shall be. We know that, when He appears, we shall be like Him, because we shall see Him just as He is. And everyone who has this hope fixed on Him purifies himself, just as He is pure." 1 John 3:1–3

First John 3:1 speaks of the love of the Father for His children (also known as the Bride of His Son). Verse 2 confidently proclaims that we will be changed into His likeness for we shall see Him as He is. This will occur when He returns for His Bride. First John 3:3 focuses our hope on Him and on our need to walk in purity as we await His return (2 Corinthians 11:2–3). Knowing He is coming soon should motivate us toward greater purity. Christ is holy and pure, and He wants us to be joined to Him in the oneness of holiness.

The Bride of Christ **DAY FOUR**

Did You Know?
THE WEDDING PROCESSION

Because every wedding was a reminder of the union of the Lord with His people Israel, the coming of a wedding procession was met with great joy. All else was secondary. People were expected to join in and if they met a funeral procession, the funeral procession had to give way to the wedding procession.

THE PRESENTATION OF THE BRIDE

Have you ever taken the time to observe the joy on a bridegroom's face as he sees his bride coming down the aisle? He knows her heart belongs to him and his heart belongs to her. We know the Lord wants to present us to Himself holy and blameless, walking in oneness and in the beauty of holiness. How is this presentation pictured in the Jewish wedding and in Scripture? When the place at the father's house was fully prepared the bridegroom would again leave his home at the directive of his father. This time he would go with the "friend of the bridegroom" and many companions, and travel to the home of the bride. This was often done at night in a torchlit procession. As they neared the home of the bride, a trumpet (*shofar*) would be sounded, and there would be a shout, perhaps announcing the coming of the bridegroom or even the name of the bride. The bride would come out to meet her groom and with her companions they would return to the prepared place and enjoy the Marriage Supper or Wedding Feast.

📖 Read 1 Thessalonians 4:13–18 and note any similarities to the customs of the Jewish wedding.

_____

_____

_____

_____

Paul was seeking to comfort the Thessalonians who were concerned that some of the believers there had died before the promised return of the Lord. He assured them that they, too, would experience the Lord's return for His Church (Bride). There will come a processional, a shout, a trumpet, and a meeting between the Bride and the Bridegroom during the Rapture of the Church. The dead will rise first and then we who remain will join them in the air and all of us will be with the Lord forever (1 Thessalonians 4:16, 17).

📖 What does 1 Corinthians 15:42–58 have to say about this change that will take place for those who know Jesus Christ as their resurrected Lord and Savior? (You may want to look at Philippians 3:20–21 as well.)

_____

_____

_____

_____

In light of these truths, how does 1 Corinthians 15:58 urge us to get ready for this time?

_____

_____

_____

_____

First Corinthians 15 says we will be changed in a moment, in the twinkling of an eye. This perishable, weak, dishonorable body will be changed into an imperishable, strong, glorious body. In Philippians 3:20–21 this transformation is spoken of as a manifestation of the power Christ has as Lord over all things. Knowing these truths, Paul encouraged the believers to walk steadfast, abounding in the work of the Lord, because that work would not be in vain (1 Corinthians 15:58); it would certainly be rewarded.

According to the pattern of the Jewish wedding, the couple returned to the father's house for the wedding feast. The bride and bridegroom were dressed in their best garments and were led into the feast by the friend of the bridegroom. It appears that there was also a friend of the bride who accompanied her and brought her to the bridegroom. These two "friends" were responsible for various aspects of the marriage arrangements, including the betrothal ceremony, communication during the interval until the wedding, preparations for the wedding feast, and the overseeing of all the details for the bridal chamber where the marriage was consummated at the end of the feast. We have already seen that John the Baptist and Paul fit the roles of the friend of the Bridegroom and the friend of the Bride. They both longed to see the Bride and the Bridegroom coming together in a pure and holy oneness, in the beauty and majesty of holiness.

The Wedding Feast, also known as the Marriage Supper, was a time of great rejoicing. It usually lasted seven days. Let's see what we can learn from Scripture about this feast time.

📖 Read Revelation 19:7–10 and Ephesians 2:10. How is the bride clothed?

_____

_____

_____

_____

📖 What is her clothing according to verse 8 and how does Ephesians 2:10 relate to this?

_____

_____

_____

_____

At the marriage supper of the Lamb we see that the bride has made herself ready. She is clothed in fine linen, *"bright and clean"* indicating a purity and holy character to what she is wearing. Verse 8 says that this *"fine linen is the*

righteous acts of the saints." The preparation of her garments has been going on during the time of her stay on earth through those deeds done in faith and obedience to her Lord. Those are the *"good works which God prepared beforehand"* for her to walk in day-by-day, according to Ephesians 2:10.

📖 First Corinthians 3:10–15 and 4:5 appear to be part of the period of time at the very beginning of the feast. What do you discover in those passages?

_____

_____

_____

_____

_____

What do you learn from 2 Corinthians 5:9–10?

_____

_____

_____

_____

_____

THE SPLENDOR OF THE BRIDE OF THE MESSIAH

"The King's daughter is all glorious within; Her clothing is interwoven with gold. She will be led to the King in embroidered work; The virgins, her companions who follow her, Will be brought to Thee. They will be led forth with gladness and rejoicing; They will enter into the King's palace." Psalm 45:13–15

Paul makes it clear we will be rewarded or suffer loss of reward at the judgment seat of Christ which apparently takes place during the time after the Church is taken up to be with the Bridegroom. We are not judged as to our salvation. That is a certainty for anyone who has trusted Christ as Lord and Savior. This judgment concerns our works while we are awaiting the return of the Bridegroom. Those who have built with righteous materials (by faith and obedience and love) will have a reward. Those who walked fleshly have used wood, hay, and straw and their works will burn, though they themselves will be saved.

Apparently there will be a difference in the garments worn at the wedding feast. Some will be clothed in great splendor because they obeyed their Lord. Others will be clothed as though they have just escaped a fire. The clothing of splendor will reflect the majesty of the Bridegroom, because all will know that only He could provide such garments. Only by His strength, grace, and ability could such garments have been woven. Ephesians 2:10 says we are His workmanship. The word workmanship could be translated "masterpiece." When people see the clothing of the saints, they will recognize two things: the awesome work of the Master and the faithful walk of His servant. The Bridegroom will receive the honor and the Bride will enjoy the reward. After the wedding feast comes the majestic return of Christ with His saints, His Bride, to establish His Millennial Kingdom when we will reign with Him (Revelation 19:11–21; 20:1–6). Ultimately, the Bride of Christ will include all the redeemed from all ages dwelling with Him in the New Jerusalem, the place prepared by the Lord for His Bride, and marked by the beauty of holiness (Revelation 21:1–5).

FOR ME TO FOLLOW GOD

Are you beginning to see what God is saying through the "Bride of Christ"? He is communicating that He has purposed a special relationship of oneness for us with Him. Titus 2:11–14 reflects what we have seen as we have looked at the relationship between the Lord Jesus and His Bride. It says:

"For the grace of God that brings salvation has appeared to all men, teaching us that denying ungodliness and worldly lusts, we should live soberly, righteously, and godly in the present age, looking for the blessed hope and glorious appearing of our great God and Savior Jesus Christ, who gave Himself for us, that He might redeem us from every lawless deed and purify for Himself His own people, zealous for good works." (NKJV)

We are His own possession. We belong to Him, secure, loved, and destined to reign by His side. What an awesome privilege!

📖 As we think of our relationship to the Lord Jesus, what applications do you see in 1 Corinthians 6:19–20? You may want to read the entire context of 6:12–20.

_____

_____

_____

_____

_____

> **"For you have been bought with a price; therefore glorify God in your body."**
> **1 Corinthians 6:20**

We have been bought with a price and therefore are not our own. We belong to the Lord. In the context of 1 Corinthians 6, Paul is dealing with walking in purity and holiness, not in immorality. The Lord wants to see and wants others to see the beauty of holiness in all we do. His very Spirit, the **Holy** Spirit, indwells us as His temple. Since He now indwells us as His very own, He wants us to reveal Him as He truly is, so that others will have a right opinion and give true honor to Him. The Lord has given all His life, and He wants His Bride-to-Be to live in such a way that others have a good idea of what kind of Bridegroom He is.

 Sometimes the best way to know what to do is to find out what not to do. Proverbs has some very practical applications to our relationships with one another. Some of those are directed to the husband-wife relationship or life at home. Read the verses given below and make applications to yourself as part of the Bride of Christ. How should you act in your daily relationship with Him in light of these verses?

Proverbs 11:22

_____

_____

Proverbs 12:4

_____

_____

_____

Proverbs 15:16–17

_____

_____

_____

Proverbs 17:1

_____

_____

_____

_____

Proverbs 19:13–14

_____

_____

_____

_____

WHAT A SAVIOR!

When all is said and done, the glorious work of Christ will be clearly seen through His Bride, holy, pure, and without any sort of blemish whatsoever. No longer poor, diseased, ugly and forsaken, she (we) will be known as His, rich in Him, made whole and beautiful in Him, forever by His side. How grateful we should be! What a Savior!

Proverbs 21:19

_____

_____

_____

The Apostle Peter also has some counsel for husbands and wives. We know that as our Bridegroom the Lord Jesus will always act according to His Word. What should we do **as His Bride** according to 1 Peter 3:1–6? Note that this applies to all of us in the Body of Christ because we are all part of His Bride.

_____

_____

_____

_____

📖 How would you apply Ephesians 5:33 as His Bride?

_____

_____

_____

_____

In 1 John 2:28 we find these words, _"And now, little children, abide in Him, so that when He appears, we may have confidence and not shrink away from Him in shame at His coming."_ Abiding in Him refers to an obedient, surrendered walk.

APPLY How is your walk? What things might make you ashamed at His coming?

_____

_____

_____

_____

Spend some time with the Lord in prayer.

Lord, I want to recite the words of Ruth as my vows of surrender to You: *where You go, I will go, and where you lodge, I will lodge. Your people shall be my people, and your God, my God.* (1:16). Thank You for Your unconditional love for me. May I walk in the truth that *"I am my beloved's and my beloved is mine"* (Song of Solomon 6:3). Thank You for Your promise, *"I will never leave you nor forsake you"* (Hebrews 13:5 NKJV), that I am secure in You and that You will ever nourish and cherish me. May I walk in the honor of bearing Your Name, the Name above all names. Strengthen me with Your power that I may walk in obedience so that I will *not be ashamed* before You at Your coming. May my oneness with You continue to grow that I might grow in the beauty of holiness. In the Name of Jesus, Amen.

Write a letter to the Lord, your Bridegroom.

_____

_____

_____

_____

_____

_____

_____

_____

_____

_____

_____

_____

_____

_____

I AM COMING QUICKLY

"And the Spirit and the Bride say 'Come!' Let him who thirsts come, Whoever desires, let him take of the water of life freely. . . . He who testifies to these things says, 'Surely I am coming quickly.' Amen. Even so, come, Lord Jesus!" Revelation 22:17, 20 (NKJV)

A Bride to Be

Take us to the mountain, O Glorious King.
There let us hear Your truth joyfully ring.
Show us Your Bride clothed in glory.
There tell us the wonderful story

Of a Bride You chose,
Of a heart that knows
Of the price You paid,
Of the call You made.

Tell us the story of a needy Bride,
Of the garments soiled, by sin defiled.
Tell us of the touch of Your pure grace,
Of the love You showed her face to face.

Tell us how You gave her Your covenant cup,
Of the death You died to raise her up.
Tell us about the place You have made,
The place of costly stones You have laid.

Tell us the story of Your coming again,
Of the waiting Bride not knowing when.
Show us her heart longing to go,
Your Bride made ready in garments aglow.

Tell us of the joy of Your pure Bride
Standing in holy beauty by Your side.
Tell us of the glory we will forever see,
And in that Bride may we be.

Then let us forever exalt and praise
Our majestic Bridegroom, His Name raise.
In the New Jerusalem our chosen place,
We will ever follow walking in Grace.

RLS and LGS

Notes

Notes

How to Follow God

STARTING THE JOURNEY

Did you know that you have been on God's heart and mind for a long, long time? Even before time existed you were on His mind. He has always wanted you to know Him in a personal, purposeful relationship. He has a purpose for your life and it is founded upon His great love for you. You can be assured it is a good purpose and it lasts forever. Our time on this earth is only the beginning. God has a grand design that goes back into eternity past and reaches into eternity future. What is that design?

The Scriptures are clear about God's design for man—God created man to live and walk in oneness with Himself. Oneness with God means being in a relationship that is totally unselfish, totally satisfying, totally secure, righteous and pure in every way. That's what we were created for. If we walked in that kind of relationship with God we would glorify Him and bring pleasure to Him. Life would be right! Man was meant to live that way—pleasing to God and glorifying Him (giving a true estimate of who God is). Adam sinned and shattered his oneness with God. Ever since, man has come short of the glory of God: man does not and cannot please God or give a true estimate of God. Life is not right until a person is right with God. That is very clear as we look at the many people who walked across the pages of Scripture, both Old and New Testaments.

JESUS CHRIST came as the solution for this dilemma. Jesus Christ is the glory of God—the true estimate of who God is in every way. He pleased His Father in everything He did and said, and He came to restore oneness with God. He came to give man His power and grace to walk in oneness with God, to follow Him day by day enjoying the relationship for which he was created. In the process, man could begin to present a true picture of Who God is and experience knowing Him personally. You may be asking, "How do these facts impact my life today? How does this become real to me now? How can I begin the journey of following God in this way?" To come to know God personally means you must choose to receive Jesus Christ as your personal Savior and Lord.

- First of all, you must admit that you have sinned, that you are not walking in oneness with God, not pleasing Him or glorifying Him in your life (Romans 3:23; 6:23; 8:5-8).

- It means repenting of that sin—changing your mind, turning to God and turning away from sin—and by faith receiving His forgiveness based on His death on the Cross for you (Romans 3:21-26; 1 Peter 3:18).

- It means opening your life to receive Him as your living, resurrected Lord and Savior (John 1:12). He has promised to come and indwell you by His Spirit and live in you as the Savior and Master of your life (John 14:16-21; Romans 14:7-9).

- He wants to live His life through you—conforming you to His image, bearing His fruit through you and giving you power to reign in life (John 15:1,4-8; Romans 5:17; 7:4; 8:29, 37).

You can come to Him now. In your own words, simply tell Him you want to know Him personally and you willingly repent of your sin and receive His forgiveness and His life. Tell Him you want to follow Him forever (Romans 10:9-10, 13). Welcome to the Family of God and to the greatest journey of all!!!

WALKING ON THE JOURNEY

How do we follow Him day by day? Remember, Christ has given those who believe in Him everything pertaining to life and godliness, so that we no longer have to be slaves to our "flesh" and its corruption (2 Peter 1:3-4). Day by day He wants to empower us to live a life of love and joy, pleasing to Him and rewarding to us. That's why Ephesians 5:18 tells us to *be filled with the Spirit*—keep on being controlled by the Spirit who lives in you. He knows exactly what we need each day and we can trust Him to lead us (Proverbs 3:5-6). So how can we cooperate with Him in this journey together?

To walk with Him *day by day* means ...
- reading and listening to His Word day by day (Luke 10:39, 42; Colossians 3:16; Psalm 19:7-14; 119:9).

- spending time talking to Him in prayer (Philippians 4:6-7).

- realizing that God is God and you are not, and the role that means He has in your life.

This allows Him to work through your life as you fellowship, worship, pray and learn with other believers (Acts 2:42), and serve in the good works He has prepared for us to do—telling others who Jesus is and what His Word says, teaching and encouraging others, giving to help meet needs, helping others, etc. (Ephesians 2:10).

God's goal for each of us is that we be conformed to the image of His Son, Jesus Christ (Romans 8:29). But none of us will reach that goal of perfection until we are with Him in Heaven, for then "we shall be like Him, because we shall see Him just as He is" (1 John 3:2). For now, He wants us to follow

Him faithfully, learning more each day. Every turn in the road, every trial and every blessing, is designed to bring us to a new depth of surrender to the Lord and His ways. He not only wants us to do His will, He desires that we surrender to His will His way. That takes trust—trust in His character, His plan and His goals (Proverbs 3:5-6).

As you continue this journey, and perhaps you've been following Him for a while, you must continue to listen carefully and follow closely. We never graduate from that. That sensitivity to God takes moment by moment surrender, dying to the impulses of our flesh to go our own way, saying no to the temptations of Satan to doubt God and His Word, and refusing the lures of the world to be unfaithful to the Lord who gave His life for us.

God desires that each of us come to maturity as sons and daughters: to that point where we are fully satisfied in Him and His ways, fully secure in His sovereign love, and walking in the full measure of His purity and holiness. If we are to clearly present the image of Christ for all to see, it will take daily surrender and daily seeking to follow Him wherever He leads, however He gets there (Luke 9:23-25). It's a faithful walk of trust through time into eternity. And it is worth everything. Trust Him. Listen carefully. Follow closely.

Other Books in the *Following God* Bible Character Study Series

Life Principles from the Old Testament

Characters include: Adam, Noah, Job, Abraham, Lot, Jacob, Joseph, Moses, Caleb, Joshua, Gideon, and Samson
ISBN 0-89957-300-2   208 pages

Life Principles from the Kings of the Old Testament

Characters include: Saul, David, Solomon, Jereboam I, Asa, Ahab, Jehoshaphat, Hezekiah, Josiah, Zerubbabel & Ezra, Nehemiah, and "The True King in Israel."
ISBN 0-89957-301-0   256 pages

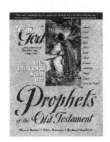

Life Principles from the Prophets of the Old Testament

Characters include: Samuel, Elijah, Elisha, Jonah, Hosea, Isaiah, Micah, Jeremiah, Habakkuk, Daniel, Haggai, and "Christ the Prophet."
ISBN 0-89957-303-7   224 pages

Life Principles from the New Testament Men of Faith

Characters include: John the Baptist, Peter, John, Thomas, James, Barnabas, Paul, Paul's Companions, Timothy, and "The Son of Man."
ISBN 0-89957-304-5   208 pages

Following God Leader's Guide

Designed for small group Bible study leaders, the *Following God Leader's Guide* contains helpful notes for all five books in in the Following God Series.
ISBN 0-89957-306-1   224 pages

Women of the Bible Book Two available January, 2002
Call for more information (800) 266-4977 or (423) 894-6060.
Log on to **followingGod.com** for more information about these books.

New Following God Release from AMG Publishers

Life Principles for Worship from the Tabernacle

ISBN 0-89957-299-5

This Bible study is designed in an interactive format, incorporating important scriptural points of interest and will help you understand all that God says to us through the components found in Israel's Tabernacle. Important historical and symbolic details will leap from the pages and into your heart. Inside the pages you'll also find the special helps sections you've come to rely on from the best-selling "Following God" series; Word Studies, Doctrinal Notes, Did You Know?, and Stop and Apply. Each help section will add to your understanding and ability to share these new-found truths with those you know and/or teach.

In the pages of this "Following God" study on the Tabernacle you'll learn to:

✓ Focus on the fence, the gate and the outer court with the bronze altar and bronze laver;

✓ Focus on the Holy Place with the golden lamp stand, the table of showbread, and the altar of incense;

✓ Move into the Holy of Holies through the veil, and look at the ark of the covenant with the golden jar of manna, Aaron's rod that budded, the tables of the covenant, the mercy seat and, ultimately, the cloud of glory.

Most importantly, you'll discover how God has provided a way for man to draw near to Him.

To order, call (800) 266-4977 or (423) 894-6060.
www.followingGod.com

Leader's Guidebooks for *Life Principles for Worship from the Tabernacle* now available. Watch for new Following God titles to be released soon!

New Following God Release from AMG Publishers

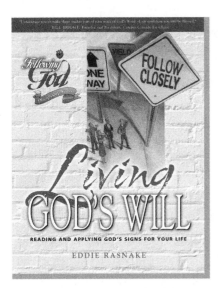

Living God's Will

ISBN 0-89957-309-6

How can I follow and identify the signs that lead to God's will? *Living God's Will* explores the answer to this all-important question in detail. It is Eddie Rasnake's deeply-held conviction that the road to God's will is well-marked with signposts to direct us. Each lesson in this twelve-week Bible study takes a look at a different signpost that reflects God's will. You will be challenged to recognize the signposts of God when you encounter them. But more importantly, you will be challenged to follow God's leading by following the direction of those signposts.

In the pages of this "Following God" study on finding and obeying God's will, you will find clear and practical advice for:

✓ Yielding your life to the Lord

✓ Recognizing God's will through Scripture, prayer and circumstances

✓ Seeking godly counsel

✓ Discovering how God's peace enters into the process of following His will

✓ Determining God's will in areas not specifically addressed in Scripture, such as choosing a wife/husband or career path.

Throughout your study you will also be enriched by the many interactive application sections that literally thousands have come to appreciate from the acclaimed **Following God** series.

To order, call (800) 266-4977 or (423) 894-6060.
www.followingGod.com

Leader's Guidebooks for *Living God's Will* are now available. Watch for new Following God titles to be released soon!